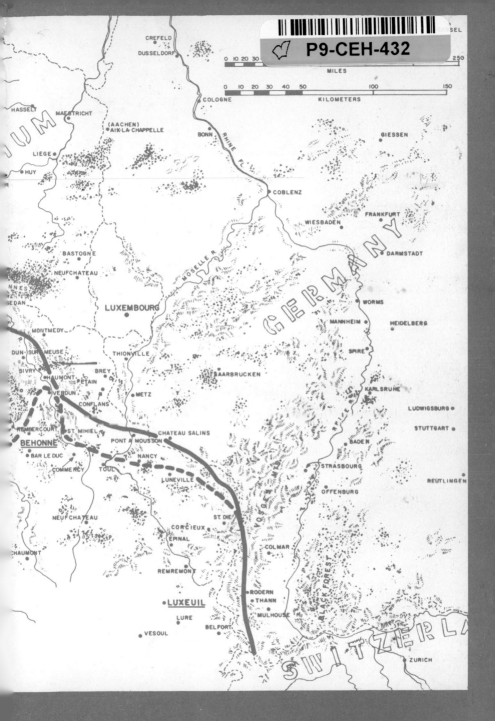

MILES

KILOMETERS

PERATIONS AREAS OF ESC. N.124

LEGION OF THE LAFAYETTE

by Arch Whitehouse

WINGS OF ADVENTURE
POOR BLOODY OBSERVERS
HELL IN HELMETS
CRIME ON A CONVOY CARRIER
THE REAL BOOK OF AIRPLANES
FIGHTERS IN THE SKY
BOMBERS IN THE SKY
COMBAT IN THE SKY
ADVENTURE IN THE SKY
THE YEARS OF THE SKY KINGS
TANK
THE YEARS OF THE WAR BIRDS
SUBS AND SUBMARINERS
SQUADRONS OF THE SEA
BILLY MITCHELL
LEGION OF THE LAFAYETTE

LEGION OF
THE LAFAYETTE

by *Arch Whitehouse*

ILLUSTRATED WITH PHOTOGRAPHS

1962 Doubleday & Company, Inc., Garden City, New York

LIBRARY OF CONGRESS CATALOG CARD NUMBER 62-11302
COPYRIGHT © 1962 BY ARCH WHITEHOUSE
ALL RIGHTS RESERVED
PRINTED IN THE UNITED STATES OF AMERICA
FIRST EDITION

Dedicated to

COLONEL PAUL AYRES ROCKWELL

Patriot

Legionnaire

War Correspondent

Military Aviator

Author

Historian

  and

Gentleman

Contents

INTRODUCTION   ix

I HOW IT ALL BEGAN   1

II THE BIRTH PANGS   13

III FIRST SORTIES   32

IV THE ROAD OF THE PATRIOTS   52

V CHAMPAGNE AND ORANGES   69

VI PETS AND PRACTICAL JOKES   87

VII THE TWO ROCKWELLS   109

VIII THE DEATH OF NORMAN PRINCE   126

IX DOWN ON THE SOMME   146

X AMERICA GOES TO WAR   179

XI CASUALTIES AND COMEDIES   202

XII IN FLANDERS FIELDS   227

XIII PILOTS WITHOUT HONOR   245

XIV THEY ALSO SERVED   268

 XV PRISONERS OF WAR   292

CONCLUSION   311

APPENDIX

   *Complete List of American Volunteers Who Served
     with the Lafayette Escadrille*   318

   Official Victories of Lafayette Flying Corps   320

   *Complete List of Lafayette Flying Corps Pilots
     in Order of Enlistment in the French Aviation*   321

   *List of Volunteers Released by the French Government
     Before Serving at the Front*   324

ACKNOWLEDGMENTS   326

BIBLIOGRAPHY   328

INDEX   331

INTRODUCTION

Yet sought they neither recompense nor praise
Nor to be mentioned in another breath
Than their blue-coated comrades whose great days
It was their pride to share, ay share even to death.
Nay, rather, France, to you they rendered thanks
(Seeing they came for honor, not for gain)
Who, opening to them your glorious ranks,
Gave them that grand occasion to excel,
That chance to live the life most free from stain
And that rare privilege of dying well.*

— ALAN SEEGER

In retracing the footsteps and air trails of the American
volunteers who took up France's cause during World War I,
we are struck immediately by these words of Alan Seeger,
himself a Legionaire, and we sense how aptly and beautifully
they proclaim the goals and ideals of this little-remembered
band of heroes.

The words "volunteer" and "patriot" have all but vanished
from our vocabulary. The advent of national conscription,
made necessary in order to withstand enemy ideology and
the continued posturings of militant dictators, has all but
denied men the right to volunteer. To the many pacifists,
patriotism is the unrealistic gesture of a deluded individual
who may enjoy some small measure of regard if he lives

* Part III, "Ode in Memory of the American Volunteers Fallen in France"
from *Poems* by Alan Seeger. Copyright 1916 Charles Scribner's Sons; re-
newal copyright 1944 Elsie Adams Seeger. Reprinted with the permission
of Charles Scribner's Sons and Constable and Company Limited.

through his campaign, but will be considered a "sucker" if he does not. Their creed has been stated: "I would rather be a live coward than a dead hero."

But these patriotic volunteers wove a tapestry of heroism with which few war stories or action novels can compare. The plain, simple tale of this modest group of American citizens will long remain a classic. No chapter in the story of the professional soldier can be more stirring than the experiences of this handful of winged Galahads. Fatigue, frustrations, and defeats were their daily lot. Previous to their enlistments they had had no conception of what trials modern warfare could produce, but they could laugh in the face of adversity, for humor, recreation—and romance—enlivened and leavened their trials.

They came from mansion and tenement, and from every section of the country. It is often presumed that most of the men of the Lafayette Flying Corps were the sons of wealthy fathers, products of Ivy League campuses, schools that bred and nurtured the aristocratic customs of the Old World. Such was not the case. They volunteered from all walks of life, from every stratum of society. One was a third-rate boxer, another a lumberman, one or two had actually learned to fly before the outbreak of the war—and had to learn all over again.

The motives that inspired their beliefs and guided their footsteps were many and varied, but practically all had one instinct in common, an unconscious idealism and manly courage, backed by an abundant measure of sacrifice that seems idiotic in these materialistic days.

Many were plainly unfit for military service in the strictest sense, but they were spiritually attuned for the defense of their civilization. Some were writers, poets, artists, architects, musicians, and even geniuses. Some were eccentrics, men who, once they had an idea, did something about it. Who knows, one or two may have been outside the pale of the law, but they eventually produced more laudable qualifications that canceled out their wild-oat sowing and previous waywardness.

Today, few of them would match up to the male-magazine editor's concept of the All-American, two-fisted, hairy-chested hero who is usually provided with a rampaging Irish ancestry. There were no Butchs, Pappys, Jakes, Mickeys, Bulls, or Killers in the Lafayette Escadrille. The Macs or Mcs listed on its roster appear to have sprung from Scottish ancestry, as shrewd and calculating a breed as one will encounter anywhere.

If the reader will turn to the complete list of these volunteers in a latter section of this book, he will be struck by the ethnic composition of the force. Of thirty-eight names on the roster of the Lafayette Escadrille we find two brothers of the Prince family, two Halls (not relatives), and two Rockwells. But investigating further, the reader will notice the number of early colonial names that make up the complete Lafayette Flying Corps. It reads like a page from the manifest of the *Mayflower*.

In later years when myriad magazines presented the victories and exploits of the aces of World War I, few of these men were ever considered, for they in no way filled the role of the professional hero. Instead of being swashbuckling braggarts, they were mild-mannered idealists who, before their country had joined the Allies, shunned national publicity, and once a few U. S. Air Service squadrons appeared on the Western Front, were completely ignored. As a matter of fact, there was some question as to whether they had forfeited their American citizenship by taking up civilization's cause before the U. S. Congress had decided on the right or wrong of the conflict. They were an unusually modest group, and I like to think that if you will glance over their photographs and read their histories, you will note that here and there you will find one who bears a haunting resemblance to someone you know.

In the beginning few of these men had even dreamed of meeting an enemy in aerial combat. Such fantastic warfare had not entered their minds. The airplane was but eleven years old, and the romance of mile-high battle had not yet been penned—except by such visionaries as H. G. Wells and Jules Verne. Most of them first went into action with rifle and bayonet, but as soon as the entrenching tool became a vital military implement, and mud took as great a toll as high explosive, it was natural that their eyes should be raised to the blue skies and golden sunshine that promised surcease from the mire. This heavenward appeal brought into focus darting aircraft, the song of engines, and the geometric patterns of tracer fire. It was as simple as that, and many of these volunteers sought their goal above the ground, rather than in the murky tunnels beneath. This resulted in the first American aviation service to engage in combat, but many who made any mark on the history of the Lafayette Escadrille, were first blooded in the trenches of the Marne or Verdun.

The original roll of American volunteers carries many recognizable types. Victor Chapman, Alan Seeger, and Henry Farnsworth were idealists of the most admirable stripe. Who can argue whether Seeger, a well-known poet of the war, had any right to leave his home and family to die with six dumdum bullets in his chest? Chapman was the first American to be lost in an air battle. He had been a student of architecture and had no particular reason to take up the gauntlet. Farnsworth never saw an airplane. He didn't live long enough, but went down with a bullet in his spine just as his infantry company reached some shell-torn objective.

Dr. David E. Wheeler, who served first as a surgeon near the front, became so inflamed by what he saw that he tore off his surgical mask, stripped himself of his gown, and fought as a private soldier in the Foreign Legion. A youth named Ivan Nock had a lucrative post in a Peruvian silver mine thousands of miles from the thunder of war, but his conscience kept his breast throbbing with shame, so he went to France, volunteered, and was killed in action.

Edmond Genet, a great-great-grandson and namesake of Citizen Genet whom the revolutionary government in France sent as its first minister to the United States in 1792, volunteered at the age of eighteen, and after many months as an infantryman, eventually flew for France. Young Genet died in an air action, the first American to be killed after the United

States declared war on Germany. Brooke Bonnell and Joseph Lydon left legs, but no regrets, on the battlefield. Jack Casey volunteered simply to repay France for the hospitality he had enjoyed while an art student in Paris. Frederick Zinn, after finishing college, went to Europe for a summer holiday, but stayed on to fight the common enemy, spending nearly two years in the trenches. He transferred to the Lafayette later and was posted to a French squadron as a photographer-observer, with which he served with distinction. He eventually was commissioned in and served with the U. S. Air Service.

Dennis Dowd, a typical New Yorker, played his Foreign Legion role to the hilt, following a pattern that might have been drawn by novelist Percival Wren. When a pretty girl refused to marry him, Dennis gave up his job, took his heartbreak abroad and joined the Foreign Legion. After a year of active service in the front line, he transferred to the French Aviation and was killed in a flying accident while completing his final training.

Many of these flying men began as volunteer ambulance drivers, serving in the American Field Service, a renowned organization that is frequently and incorrectly called the American Ambulance Service or the Red Cross Ambulance. The American Field Service, which was revived in World War II, furnished untold aid and comfort to Allied fighters in all theaters of war. It always attracted those who wished to serve without risking the loss of their citizenship, and it was while they were driving these missions of mercy that dozens of Americans came to realize the full significance of the French cause, and determined to contribute more of themselves. They enlisted in the Foreign Legion, which in many cases led to appointments in the French Air Service.

But what was their real objective? Why did they leave the halls of ivy, paying professions, promising careers, Southern plantations, or important posts in our great industries to serve for the proverbial sou a day in an army that had had few triumphs to recommend it? Why did they assemble publicly at the Hôtel des Invalides in Paris and demand to serve in the Foreign Legion, at the time a ragtag organization of ne'er-do-wells, men of disreputable character and record, the dregs of the world's slums, the sweepings-up of foul prisons, or undesirables who had been drummed out of other regiments? How did they expect to fit into such a renegade rabble? What could their sincere aims and ideals add to such a conglomerate group of human misfits?

It was a very complicated conflict they had taken on, but they did not huddle behind the World War II chestnut of "Why should I get involved? I haven't the slightest idea what this war is all about." They were not puzzled by the causes and effects, the right or the wrong. They presented no arguments that it was a capitalistic war, a pointless carnage subsidized by the merchants of death, the armament barons, or that it was a sordid political readjustment set up to deal with the balance of power.

Theirs was no hybrid intelligence. They were proud and true Americans, claiming no reservations or qualifications on their enlistment papers. They applied no "old country" prejudices or religious strictures. They knew what they were fighting for and did not need a psychological warfare officer to interpret the war for them. They willingly discarded the comfort of a high standard of living for a foreign uniform, for it mattered little under which flag they fought; they had a goal, a determination to retain all the human decencies laid down by their forebears. The guide rails of their ancestry were straight and clear and led to the highest ideals of modern civilization.

Theirs was not an impulsive, emotional, patriotic gesture to halt a goose-stepping invasion by a Prussian emperor; it actually was a revolt against their homeland's apathy to an armed threat that was aimed at the heart of mankind. Their principles and sentiments were those of simple men who knew right from wrong. They were in no way brutalized by their background or environment; on the contrary few of them had any military training or service traditions to maintain. Their Grail was more important than that. They volunteered to fight for humanity, not necessarily to repay a debt to France, not in defense of a flag, not for any special country, not for any race of people. Theirs was the Great Crusade of modern times.

Today we know how right they were and how little they were understood or appreciated. But if further evidence of their inherent fear is necessary, we need only be reminded that a man named Hitler preached the cult of Nazism, and a reborn Germany once more swept across the same battlefields of Europe, making a second attempt to subjugate the world.

Who will be next, and who will willingly take up the cudgel and block the path? From where shall we recruit our next Legion of Volunteers?

ARCH WHITEHOUSE

October 20, 1961
Montvale, New Jersey

LEGION OF THE LAFAYETTE

Chapter I

HOW IT ALL BEGAN

The first American airman to destroy an enemy airplane on the old Western Front was an unsung hero named James J. Bach. When lists of ranking aces or outstanding heroes of those days are published, Jimmy Bach is seldom mentioned. Few people today know who he was or where he came from, but it was the spirit of Jimmy Bach that inspired the famed Lafayette Escadrille. He was never actually a member, for that legendary organization did not come into being until April 20, 1916, and by that time Jimmy Bach had been a prisoner of war for more than six months. But he had racked up a victory against the common enemy, the first to go down before the guns of an American volunteer.

Bach's military career so represents the course of events that marked the path of the Legionaire that it is worth offering as an introduction to this book. He was born in Paris of American parents, and had spent a great deal of his life in European cities where he worked as a mechanical engineer. At the outbreak of the war he enlisted in the French Foreign Legion along with such immortals as William Thaw, James Stewart Carstairs, Edgar John Bouligny, Kiffin Yates Rockwell, Paul Ayres Rockwell, Charles Sweeny, Dennis Dowd, Robert Soubiran and Charles Trinkard.

The French poilu's pay in those days was one sou, approximately one cent a day, and payday came every ten days. Whether the men smoked or not, three cents of their pay was deducted for tobacco, leaving only seven cents for comforts and riotous living. Bach, Thaw, and Carstairs had some savings when they joined, but since all three were overly generous to their less fortunate comrades, the whole American contingent was soon on the indigent list. Jimmy Carstairs was particularly liberal with what he had, but eventually learned to hoard and sell his *tabac* ration at double its value.

Many of the American volunteers who had even a smattering of French were soon promoted, and Bach, Thaw, Sweeny, and one or two others were made first-class privates. Their service in the line was no better and no worse than that endured by any infantryman in those early days. They had all put in about four months amid the hottest fighting along the Marne, and could be considered cootie-bitten veterans, but most of these Americans were shrewd enough to realize that there was little future in trench warfare and the only way to get out of the mud was to be hoisted clear in some manner. Eventually the airplanes of the French Aviation Service furnished the key to the situation, and within a short time, one by one, the volunteers were applying for transfers to the military air squadrons.

It should not be assumed that because they were Americans and willing volunteers they were quickly and warmly accepted. Physically, they were no better than any other young service group. They brought no natural inheritance for flying. The United States did not hold a particular position as an aviation power. On the contrary, aviation had been almost ignored as a factor of military strength in the land that had produced the first successful heavier-than-air machine.

On the other hand France had hundreds of first-class candidates, many young soldiers of various ranks who had served honorably during the opening weeks of the war. But at the same time it was realized that a great pool of trained manpower was being wasted in the classic cavalry regiments. All these men were Frenchmen, experienced soldiers, candidates who spoke French and were inherently loyal to their homeland. By now the Aviation Service had become the *élite* force in the French, British, and German armies, for only the airmen were visibly active enough to afford headlines for the war correspondents. The infantry was wallowing deep in the mud and mire of the trenches. The navies had little opposition other than the German submarine menace to intrigue the historians.

Although there was some natural hesitation about allowing the "foreign" volunteers to take flight training, high government officials soon realized that such a move eventually would have important political implications. If it could be shown that a number of Americans were willing to serve with the French, it would first of all convince the neutral world of France's honorable aims in the conflict. Next, it was hoped that any success these American volunteers might have, would be played up in the United States press and perhaps have some influence in attracting America to join the Allies. This last viewpoint turned out to be more important than the sinking of the *Lusitania* or the unrestricted U-boat warfare that raged all through the vast waters of the Atlantic.

History records that in November 1914 an aerial combat near the village of Vailly on the River Aisne was witnessed by a small platoon of American volunteers. Previously they had seen airplanes in normal flight and had watched aircraft of both sides being shelled by antiaircraft fire, but this was the first time any of them had seen two airmen locked in mortal struggle. What type airplanes they saw has not been explained, but, considering the time, they had to be aircraft that carried a machine gunner as well as a pilot, for up until November 1914 there had been no fighter planes, as such. The machine gun had not been synchronized to fire through the propeller. What engagements were fought had to be staged by observers or gunners using light machine guns set on primitive mountings.

As the story goes, Bill Thaw, one of the leading lights of the American group, knew a Lieutenant Brocard who was then in charge of a French squadron operating in that area. Bill actually hiked a distance of thirty-two kilometers to Brocard's field to ask him to intercede for the Americans. Ap-

parently the trip was worth it, for, by mid-December, Bill
Thaw, Jimmy Bach, and Bert Hall left the Foreign Legion and
reported to the Air Service headquarters. There was one solemn moment. Bill who had grown a luxuriant beard in the
trenches and looked for all the world like King Henry VIII,
was ordered to remove it.

Jimmy Bach made the routine trip through the red tape
and tribulation of a headquarters' obstacle course. He was
taught map reading, given a lesson on engine mechanics, and
some primary instruction in aircraft rigging. He did not get
to a flying school until March 10, 1915, when he found himself at Pau. This was a primary field where students ran up
and down the turf aboard "penguin" aircraft, old Blériot
monoplanes with sharply clipped wings. These trainers would
not get off the ground, but gave the pupil some idea of the
controls, how to run the engine, and get the feel of flying. By
the Fourth of July Jimmy had been passed on the old Caudron and given his pilot insignia. He had now reached the
rank of corporal, and, on being transferred to Escadrille
M.S.38 (flying Morane Saulniers), he was sent to the front
on August 29.

The Morane Saulnier was a two-seater monoplane that had
the wing mounted high above the body for "visibility purposes," resulting in its being called the Parasol. It was intended originally for a reconnaissance machine, bearing a
pilot and a trained observer, but gradually a few models were
fitted with two machine guns. One was mounted to fire forward over the wing, and set so the stream of bullets would
clear the arc of the propeller. The second gun, intended for
the use of the passenger, was fitted to a primary type of
flexible mount and could be fired over a fairly wide arc at
enemy planes attacking from the rear or broadside.

Up till the early summer of 1915 air duels as such were rare.
The idea of single combat was not fully appreciated, but here
and there an encounter took place.

It was the destiny of Corporal Jimmy Bach to strike such a
blow for the American contingent. He had been on a long-

distance reconnaissance that had taken him into the vicinity of Mézières and on the way back he met a German Aviatik, homeward bound from a similar mission. Jimmy's observer was a Lieutenant Giroux. In those early days piloting was not considered the premier duty; it was more important that intelligent and accurate information be gathered, and this could be collected only by commissioned officers. The pilot was simply a chauffeur. This was the pattern in the beginning of aerial warfare.

The observer in the German plane fired a long-range burst at the dainty Parasol, a gesture that enraged Jimmy. A second burst was more accurate and slugs ripped through the linen fabric, battered at the engine cowling, and one hissed through the cockpit, nipped at Jimmy's coveralls and made him jump against the snug seat belt.

"Get your gun ready," he yelled at Lieutenant Giroux. The monoplane peeled over into a tight bank and the 80-hp Le Rhone engine screamed under full throttle.

The Aviatik nosed down to get away, but the Parasol was somewhat faster, and as they both continued the dive, Jimmy's Lewis gun snarled in short bursts. The chase was maintained until the French observer was concerned that his pilot would follow the enemy machine all the way back to Berlin if necessary. But Jimmy ignored his entreaties and poured burst after burst into the fleeing Aviatik.

When he had crept up to within seventy-five yards of his target, Jimmy's gun jammed, and he struggled in his seat to reach up and replace the drum, or haul back on the cocking handle to clear the stoppage. As he flew with the stick between his knees he noticed that the German airplane was acting erratically. He took another look and saw that the observer had been hit and was sprawled over his gun.

Jimmy's officer passenger tapped him on the shoulder and pointed at his own weapon. "I'll finish him for you!" Lieutenant Giroux yelled.

Jimmy took the long chance with the frail Morane. Getting the last few revs out of the clanking Le Rhone, he nosed down steeper to gain speed, and then risked everything by hauling up to give Giroux a shot. With every wire strained to the limit and the monoplane wing creaking and showing signs of cruel distortion, Jimmy forced her into a position from where his observer could pour in the finishing touch.

Two short, but accurate, bursts slammed into the Aviatik, the propeller on the Mercedes started to splinter, finally broke up, and the hub ran wild.

"Don't let him get away!" Jimmy pleaded.

Giroux took another careful shot and the Aviatik bounced under the fusillade, pieces of wood, strips of linen, and spatters of dried paint flew off. Another burst and the wings collapsed as if battered by a massive hammer. The plane rolled and the body ripped itself from the tangle and raced on through like a berserk dart. Once clear, the body began to spin, and the runaway engine told its mournful story as it dragged a long greasy plume of smoke down with it.

By now Jimmy Bach was praying that his own fuselage would stay with his wing as he moved to ease down the engine and bring the Morane back to a safe pullout. The Parasol had not been designed for this type of action, but he managed to keep her together and turn back for his own lines. When he opened the throttle again the Le Rhone engine sniffed, choked, and coughed. He possibly had fouled his plugs while easing out of his wild dive, as had happened to so many pilots before. The chase had taken them well inside the German lines, and as matters stood, with the prevailing wind against them, Jimmy knew that he had a long dead-stick glide ahead if he hoped to get into friendly territory.

"You chased him too far," Lieutenant Giroux complained.

"I had to. He would have gotten away."

"Well, I'll admit you got him, but now they'll get us."

"Don't give up so easily," Bach grumbled, and turned back to his controls.

The jagged pattern of trenches and sapheads that was the front line seemed miles away, as the wind blew telltale ground smoke toward the enemy back areas. Risking everything, even a deadly spin that comes with losing flying speed, Jimmy stretched his glide mile after mile. The French lines were ahead now, marked plainly by the dull browns and whites of the various excavations where thousands of infantry-men huddled and watched this little airplane as it fluttered on in its effort to reach safety.

Somehow they made it and their wheels crossed the friendly line with only feet to spare. There was no flat or cleared area anywhere and they thudded and bounced through tangles of barbed wire, and floundered into a number of water-filled shellholes which finished their undercarriage; what was left slithered along on the belly and finally came to a halt. Lieu-tenant Giroux who had been standing up telling Jimmy how to handle this situation, was tossed out and received a broken arm. Jimmy who was well belted in had not a scratch.

On their return to their squadron, after full details had been written out and assayed by the squadron commander, credit for the exploit was given to Corporal Bach who had given chase, delivered the first telling blow, and had "courageously" stayed in action until his observer could destroy the enemy.

This was a great beginning and it was unfortunate that Jimmy could not continue to add to this reputation, but such was not to be.

One of the more unpleasant duties assumed by two-seater squadrons of those days was the delivery of intelligence agents into the enemy lines. These were important missions, but in so many cases ended disastrously.

At dawn on September 23, 1915, Jimmy Bach and a Ser-geant-Pilot Mangeot each took off with two soldiers in their passenger seats, who, wearing civilian clothes and carrying boxes of explosive, were to be dropped near Mézières, with orders to destroy a length of railroad line between Mézières and Hirson. After collecting other vital information they were to make their way back through their own lines as best they could.

Jimmy made sure that all plans were carefully drawn and

that both he and Sergeant Mangeot knew exactly where the landings were to be made. On the map the areas looked reasonably safe, but since the two soldiers had decided where they wished to be dropped, they had considered only their own situation, and had given little thought to the problems of landing aircraft.

When Bach and Mangeot arrived over the drop-spot they saw that the field was very rough with much low brush and several small trees, but they both made good landings and the agents were put down exactly where they wished to be. Jimmy wasted no time since he knew that if he were caught, he could be brought up on serious charges of aiding saboteurs or spies. He was lucky and made a clean take-off, but once in the air he glanced back and was alarmed to see that his sergeant-pilot comrade had wrecked his airplane. He immediately throttled back, curved around again into the wind and decided to pick up his companion. All went well; the sergeant-pilot clambered aboard with real gratitude in his eyes, and settled back for Jimmy's second take-off.

This time their luck ran out. In taxiing over to reach Mangeot, Jimmy had placed himself in a difficult position and in trying to get away quickly, failed to select a clear runway. The Morane Saulnier was just about airborne when a wing tip tripped against a large tree branch. They crashed, but neither was hurt. Realizing what a serious position they were in, they decided to lie low in a hedge until they were certain that the two soldier agents were well clear of that area.

There was plenty of cover and they stayed hidden while they listened to the shouting and general activity of some enemy troops that had been rushed to the area. They sensed that the Germans had found the wrecked planes and were searching for the pilots.

"I hope those agents get away," Jimmy muttered.

Sergeant Mangeot contributed to the concern. "If they find all four of us in the same area, *kaput!* Those soldiers in civilian clothes will be considered spies, and we'll be so judged for flying them in."

"I know, but they get special pay," Jimmy added. "They can afford to take the risk."

Corporal Bach and Sergeant Mangeot crept deeper into the forest. When they became tired and hungry they climbed up into a small bushy tree and rested there for many hours with every muscle screaming for relief from the cramped quarters.

When night fell they crawled down quietly, crept away and found a plowed field. They followed the furrows that led them to the high wall of a farmyard, which they risked entering in the hope of finding a friendly French family and at least obtaining a drink of water. Instead, they stumbled into a group of German soldiers who were huddled around a small campfire.

Mangeot was nabbed before he realized what they had walked into. While he stood bewildered, seven or eight Prussian infantrymen bore him to the ground. Bach, who was in a position to judge what was happening, darted back into the shadows, reversed his field and began to run down a road. Encumbered with heavy boots, a coverall and other flying gear, he was soon exhausted and turned to slip through an opening in a hedge where he walked smack into a whole platoon of German soldiers, ready and waiting with bayonets fixed.

Jimmy had no argument for any of this and surrendered. After some general conversation and inquiry he was marched back to the farmhouse where Mangeot was undergoing a rough interrogation.

"I thought you'd made it, Jimmy," the sergeant-pilot greeted. "I never had a chance."

"I didn't make much of mine," Jimmy growled. "I ran like hell—straight into the muzzles of these jerrys. We're in a sweet mess, eh?"

"I've been praying for several minutes," Mangeot said to reassure the American.

"We'll need all the friends you have—up there."

Bach was in a particularly tough spot for he was an American, a national of a neutral country, and in being captured while wearing a French uniform under his flying coverall, had branded himself as a franc-tireur, a mercenary. The penalty for the conviction of a franc-tireur was the firing squad!

At the time of their capture, regardless of the object of their mission, both Bach and Mangeot were wearing regulation uniforms. Mangeot's indicated that he was a sergeant-pilot, but Bach never bothered to wear any insignia of rank— after all, he was only a corporal. His German captors assumed therefore that any American mercenary would insist on a commission, so he was treated as such for a time, and both men were made comfortable at a German corps headquarters in the ancient French city of Laon.

In the initial interrogations both admitted that the wrecked Moranes were their planes but made no mention of their passengers or the object of their flight. The Germans, however, naturally wondered why two two-seaters could be in the same area, and wrecked in much the same manner but with no evidence that regulation observers had been carried.

Between September 23, when they were captured, and October 20 when a first trial was held, both Bach and Mangeot were kept under heavy guard. By the night of that fateful September 23 their two agents who had eluded capture carried out their task of blowing up a sector of railroad track. It was easy, then, to presume that this had been done by French agents who had been brought into the area by airplane. Bach and Mangeot had admitted flying the two wrecked planes, and there was little they could do but maintain a strict silence.

The first trial was fairly routine, and when Jimmy got up and pleaded his own case, he put on such a show that the court had no basis for convicting either man. It was agreed that the circumstantial evidence was not strong enough, so both were remanded for a second trial slated for October 30. This time the prosecutor was determined that these two spy fliers would not wriggle out of his clutches.

Jimmy Bach knew that they were going to concentrate on him as the American franc-tireur. Fortunately, he managed to gain access to some of his French funds, and he used the money to hire a well-known Berlin lawyer to defend him. While willing to take the American's cash, the German lawyer admitted he could do very little in Jimmy's behalf. During the days between the two trials both Bach and Mangeot dreaded the news that the two railroad-cutting spies had been caught and would implicate them. Fortunately, when the German court convened for the second trial, they were still at large, or had returned to their own side of the line. This left the field clear for the Berlin lawyer, and, to give him credit, his impassioned plea won the day. The judge advocate closed the trial with these words, "By unanimous verdict of this court, the French aviators Bach and Mangeot, accused of espionage, are found not guilty. It is then directed that they be held and confined as honorable prisoners of war."

Whether this came as the result of the Berlin lawyer's convincing plea, or whether the German government decided not to antagonize neutral America, may be debated. The United States government could have protested, had Jimmy been convicted, but there would have been little hope for him. By the time routine and red tape had been overcome and a formal protest worded and delivered, he could have been in his grave for weeks. Jimmy was an enlisted French soldier, regardless of his national status, and any plea that America might have made would have been only a token gesture.

The case possibly set a precedent for all other American citizens who were to serve with the French and British later on. In this, Jimmy Bach contributed more than his own effort —the first enemy plane credited to an American, and a few weeks of front-line service—he also paved the legal path for others to tread when they offered their aid in this Great Adventure.

Once the strain of the trial was over and the two airmen were locked up in a Laon prison, they made plans for their escape, but the day before they had decided to make the break, they were separated. Jimmy wound up in a military prison located in Bavaria, and once more began to figure a way out. His jail was an old fortress-like château built on a high hill, three sides of which were protected by almost perpendicular cliffs, and the one entrance closely guarded. Although getting out of his cell was not too difficult, Jimmy knew that discovery would come soon, and that to escape down that mountain road was almost impossible. Nevertheless, he gave it a try.

A few days later he managed to get a menial job driving a supply wagon into town. He, of course, was guarded closely by an armed soldier, but after playing dumb and docile for several days he had convinced the guard he was harmless, and that continued vigilance was not necessary. The minute the guard's head was turned, Jimmy gave the horses a sudden lash of the whip and leaped down from the seat. Taken unaware, the guard tried to fire after the escaping prisoner, but the horses had broken into a wild gallop, and his aim was very unsteady. Jimmy disappeared into the gloom of the oncoming evening.

Moving carefully, he made his way to a nearby village and took refuge in the house of a woman who had been carrying out some form of underground prisoner-escape system. Jimmy had learned of her through a fellow prisoner at the fortress château. Unfortunately, Jimmy arrived at a time when this Alsace-Lorraine woman had come under suspicion. After receiving a good supper and full details of the safety route out to the Swiss border, he was preparing to leave when suddenly the house was surrounded. Once more Jimmy Bach was in the toils of his captors. Before they marched him away, he was forced to stand shackled while a firing squad executed the woman who had tried to guide him back to the French lines. It was a sight Jimmy Bach never forgot.

On being returned to the Bavarian fortress, he was placed in solitary confinement and then removed to a new prison located at Nuremberg where he made several more unsuccessful attempts to escape. He remained there for the rest of the war, and because of his seniority became Herr Direktor of the Amerikanischer-Kriegsgefangenen Klub. Over the long months of privation Jimmy's once black thatch of thick curly hair thinned away to almost baldness, and what hair remained was snow white when he was finally returned to his comrades.

In February 1959 a man by the name of J. James Buck died in the Latter-day Saints Hospital in Salt Lake City, Utah. He was seventy-four years of age. Mr. Buck had been teaching French at the University of Utah for more than fifteen years. In his obituary it was disclosed that Mr. Buck had used the name of Bach during World War I when he had been a pilot in the French Air Service. He was of Danish descent and had changed his name to the less Germanic Buck at the outset of World War II. The French Government had awarded him the Legion of Honor, the Médaille Militaire, and the Croix de Guerre.

Chapter II

THE BIRTH PANGS

The organization that became the Lafayette Escadrille endured many months of anxious birth pangs. It was not conceived and organized overnight, nor did it evolve as the result of any sudden emotional upheaval. It is a wonder that the French encouraged it in the first place, for any such organization of foreign volunteers was certain to arouse political implications. The United States was jealous of its neutrality, and in many of its industrial cities the populace was pro-German. When scraps of news turned up, official Washington frowned on the idea of Americans volunteering to fight for either side. It was obvious that if any of these "headstrong youngsters" enjoyed success, their exploits would have considerable influence on public opinion in America. For a time this attitude discouraged the French from permitting enlistments in their Air Service. Volunteers for the Foreign Legion could be glossed over, since that bobtail organization for years had been the catchall for drifters from all over the world.

Bill Thaw of Pittsburgh, Pennsylvania, who held an American hydroplane license naturally thought that the Aviation Service would welcome him with open arms, but despite his previous flying experience the French could find no place for him. They had plenty of flying men, 1273 licensed pilots to be exact, but less than one thousand planes of all types.

Bill took this initial rebuff philosophically, and walked out into the street again where he came upon a number of proclamations signed by a group of European writers. They were dated July 31, 1914, and commanded the attention of a number of foreigners, particularly Turks, Russians, Greeks, Belgians, British, Poles, Rumanians, Armenians, Syrians, and a number of Negroes from Martinique. All these men were appealed to to support France in her hour of travail. The impact of these notices struck Bill at once and he immediately gathered a few cronies together and had another proclamation drawn up; one that appealed to all able-bodied Americans in Paris. This was signed by René Phélizot of Chicago, Jules James Bach of St. Louis, James Stewart Carstairs of Philadelphia, and William Thaw of Pittsburgh. It was dated August 5, 1914.

Over the next two weeks, during which time the French Army crossed into Alsace, Britain's Contemptible Little Army landed at Ostend, Dunkirk, and Calais, and the Belgian capital was hurriedly moved from Brussels to Antwerp, foreign patriotic groups swarmed to the French colors. To the amazement of everyone more than eight hundred Germans volunteered to fight in the Foreign Legion against their emperor and homeland. Few of these groups could muster enough men to form a separate corps, and the first American rally brought a wild mixture of self-appointed volunteers of which less than one third were American citizens. More than half of them did not speak English and it was soon evident that a severe weeding-out would have to be done before a reputable offer could be made to the French Government.

At first the French were suspicious of this gesture. Soon after the war broke out both they and the British had had to exercise ceaseless vigilance against German spies who masqueraded as American citizens. Before allowing any so-called neutral access to her flying schools, depots, or front-line squadrons, France gave every candidate a comprehensive examination. As pointed out before, there never was a shortage of applicants for aviation in any of the belligerent countries, and it was natural that preference was given to volunteers who were known, who had some military training, and a reliable national status.

However, there long had been a warm friendship between the United States and France since the days of the Marquis de Lafayette who had fought with the American colonists against the British during the Revolutionary War. This young patriot's experience paralleled somewhat that of the American's 138 years later. A born soldier, Lafayette became a cadet even though his father had been killed at the Battle of Minden in 1759. When the colonies proclaimed their independence he was a captain of dragoons, and "his heart was enrolled in it." Through an American agent, Silas Deane, Lafayette was permitted to join Washington's forces as a major general. Before he could pack up and sail for America, news of grave dangers to the colonial forces was received, and many of Lafayette's friends, including Benjamin Franklin, urged him to abandon his plan. The British then seized the ship he was fitting out at Bordeaux and he was placed under arrest. Later the ship was sent to a port in Spain and Lafayette, in disguise, escaped from custody. A few weeks later he arrived at Georgetown, South Carolina, and offered his services. He was nineteen years of age at the time.

With this in mind the French finally looked with favor on the American volunteers. Thus, when we consider the historical significance of the Lafayette Flying Corps we must bear in mind that the motive that actuated France in permitting its establishment was largely political, but this in no way detracts from the spirit of the men who were to make up this legendary force.

As Emerson once said: "The heroic soul does not sell its justice and its nobleness. It does not ask to dine nicely and to sleep warm. The essence of greatness is the perception that virtue is enough. It does not need plenty, and it can very well abide its loss."

It is generally conceded that Norman Prince of Prides Crossing, Massachusetts, first conceived the idea of forming a squadron of American volunteers to fly with the French. He was a small, compact man with powerful shoulders, blond hair, blue eyes that were far from the 20/20 standard, and at the time sported a shaggy yellow mustache. Prince had a ready smile, tremendous energy, and a winning personality. The scion of a distinguished New England family, he had passed much of his life abroad, and was an indefatigable huntsman. Before the war he had spent several hunting seasons at Pau in the Basses-Pyrénées area, and during those holidays had made many friends and spoke the language fluently.

Like so many others of his stripe he felt he ought to offer his services when war broke out, for he had grown to love France and its people almost as much as his own. He did not take up the cause with the American Field Service, or in the ranks of the Foreign Legion. Norman Prince immediately reacted to the lure of aviation as did so many others who were fine horsemen or keen yachtsmen. For a short time he dallied with the idea of volunteering for the French Air Service, but on second consideration—knowing the real situation—he decided first to become a pilot and then offer his services.

He returned to America and signed up for flight training at the Burgess Flying School at Marblehead, Massachusetts, where he became acquainted with Frazier Curtis, a thirty-year-old enthusiast who also had ideas of helping out the Allies. Curtis had a problem, however. He did not speak French and the idea of joining a force that spoke a foreign language seemed ridiculous, so he decided that it would be simpler to volunteer with the British.

In the meantime Prince and Curtis completed their training on hydroplanes and were fairly proficient as civilian fliers, and took up the Allied cause once more. By then Curtis had already tried to enlist in the British Army but had been turned down because of his citizenship. In those days anyone signing up for any of the British services took a routine oath to "serve the King" as his sovereign. Many Americans assumed this meant relinquishing their own citizenship and thought twice about taking the oath. Later, the phrase "for the duration of the war" was inserted in the enlistment papers, which seemed to satisfy all concerned.

However, Curtis had shied off the British idea, although he did try once more to join the Royal Naval Air Service where he again faced the "loss of citizenship" problem. With that he crossed the Channel and went to Paris to see what could be done in France.

On March 4, 1915, Prince signed enlistment papers for the French Air Service and then hung around for about five weeks awaiting an opening at the Pau flying school. During that time he and Curtis worked day and night to foster their idea of an all-American flying squadron to be attached to the French service. They first sought the interest and aid of several Americans living in Paris, among whom were Robert W. Bliss and Robert Chandler, two enthusiasts who got interviews with important members of the French Ministry of War Office. During one of these busy days Prince encountered Curtis in the lobby of the Hôtel Palais d'Orsay. Frazier advanced the idea of appealing to Jacques and Paul de Lesseps, members of the Air Guard, organized to defend the skies over Paris. The de Lesseps brothers took up the cause with enthusiasm and planned a dinner at which a letter was composed for M. Alexandre Millerand, then Minister of War, offering the services of a group of American airmen.

M. Millerand dashed their hopes with the explanation that no foreign volunteers could be admitted to the flying service, pointing out that owing to its popularity, hundreds of experienced soldiers were already applying for training as pilots.

Both Prince and Curtis realized the hopelessness of their quest and began to reconsider the British situation, but at this point Bliss arranged a meeting with M. Jarousse de Sillac, which turned out to be most fruitful. It was de Sillac, a government official, who saw the important political significance of such an organization and he wrote a letter to a Colonel Bouttieaux at the French Ministry of War Office. In it he explained:

I beg to transmit to you, herewith attached, the names of six young men, citizens of the United States of America, who desire to enlist in the French Aviation—an offer which was not accepted by the Minister of War. Permit me to call your attention to this matter, insisting on its great interest. It appears to me that there might be great advantages in the creation of an American Squadron. The United States would be proud of the fact that certain of her young men, acting as did Lafayette, have come to fight for France and civilization. The resulting sentiment of enthusiasm could have but one effect: to turn the Americans in the direction of the Allies. There is a precedent in the Legion of Garibaldi, which has had an undeniably good influence on Franco-Italian relations. If you approve of these considerations, I am confident that it will be possible to accept these young men and to authorize their enlistment in such a manner that they may be grouped under the direction of a French chief. In doing this you will contribute to the happiness of these six Americans.

The six Americans to whom M. de Sillac referred were Norman Prince, Frazier Curtis, Elliott Cowdin, William Thaw, Bert Hall, and James Bach.

The letter brought the following response from Colonel Bouttieaux by February 24, 1915:

I think that your candidates will be welcomed. They should contract an engagement in the French Army for the duration of the war, and should agree to fly only the aeroplanes customarily used in the French Aviation Service.

Bach, Hall, and Thaw were already serving in the French Army, and had effected their transfer to the Aviation Service after about four months of front-line service in the Foreign Legion. Furthermore, they had been under training at Buc (Seine-et-Oise). Prince, Curtis, and Cowdin were sent to Pau where training facilities had been set up for them. They were soon joined by Jimmy Bach and Bert Hall, after Prince had requested their transfer. Bill Thaw had flown as a civilian before the outbreak of war, and on his transfer from the Foreign Legion naturally made fast progress. By Christmas Eve, 1914, he had been relieved of further flight training and posted to the French D.6 Squadron then flying Deperdussin two-seater monoplanes, a prehistoric kite powered with an 80-hp Gnome rotary engine. By no stretch of the imagination could this be considered a military plane, but it did carry a machine gun for the use of the observer-gunner. The term "machine gun" in this case meant light carbines or automatic pistols. Thaw began his interesting career as an aerial gunner but soon tired of this unrewarding business and requested pilot duty.

He was sent to the Saint-Cyr-l'Ecole where he had some training on the old Caudron G-II, another prewar biplane, powered with the same 80-hp Gnome. Bill Thaw quickly mastered this two-seater and was moved on to Le Bourget where he was retained for some time as a corporal pilot, flying commissioned officers who were learning to be aviation observers.

By March 20, 1915, Thaw had learned that Norman Prince had set up plans for the origination of an American squadron. Thaw has never claimed credit for the formation of the Lafayette Escadrille; instead, he was uninterested at first and moved to be posted to a front-line squadron where he could get real action. When he was ordered to join the Americans at Pau, he thundered into the French Ministry of War Office and again demanded to be sent to the front, and was so vehement he was assigned immediately to C.42 Squadron which was operating outside Nancy, and later from Lunéville.

There he flew regularly, and was promoted to sergeant and cited twice in Army Orders.

Norman Prince and Elliott Cowdin were also sent to the front as pilots in a Voisin squadron. Cowdin, who had been in the American Field Service, met Prince in Paris, and caught Prince's enthusiasm for the Escadrille Américaine idea. On his next trip up to the line to drive back wounded soldiers, Elliott encountered a Colonel Barrés, then Chief of Aeronautics in the Army Zone. Colonel Barrés promised to lend his full support to the plan of assembling a group of Americans into one unit. Cowdin relayed this news to Prince who by this time was becoming discouraged with the way things were going. Cowdin, who was completely sold on the idea, also worked his transfer to the French Aviation, and by April 29 had won his wings on the Voisin. On May 3 he was assigned to VB.108, a so-called bombing squadron. Between that time and April 28, 1916, he served with three Nieuport fighter squadrons.

In December 1915, Cowdin, along with Thaw and Prince, went on leave to the United States. Their visit home had considerable impact on American opinion. At first all three fliers were lauded, publicized—and then denounced. Supporters of the Allied cause used them as fine examples of what America could do against the common enemy. On the other hand German sympathizers—and there were thousands of them—asked that all three men be interned because of their violation of American neutrality. The sinking of the *Lusitania* the previous May had been all but forgotten.

Meanwhile the French government, mindful of the great interest created by these three Americans, regarded the furlough as excellent diplomacy and realized that a full squadron of American volunteers at the front would have an important influence on public opinion in the United States. A few months later, April 20, 1916, when the first squadron, listed as the Escadrille Américaine, reached the front as Nieuport 124, Elliott Cowdin was included. Within a week he had won the Médaille Militaire for his showing in combat

against a large German patrol formation, one of which he
shot down. He was the first American to win this French
honor.

Over the dreary weeks and months as Prince and his comrades awaited some response to their original request, another
American civilian, Dr. Edmund L. Gros, then one of the heads
of the American Field Service, had been thinking, quite independently, of the possibility of forming a squadron of
American airmen. A number of his countrymen had already
distinguished themselves in the Foreign Legion, and there
were many more in his ambulance group who were eager to
be in a more active branch of service.

Dr. Gros learned one day that Frazier Curtis had been
making a canvas of American ambulance drivers to learn if
any of them were interested in volunteering for the proposed
Escadrille Américaine. Later on Curtis wrote the following letter to him:

Dear Dr. Gros,

I went to the Ambulance today to see if I could find any drivers
who wanted to join the French Aviation Service. The government
is willing to train 100 American flyers and to keep them together
in one corps. Men of flying experience would be preferred, but
those of apparent aptitude (knowing French, gas engines, etc.)
will be acceptable. Mr. Frechon tells me you are keen on getting
up a big corps, so we ought to be able to work together. I would
like to introduce you to one of my friends who is running this
enlarged corps. I am here on sick leave, three accidents having
left me pretty well jarred up. I expect to go to the seaside for a
good rest in a day or two, but I am anxious to see you first.

Sincerely yours,
FRAZIER CURTIS.

Thus, it was through Curtis that Dr. Gros learned of Prince's
trials and tribulations. He was also introduced to M. de
Sillac. Because the good doctor's duties kept him in Paris and
he was fluent in French, he naturally became the spokesman
for the aviation volunteers, and his home at 23 Avenue du

Bois de Boulogne became an unofficial headquarters for the organization. Gros and de Sillac interviewed French authorities, aroused the interest of other prominent Americans, and kept the project moving toward realization. Later on, a committee was formed with M. de Sillac as president, Dr. Gros as vice-president, and Frederick Allen to represent the organization in America.

Another American seldom mentioned in Lafayette history is William K. Vanderbilt who began as a guiding light in the early days of the American Field Service and furnished funds that established a rest house in Paris for the volunteer workers where Mrs. Vanderbilt devoted much time and personal attention to the men who but a few hours before had been under heavy shellfire along the Marne.

Mr. Vanderbilt had spent much time abroad, realized the significance of the French cause, and was strongly opposed to America's neutrality. He admired the young Americans who were fighting in the Foreign Legion and took great interest in their welfare.

In December 1915, Dr. Gros presented the plan for the formation of an American flying squadron, and the Vanderbilts immediately agreed to support the work, and made a generous contribution to the committee's funds. From that time on until long after the Armistice Mr. Vanderbilt assumed most of the financial responsibilities of the volunteer organization. Monthly allowances were given to those who turned up with no personal funds, and some were given money with which to order suitable uniforms and underclothing. He appreciated the influence the group would have on public opinion in America, particularly if his country were drawn into the conflict. Right from the start he planned to enlarge the organization, regardless of the cost, and as the numbers grew he assumed willingly the added financial burden. Dr. Gros said that Mr. Vanderbilt's generosity must have brought in at least one hundred pilots to the Lafayette group.

On October 9, 1918, the French Government conferred upon Mr. Vanderbilt the Cross of the Legion of Honor, the citation stating: "The Government of the Republic is happy to express its appreciation and gratitude to one of the citizens of America, who, from the very first hour, has been a warm and valued friend to France."

Despite this organization's effort and long hours of work, very little was accomplished; week after week passed with little or no progress to report. Finally, on July 8, 1915, General Hirschauer, Chief of French Military Aeronautics, was tendered an invitation to a luncheon at the home of Senator Menier, and it was here that General Hirschauer was persuaded to use his influence in the formation of an American squadron. The proposed name, Escadrille Américaine, was also accepted. But with all this, matters continued to move with the speed of sluggish molasses, and it was not until August 21, 1915, that the Ministry of War and the Ministry of Foreign Affairs agreed that the Escadrille Américaine should be handled by a Franco-American committee composed of General Hirschauer, Colonel Bouttieaux, Senator Menier, Leon Bourgeous, Robert M. Bacon, M. de Sillac, Dr. Gros, and Dr. William White of Philadelphia.

By October 28 some further advance was made when M. René Besnard, Sub-Secretary of State for Military Aeronautics, wrote asking for more details on the committee's plan of action. From that point on progress was marked by the continued exchange of polite notes, formal requests and dignified responses, but little actual advance was made until December 1915, when a letter from M. Besnard disclosed that after considerable correspondence with the officials of the infantry some concessions had been made concerning the many American volunteers who were serving with the Foreign Legion. In this letter was a plan that allowed them to transfer to the Aviation Service if they could pass the required physical examination. The transfer was to be rescinded on the demand of the military authorities in the case of proven inaptitude for service with the flying personnel of the Military Aviation.

General Hirschauer had promised to give orders for the

formation of an American squadron in July 1915, but the
months rolled along and the war continued its doleful course.
The American steamer *Leelanaw* was torpedoed off Scotland.
Warsaw was captured by the Germans. The ill-fated Gallipoli
campaign was entering its second phase with British troops
scrambling into Suvla Bay. The White Star Line steamer *Arabic* was torpedoed and sunk off Fastnet Light, Ireland, and a
force of Austro-Germans had taken the Russian fortress of
Brest-Litovsk.

That September every day brought news of new defeats
and setbacks. In Belgium the Germans shot Edith Cavell, a
British nurse who had been aiding British prisoners of war to
escape. London was again bombarded by Zeppelins. Henry
Ford, with a large party of American peace advocates set sail
for Europe aboard the *Oscar II*, hoping to bring an end to the
carnage. Eighteen days later the automobile manufacturer returned to America, leaving the group and the Peace Ship in
Christiania—now Oslo—Norway.

The year 1915 passed and 1916 saw the bombing of both
London and Paris by Zeppelins. Fort Douaumont near Verdun
fell to continued German onslaughts, and the enemy stepped
up his U-boat campaign, sinking anything that came within
the scope of his torpedoes.

A special plea was made to have Robert Soubiran, Wil-
liam E. Dugan, Jr., Pierre Boal, Marius Rocle, and Frederick
Zinn, young Americans who were still serving with various
French infantry regiments, transferred for aviation training.
At this point all planning had to be reconsidered when a
Colonel Régnier was made Director of Aeronautics, filling a
new post in the bureau.

Fortunately, Colonel Régnier welcomed the idea and by
March 14, 1916, sent a note to the committee in which he
said that he had known of the proposed American squadron,
and had made further inquiries with the Commander-in-Chief.
"General Headquarters has just replied, informing me that an
American squadron will be formed with the pilots whose
names follow: William Thaw, Elliott Cowdin, Kiffin Rock-

well, Norman Prince, Charles C. Johnson, Clyde Balsley, Victor Chapman, Laurence Rumsey, and James R. McConnell. I have every reason to believe that the squadron will be constituted rapidly, and I will keep you posted as to what is done in this matter," Régnier concluded.

A short time later the pilots, some of whom were in service with French squadrons, were ordered to Le Plessis-Belleville, then one of the important aviation depots a short distance north of Paris. On April 20, 1916, the Escadrille Américaine, as it was first known, was placed officially on the French roster as N.124 Squadron and ordered to the front.

The training provided the American volunteers was unlike that experienced by student pilots of any other flying service, before or since. From all accounts, once they were accepted for flight training, that is exactly what they got—nothing more. Those of us who volunteered to serve with the British in those early days may be pardoned if we appear perplexed at the simplicity of their routine.

Students in the Royal Flying Corps, no matter what their previous service, first went through a six-weeks' ground school course that included stiff physical training, the rigging of an airplane, Morse telegraphy, theory of aviation engines, aerial navigation, map reading, and interior economy. Once that was out of the way several weeks were spent at a special machine-gun school where the intracacies, repair, and handling of both fixed and movable guns were learned. Before even touching an airplane we were taught practically all there was to know about all types of aircraft engines, and had much experience in running radials, rotaries, and in-line engines while sitting in test cockpits on the ground. Thus, when we were finally allowed to get aboard a training plane, we were reasonably familiar with the power plants, instruments, the controls of an aircraft, and any armament we might encounter in our primary training.

The German student pilot had much the same routine, and

later on when the United States entered the war, American flight training followed this general pattern.

Not so with the French Aviation.

Once the American candidates arrived at Avord aviation school they apparently enjoyed comparative freedom of action. Beyond appearing at the hangars at stipulated hours for flight training, they had little to do except make themselves comfortable. There was no parade-ground drill, no guard duty, no sharing the work of the kitchen staff or any of the manual toils of the average recruit. At least, no mention is made by any of the candidates of those days, and it can be presumed that none of these chores was endured, since much would have been made of such indignities.

On arrival at Avord the volunteers usually reported to a primary instructor who was generally found reclining in a deck chair. Here the recruits seem to have trained themselves, beginning with the Blériot "penguin" aircraft that had clipped wings. Once the engine was started, the propeller would pull the clipped-wing device up and down the field. Actually, this was not easy since the slightest irregularity in the ground, or cross wind would make the "penguin" almost unmanageable, but it gave the students a chance to handle an aircraft engine—a three-cylindered Anzani—and learn how to control the *avion* on the ground. Some students experienced considerable difficulty in this craft, while others, indicating a sure touch and instinctive feel, soon passed this test.

From the "penguin" they graduated to a "roller," another training device that had larger wings, and once brought up to full speed might conceivably get off the ground. The students were told not to fly them, but the French instructors usually winked when they made this admonishment; as a result many got their first actual flying experience while racing these "rollers" up and down the wide acreage, and unquestionably enjoyed some true feel of aircraft controls.

It may seem unbelievable today, but the American volunteers seldom had any dual-control training with an instructor.

Once they had a few "unauthorized" flights with the "roller" they passed into a period known as *tour de piste,* which meant they were allowed to fly a full-scale Blériot monoplane—actually a model of the type first flown by Louis Blériot across the English Channel in 1909—and were encouraged to cruise about the field at an altitude of six hundred feet. In this they learned to use rudder and ailerons, make simple turns, and gain more confidence. What crashes they suffered were usually the outcome of careless sideslips, but seldom resulted in personal damage. The student soon learned to avoid these mistakes and probably learned fast. Whether he developed serious flying habits that might have been noted and checked by an instructor is a question. However, those who were to go to two-seater observation or bomber squadrons probably had to get their final training under competent instructors who soon corrected any bad flying habits their pupils had developed.

Before the Avord course was finished all students had to make two triangular cross-country flights of approximately one hundred fifty miles each. The route was flown from Avord to Châteauroux to Romorantin. The countryside was beautiful to the eye, but the area became the graveyard of more than fifty students, many of them American volunteers. Some explanation will be found in the fact that on these cross-country exercises the beginners found themselves away from familiar landmarks, and easily became lost. Some were trapped by sudden changes of weather, for meteorology was not the science it is today. Others experienced engine trouble, lost their heads and set up crashes that need never have happened.

Once the primary training had been completed, small groups were moved off to Pau in southern France where they were given more advanced flying, a course that included some military acrobatics. Here, too, there seems to have been little parade-ground discipline and scant extra duty. Meals were furnished on a very flexible schedule, and the Americans

who had a few extra francs in their pockets usually sought out
nearby civilians who would provide hot chocolate, omelets,
and heaping platters of French fried potatoes.

At Pau the candidates were presumed to be pilots and had
earned their collar wings, corporals' chevrons, and the
wreathed-wing insignia awarded to military aviators. By now
most of them had new tailored uniforms, for after their
arduous life at Avord they were awarded seven days' leave,
usually spent in Paris. Most of this time was passed at Henry's
or at the Chatham where all wing-wearing aviators gathered
to hear the latest from the front, or to toast the newest air
hero.

It was at Pau that they encountered the eighteen-meter
Nieuports, the trainer type with more wing area than the
Nieuport Scout that was being flown at the front line at that
time. In their first lesson they were given a lecture in which
they were told *how* to do vertical spirals, sometimes called
spins or spinning nose dives. This period also took its toll, for
many students were not psychologically attuned to this tricky
maneuver and never knew when to pull out; others were
heavy-handed and literally ripped off the Nieuport's wings in
coming out of the spin. The trick was to put the machine into
a spiral and complete five turns within nine hundred feet.
These had to be spun both to the right and the left before the
student was considered to be accomplished in the feat. Most
of the training at Pau was concentrated on this maneuver,
and, once it was carried out almost automatically, the student
was given a fifteen-meter Nieuport, and all he had learned
previously, was carried out aboard this front-line type machine until the instructor—still sitting in a deck chair—was
satisfied that the candidate was making progress. If anyone
showed undue caution or outright dread, the instructor
climbed into his own personal airplane and put on a display
that left the students aghast, but convinced that practically
any maneuver could be made with the plane.

The finished pilots were sent from Pau to the Groupe des

Divisions d' Entraînement (G.D.E.), the Pilots' Pool or clearing station for all aviators destined for the front. G.D.E. was located at Plessis-Belleville in the Zone des Armées of northern France, about thirty miles from Paris. At Plessis there were fields that provided every type of war-front plane: Voisins, Breguets, Sopwiths, twin-engined Caudrons, Letords, Morane Parasols, and Nieuports. Pilots awaiting assignment could keep their hands in, or try out many other types, chiefly to add time to their logbooks. The average time the fully trained pilot spent at Plessis-Belleville before his active-service orders came through was about three weeks.

Most of the American volunteers stayed at the ramshackle Hôtel de la Bonne Rencontre located near the railroad station of the town. This ancient hostelry was noted for its hideous wallpapers, the diversity of bedbugs, dust and grime, and the most amazing collection of beds in all Europe. Everyone who stayed there retained a lifelong affection for the place, and for years the proprietress, Mme. Rodel, was deluged with letters from her wartime patrons. For those who lived through the war, the days spent at Plessis were remembered as the happiest of their lives. There they sensed the tang of battle, heard the hottest rumors and learned who had "gone west," and who had added to his bag. Life at G.D.E. was frantic, yet serene with the feeling that at last one had become part of the war. It was "just over there" where you could see those kite balloons, the smoke of battle, and at night hear the roar of the guns.

At Plessis the volunteers enjoyed the spirit of being above the routine and bog of stationary warfare. One did not have to consider the deadly snake of trenches that writhed from the North Sea to Switzerland. Flying men were the younger gods of Mars, and they gloried in their reigns, however short. Their battle gear was a suit of pile-lined coveralls, jaunty gloves, and fleece-lined boots, topped off with a soft leather helmet and glistening Meyrowitz goggles. They shouldered no rifles, bayonets, or entrenching tools; nor were they encumbered with steel helmets, gas masks, knapsacks, or mess kits. A simple leather belt filled all requirements when on leave or wandering about the back-area towns. The fields and sky lanes of Armageddon were just over the horizon.

This long-awaited climax was first celebrated with a dinner held in Paris and among those present were Norman Prince, the actual founder of the squadron; Bill Thaw, Victor Chapman, Kiffin Rockwell, James McConnell, Clyde Balsley, Charles Chouteau Johnson, and Laurence Rumsey, all proudly wearing French Air Service insignia.

After dinner that evening, Prince, Chapman, Rockwell, and McConnell left for Luxeuil-les-Bains where N.124 was to begin its active service. A short time later they were joined by Thaw, Cowdin, and Bert Hall. These seven men became the nucleus of the Escadrille Américaine. These facts and data are offered in hope they will clear up the many misunderstandings and incorrect claims concerning the origination of this American organization.

On their arrival at Luxeuil-les-Bains they were greeted by Captain Georges Thénault who had been appointed as the French commander of the squadron. Automobiles transported them from the station to the field, a luxury compared to their students days at Pau when they had to walk six miles to deliver and collect their laundry. This fact in itself gives some insight to the types these men were. Professional soldiers would have rigged up a small tub of water and laundered their own clothing.

The French, it must be said, left no stone unturned to make the volunteers welcome. The hangars and aircraft—Nieuport Scouts—were brand new, as were the fifteen Fiat trucks, the squadron office, and the rest tents. There was a young army of mechanics, chauffeurs, armorers, motorcyclists, telephone clerks, wireless operators, medical orderlies, and administration clerks. Barracks, as such, were out. The pilots were assigned rooms in a villa adjoining the hot baths of Luxeuil. Regardless of their rank they ate their meals with their officers, Captain Thénault and Lieutenant de Laage de Meux, at the best hotel in town. An automobile always was on hand to carry them back and forth from their quarters to the flying field.

James McConnell said, "Golly, I began to wonder whether I was a summer resorter or a soldier. But much of that was soon knocked out of me when we were introduced to a Captain Happe, commander of a bombardment group nearby. After shaking hands he pointed to eight boxes on a table. 'They are Croix de Guerre for the families of the men I lost on my last raid,' he explained and then added, 'It's a good thing you're here to go along with us for protection. There are a lot of Boches in this sector.'"

The French officers assigned to the Escadrille Américaine wisely motored their new pilots through several areas of the Vosges Mountains to show them the general countryside and point out spots where emergency landings might be made. From an automobile the scenery was glorious, Le Val d'Ajol unbelievable. The steep mountain sides bristled with a solid mass of giant pines, glittering cascades tumbled down through great avenues of foliage and became one roaring torrent at the foot of the slopes.

But this was a pleasant aside to the days of danger and drudgery ahead. There were to be hours of continual flying and dozens of short sorties over the enemy line to get the feel of action and learn how to face up to the barrage of antiaircraft fire. The latter was not to be ignored or laughed off. Jerry was getting more accurate every day and his high-angled equipment, for the time being at least, was superior to anything the Allies had produced. It was simple, and considered "professional" to sneer at enemy aircraft but within a few days Bill Thaw's Nieuport was hit when he was cruising about at thirteen thousand feet. More important, more than one American volunteer was to go down before German antiaircraft fire.

Chapter III

FIRST SORTIES

The Nieuport 17-C1 of 1916 that was assigned to the Americans was among the first of the Allied single-seaters designed to fire a fixed machine gun along its line of flight. Previously, machine guns had been mounted wherever convenient, their firing, efficiency, and arcs of fire not having been considered seriously.

Many American accounts of World War I give the impression that German aircraft were the first to appear on the front with a fixed front-firing gun, and careless historians have repeated over and over that the Dutch inventor, Anthony Fokker, conceived and produced the first front-firing gun, a device that gave the Germans a tremendous advantage in aerial fighting.

This is not so.

Fixed, front-firing guns were in use some time before the Fokker gear was thought of. The French airman Eugene Gilbert worked out a fixed-gun idea early in the war, and it was Roland Garros, a compatriot, who perfected and used Gilbert's invention. It was he who began the "ace" race by shooting down five German planes with a Morane monoplane that had been fitted with his device. Garros used a simple feature that allowed the gun to fire through the whirling blades of the propeller; a sleeve of thin armor plate was bolted around the boss end of the propeller, deflecting any bullets that did strike the rotating prop. This device was effective for a few weeks until Garros was forced down inside the German lines with a stalled engine and the enemy learned how his "magic" trick of firing through the propeller had been accomplished.

The British were also using a front-firing gun. All through early 1915 they employed a number of light pusher-type aircraft, notably the D.H.2, a light, fast monoplane that mounted a Lewis gun fixed to fire forward from the nacelle. Since the engine and propeller were aft, there was no need for an inter- rupter gear between the weapon and the propeller. In many cases this gun was mounted flexibly, so that the pilot was not confined to shooting dead ahead but could aim it over a fairly wide arc. This type of mounting was in use on many British and French aircraft in 1915–16. Admittedly, the Fokker gun gear was the first reliable system that controlled the rate of fire to the revolutions of the propeller, but it did not furnish as great an advantage as has been claimed.

The phrase "Fokker Fodder" was a convenient alliteration, but had little basis in fact. Germany's important advantage in the air was the result of their selecting the battleground. They seldom crossed the Allied lines on offensive patrols. A few— very few—hurried photography flights were attempted, but little daylight air bombing was made against Allied ground forces in France or Belgium. The British and French airmen therefore had to go deep into enemy lines to obtain any ac- tion, and most air fights were staged in an area where the west wind was the prevailing influence during the action.

It was easy for the Germans to run up accredited scores. What Allied planes they shot down usually fell in their ter- ritory, but German planes destroyed by Allied airmen were difficult to claim, for it was generally agreed that at least two other members of each formation would have to assert that the enemy aircraft actually had been demolished. There must have been dozens of situations where German pilots were wounded severely in air fights, but were able to with- draw from the action and attempt to get back to their fields. Perhaps they did, but in many cases they crashed some time after the original action. There must have been instances where these wounded pilots may have reached their bases, and then died of their wounds, or were so badly injured they never flew again. They were as surely out of action as if they had been shot down in flames.

From the Allied point of view, their pilots not only faced enemy air opposition, but also risked engine failure, or lack of

fuel after long flights into enemy territory, or long, drawn-out
combats with German formations. In these cases they might
land their aircraft and be uninjured themselves, but they were
lost to the cause. In some such instances German pilots would
note these lame-duck planes and follow them down for easy
shots, or escort them in and claim "victories."

A similar situation arose during World War II when great
fleets of German fighters and bombers attacked Britain, and
the "few" of the R.A.F. ran up impressive "ace" scores. As
soon the tide turned and British and American fighter and
bomber forces ranged over German cities, Hitler's airmen ran
up astronomical kills. There are several who claim to have
downed 250 planes. Many of their victories were scored
against airmen and aircraft that had been damaged by antiaircraft fire, or had run out of fuel, and had to land in enemy
or occupied territory.

In the spring of 1916 the flying equipment on both sides
was fairly well balanced. The Germans had the best fighting
scout in the Albatros D-1 biplane, a rugged machine that was
powered with a 160-hp Mercedes engine. The D-1 was the
first single-seater to be armed with two fixed machine guns,
a practice that was to become general on both sides of the
line for the rest of the war. This early Albatros had a top
speed of 110 mph, was not too maneuverable, but would take
severe punishment. Later on the Albatros D-3, a sesquiplane
with greater power was adopted, and because of the narrow-
chord lower wing, was known as a vee-strutter, since it had
a vee-type strut between the upper and lower planes, a support similar to the vee strut of the Nieuport scout. Some
French experts claimed that the Albatros had been copied
from the Nieuport, but if it had, considerable improvement in
structure and ruggedness had been added.

This Albatros enjoyed the enviable quality of often being
mistaken for the Nieuport because of the vee strut. All too
many Allied airmen mistook the D-3 for a friendly French
scout and went about their business only to discover, usually
too late, that the vee-strutter was in fact an enemy airplane

and that its bullets were cutting away wings or hammering an engine to useless junk.

Generally speaking the Albatros D-3 was "all wood" since the wings and fuselage were built up on a self-braced wooden framework and covered with three-ply. Only the small control surfaces, rudder, ailerons, and elevators were covered with fabric. This improved D-3 played an important role in the "Bloody April" offensive of 1917. The famous Baron Manfred von Richthofen scored many of his early victories in the Albatros models, but later he preferred the Fokker triplane.

Other German fighters on the front that contended with the American volunteers included the Fokker D-2, an orthodox biplane powered with the 130-hp Oberursel rotary engine. This model was produced to meet the highly maneuverable scouts being turned out by the French and British that used the Le Rhone rotary power plants. The high speed of these engines with their main weight whirling around a master crankshaft, afforded a strong torque power that was used in right-hand turns. No stationary type engine could produce this trick, and the Germans not only tried a rotary-engined scout, but completely copied the French Le Rhone engine. However, the Fokker D-2 failed to satisfy Oswald Boelcke, commander of Germany's "Boelcke's Circus," and was quickly discarded. A new model, the D-3, replaced it.

In the meantime the Halberstadter Flugzeugewerke brought out the Halberstadt biplane scout, a machine that for a time threatened to monopolize the air. This startling airplane was powered with either the 120-hp Argus or the 170-hp Mercedes. It was armed with either one or two synchronized machine guns, and had it been able to keep its tail assembly intact during violent maneuvers, or against enemy machine-gun fire, it might have become a very valuable aircraft. Later models were attempted, with no better result, and the company eventually used all the best features of the scout and built them into a two-seater, the CL-2, which late in 1917 became an important two-seater fighter and ground-attack airplane.

In 1916 the British service was undergoing a state of transition from which a number of excellent aircraft were evolved. At the same time their designers were improvising in a manner which the British deemed most competent. They were more than holding up their end with several almost obsolete models. Many R.F.C. squadrons were doing very well with the light and very maneuverable Sopwith Pup, a radial-engined biplane that carried a fixed machine gun, geared to the prop through the Sopwith-Kauper gear. This outdated model, a delight to fly under any circumstances, ran up an impressive score despite its low power and limited armament. It played a heroic role during the battles of Ypres, Messines, and Cambrai. Later on it was the nemesis of the German kite balloon squadrons. All pilots who flew the Pup during the war delighted in its ability to maintain altitude no matter how violent the maneuver.

Other single-seater squadrons did well with the de Havilland-2, the pusher fighter previously mentioned. Owing to a shortage of scout aircraft early in 1916 the British adopted temporarily the French Nieuport Scout and equipped seven squadrons with these machines. But with the advent of the Albatros planes much of the fighter work had to be assumed by the two-seater F.E.2b pusher type that carried a skilled aerial gunner as well as the pilot. Before the year was out, however, the Sopwith triplane, a valuable machine, was added to the R.F.C. fleet, disproving the popular fallacy that the triplane fighter was developed by the Germans. The Sop-Tripe, as it was affectionately known, appeared months before the Fokker Dreidekker was heard of.

The French relied heavily on their Nieuports for all single-seater missions since the much publicized Spad did not appear as an experimental model until July 1916, and the standard mount, the Spad-7, did not turn up in squadron strength until well into 1917. It was the Nieuport-17 model that was carrying the burden of the French fighter squadrons by the time the Escadrille Américaine was first established. It was not an outstanding aircraft, but it had certain features that endeared it to hundreds of airmen of the day.

However, the Nieuport was notoriously frail. Like the Sopwith Pup, it was delightful to fly in standard maneuvers and in good hands could hold its own with anything, but it had a tendency to shed its wings in high-speed dives. It had a standard wooden frame that was wire-braced and fabric-covered. The lower wings had a single main spar that gave the vee-strut design and racy appearance to the little gadfly. It was powered with a 110-hp Le Rhone radial engine that attained a maximum speed of 113 mph, and here again the high torque gave it fast, tight-turning qualities, but in the early models its fighting ability was limited by the makeshift armament system.

In the original Nieuport scouts, the type furnished by the French for the American volunteers, only one Lewis machine gun was available and this was equipped with the infantry-type ammunition drum that carried but forty-seven rounds. Later on Lewis drums for aviation weapons were deepened to contain ninety-seven rounds. Furthermore, the gun was set on a fixed bracket above the top plane, allowing it to fire clear of the arc of the propeller blades, but in some of these mountings it was impossible to tilt the weapon in order to replace an empty drum, so the fighter pilot with this early equipment went into action with only forty-seven rounds of ammunition. The bracket was improved later and given a hinge that permitted the airman to tilt it down toward him and remove the empty drum, a difficult and cumbersome arrangement at best.

By October 1916, Captain H. A. Cooper and a Sergeant Foster of Number 11 Squadron, R.F.C., then flying Nieuports, devised a rail mounting that allowed the pilot to draw back the gun and tilt it to replace the ammunition pan. The weapon was secure at all times and some Nieuport pilots, notably the famed Captains Albert Ball and Billy Bishop, used this gun device to fire up at enemy planes above them.

Considering everything, the Americans did not walk into an aerial picnic. The opposition did most of its fighting well over its own side of the line, they had better equipment, and

their planes were better armed. French training, as far as air
fighting was concerned, was not well organized. Formation
work and team tactics were not for the Gallic temperament;
their aims were more often devised along individualistic lines
rather than in general squadron effort. The British were better organized and performed in a businesslike manner, running regular patrols daily, weather permitting, and wherever
possible played down the individual and sustained the squadron effort. Teamwork and prescribed maneuvers designed to
overcome the enemy were regular features of British training,
and their fighters were more often employed on bomber-
escort, and Army-co-operation work, rather than in the hap-
hazard business of shooting down their opposite numbers just
to run up high scores. Americans who served with the British
flying services have pointed this out, and stated that they
learned more about war flying with their British cousins than
with any other Allied organization.

In spite of their inherent love for their French comrades
and their wholehearted concern for the French cause, the
original pilots of Escadrille Américaine were handicapped to
some extent by the language barrier. Although they had a
program of routine training comparable to that provided by
any other in the French service, and several of their group
spoke French fluently, they did not think in French. Whatever theories or advice were offered, were given in French
and then had to be translated mentally into English. This
was not easy and in many cases these American volunteers
sought further advice and experience from the British.

This I remember clearly for early in 1917 small groups of
the then Lafayette Escadrille landed on our field at Estrée-
Blanche to mingle with the aces of Number 56 Squadron, and
with the pilots and observers of my own Number 22 Squadron, Royal Flying Corps. I saw Raoul Lufbery, Bill Thaw, and
Didier Masson arrive at our field with their new Spads that
carried the American Indian insignia. They talked for hours,
although at the time there were no Americans in either Num-

ber 56 or Number 22. They simply wanted information and
advice. These two squadrons were experienced and had flown
hundreds of front-line patrols and were expert in all forms of
co-operation work. It was all this that they wished to know,
and whether they learned anything or not, it cannot be ignored that at this period the Lafayette Escadrille was reaching the peak of its history.

The Escadrille Américaine was soon taken on its first sortie
as a unit. Captain Thénault had decided that they should do
an early-morning patrol, and everyone was ordered out on the
line by 6 A.M. This flight turned out to be something of a
scramble for no plans had been made for maintaining a regular formation. Jimmy McConnell said he had never flown
above seven thousand feet and always had trouble keeping
other airplanes in sight, so once they were off the ground, he
pulled up higher than the others and flew along alone from
where he could keep his eyes on the planes below.

This morning of May 14, 1916, was misty with small groups
of cloud here and there, and as soon as Jimmy popped into
one of these he quickly lost the rest of the group. Flying alone
above a layer of white that reminded him of crossing an
Arctic ice field, he began to feel some concern, but gradually
his companions popped up through the layer and one by
one rejoined the so-called formation.

Over Belfort they identified the French trenches, and then,
after drawing the stragglers together, Captain Thénault took
his fledglings over the line. The cloud bank was left behind,
ahead ranged the Alsace plain stretching toward the Rhine.
Now flying at thirteen thousand feet, Jimmy McConnell
identified Dannemarie and the gaunt trench areas of the
Germans. But this delightful isolation was soon shattered.
Two blobs of black smoke appeared ahead, followed by two
crashing explosions. Jimmy crouched in his cockpit just as
more of these antiaircraft shells erupted all around them. The
smoke regurgitated stabbing jets of scarlet flame and then

gave off a telltale stain, white, yellow, or green indicating what type of shells were being fired.

"Funny thing," Jimmy said later. "After the first two or three, the roar of my engine took over, and the whole opposition business became quite impersonal."

After crossing the line Thénault turned north and the town of Mulhouse spread itself below. The twin lakes of Gérardmer sparkled in the early morning light, and as the morning lengthened, they noted ground activity and heavy guns pounding the Hartmannsweilerkopf. It was bitterly cold at this level and for the first time most of the American pilots noticed the effect of rarified air and soon learned to take long, deep breaths to feel comfortable. The patrol, interesting and instructive to the beginners, attracted no enemy aircraft, so they were not molested.

Four days later Kiffin Rockwell scored the first aerial victory for the Escadrille when, with the expenditure of only four bullets, he shot down an enemy two-seater over the old town of Thann which was clearly marked by the majestic tower and spire of its Gothic fourteenth-century church of St. Theobald.

Rockwell was the epitome of the idealistic volunteer. He was possibly the first American to offer his services to France. He also offered those of his brother Paul. Germany declared war on August 1, 1914, and, on August 3, Kiffin, a native of North Carolina, wrote to the French consul at New Orleans, Louisiana, somewhat as follows:

I wish to volunteer to serve in case of actual warfare and wish to know whether I can report to you at New Orleans and go over with the French Reservists, or would it be wiser to go to France before enlisting. I am twenty-one years old and have had military training at Virginia Military Institute. I am very anxious to see military service and would rather fight under the French flag than any other, as I greatly admire your nation. If my services can be used, I will bring my brother who also desires to fight under the French flag.

Amusingly enough, the following news item appeared in the Atlanta *Journal* of August 4, 1914, beside a portion of President Wilson's neutrality proclamation.

THREE YOUNG ATLANTANS
WOULD SHOULDER ARMS
IN DEFENSE OF FRANCE

Paul Rockwell and his brother K. Y. Rockwell and their friend R. L. Mock, three young men of Atlanta, have telegraphed to the French Consul in New Orleans offering to enlist as soldiers of France in the war against Germany.

An ancestor of the Rockwells named Rochelle, fought in the army which came from France to aid the American patriots in the War of the Revolution.

Therefore in honor of that ancestor and as evidence of their gratitude to France for the noble part she played in the winning of American independence, the young brothers have determined to fight under the Tri-Color in the present great war which threatens to engulf all Europe, and their friend Mr. Mock has joined them in the adventure.

Wilson's proclamation, in part, read:

I do enjoin all citizens of the United States and all persons residing or being within the territory or jurisdiction of the United States, to observe the laws of nations in that behalf. That no person within the territory and jurisdiction of the United States shall take part directly or indirectly, in the said wars, but shall maintain a strict and impartial neutrality.

So much for neutrality!

Paul Rockwell sent the newspaper page to the author and explained that the item had been written by a reporter who had overheard them discussing their plans for enlistment.

He added: "Rochelle is a very ancient spelling of our name. The Rockwells have been in America since 1630, coming from Somersetshire, where the family name was spelled Rockwell,

Rockewell, or Rokell since the 1400s. Our great-great-grand-father Noadiah Rockwell was a soldier in Washington's Con-tinental Army during the Revolutionary War, and may have fought alongside Lafayette's French troops.

"Mock was one of those big talkers one encounters through-out life. When he realized Kiffin and I were serious about going to France and enlisting for the war, he faded out of the picture. I never have heard of him again."

Kiffin Yates Rockwell inherited his military leanings; both his grandfathers, Captain Henry Rockwell and Major Enoch Shaw Ayres, were officers in the Confederate Army, and a more remote relative was a captain who served on General George Washington's staff during the Revolution. However, the founder of the family was an Englishman, William Rock-well. Kiffin had all the simple virtues of the medieval warrior; his pride was attuned to almost sensitiveness, but he had un-bounded energy, determination, courage, and a Galahadian faith in the righteousness of the French cause. He found it easy to enlist to fight in a war that threatened to overwhelm Europe, and he saw that France was preparing to defend her frontiers and republican ideals against an aggressor who de-spised human liberty. His course was clear; it was useless to wait until America as a nation saw the full implication of Germany's intent. The time was now. France needed him, and his flame of idealism never dimmed. Months later when some glint of disillusion may have enlightened him, after he had seen the squalor of war and the blood of battle, he wrote home: "If I die, you will know that I died as every man should—in fighting for the right. I do not consider that I am fighting for France alone, but for the cause of humanity, the most noble of all causes."

Unwilling to wait for consular red tape to unwind, Kiffin and his brother Paul sailed from New York on August 7, 1914, and on their arrival in Paris immediately enlisted in the For-eign Legion, along with twenty-nine other enthusiastic Americans. Their entry into this plodding branch of the French service was not without some moments of humor. Kiffin had had some military training and discipline at VMI, but many of the others had to invent their qualifications. One or two gravely related their experiences in the Salvation Army, others swore that they had fought in some fictitious campaign against Mexico, but when practically all of them displayed total ignorance of routine parade and ground drill, they explained that all their war service had been in fighting guerrilla skirmishes.

Kiffin, who was a rapid learner, was soon sent to the front where his record gleamed with courageous exploits, and his weeks upon weeks of dreary toil with the French infantry did not lessen his enthusiastic fighting spirit. On May 9, 1915, when the Foreign Legion made a bayonet charge at La Targette he was wounded in the thigh and stopped in his tracks. This engagement wiped out nearly half of his regiment. Although not critically wounded, Kiffin had to drag himself across an open field, pulling and clawing at tufts of grass or roots of low brush, an ordeal that took him most of the afternoon. He spent some time in a hospital and chafed with impatience when he heard that his Third Regiment once more had gone into action, and again been cut to pieces. He liked this type of soldiering and on a later occasion explained that there was nothing like a bayonet charge. He said that it took no effort, one seemed to float across the field in spite of the load of the pack and the three hundred twenty-five extra rounds of ammunition. One carried a gun, but it had no weight. If the infantryman got a bullet in his head, it was all over—there was no pain.

A particularly enlightening picture of life at the front in those early days will be found in a letter written by Kiffin to St. Elmo Massengale of Atlanta, Georgia, with whom he was associated before he went to France.

Feb. 5th. 1915
2eme Regt. Etgs.
Bon C 1 ere cie 9 eme Eod.
Bureau Central Militaire,
Paris.

Dear Mr. Massengale:

Received your letter early part of last month and wanted to answer sooner but am always either busy or too tired and sleepy. I have spent the most of this year in what was once a very prosperous village but is now a mass of ruins. I am now in the wine cellar of what was once a beautiful chateau belonging to some millionaire. It is nothing but ruins now, however, and the framework being all that is standing. To approach it in the moonlight reminds one very much of the White House. It is on the outskirts of the town and has a large brick wall around the park which covers hundreds of acres. On the other side of the wall the German trenches begin forming a half circle. We have to be very careful here as the sharpshooters are rather busy and have the advantage of higher ground. We stay in and sleep in the daytime. At nightfall the sergeant comes in and forms groups of four and six men and each group goes out to some post to stand guard in the night. We have several posts along the wall where we watch through holes made by shells; other places we have ladders against the wall and climb up and lie on top of the wall. Then every street is barricaded and guards are placed there. When we get on one of these posts each group is independent of the others. For instance, say I am at a barricade with three other men, our duty is to stay there regardless of what happens. If we are attacked, they will send reinforcements if possible, but whether reinforcements come or not, we stay there, dead or alive. At daybreak we all come in. That is the most interesting time in all the life. We all gather around, have our coffee, rum, wine and food, and tell our night's experiences. We talk for about an hour and then, half drunk with either fatigue, excitement or the wine and rum mixed, usually the three combined; we go to sleep for the day.

The firing line here has remained practically the same for so long that it has developed into a kind of guerrilla warfare, owing to the absence of real action. We send out a small bunch of men at night to prowl around the German lines, and they do the same.

If we meet, there is a scrap. We learn the location of one of their posts and go up and wipe it out or capture it. They come down to our wall and throw bombs at the sentinel or about them, if possible. One of their stunts is to come marching along one of the entrances to the town as if they were a French patrol; when the sentinel challenges them, they pour a volley in his direction, then scatter and depend on the darkness to get back to their trenches. Sometimes we fool them though, we shoot and challenge after. I have had some close calls here myself. I received your letter one afternoon; that night we came here. At that time we didn't really hold the town, it was just an advanced post and a kind of a death trap for the troops who were here. There were nine of us put on a post that we felt was a real death trap. We were so tired though, that we didn't care much. I hadn't slept for two days and nights and started the third night knowing that there would be no sleep for me then. It was cold and raining. About ten o'clock I went to take a post at a hole in the wall that had an old door propped up over it. Before taking the post I remarked to one of the fellows that I wished the Dutchmen would come, or something happen to keep me awake. I hadn't been there fifteen minutes before things began to happen. The 'swine' slipped up on the other side of the wall without my hearing them. Instead of putting a gun through a loop-hole and shooting me, they thought they would create a little confusion, so they threw a bomb at my feet. It failed to explode and as my corporal came running up they threw a second one. I jumped out of the way as it exploded. Before we recovered from the shock they pushed in the doorway and opened fire. I dropped to the ground and the corporal fell dead beside me. The woods and cover were about ten yards to the rear. I didn't lose much time getting there with them shooting at me from three directions.

But I could write all day on little exciting incidents. What time we are not having them, we are working. Last night I didn't do any guard duty but went about two miles to the rear and brought back a heavy load of stakes for barbed wire. Then I went about three miles along the front to another regiment where we borrowed some barbed wire and brought it back. Then we put it up. Tonight I am on the same post. You remember those pictures about "Nothing to do until tomorrow!"? Well that's the kind of job I have now. But I don't mind it. I am in fine physical condition and have reached the point where I don't give a damn. I had a chance last week of being transferred to the English Army. I would have a good chance there for a commission, whereas here I will never get above a common soldier owing to lack of knowledge of the French language, if for no other reason. Yet I didn't go. Decided as I came over to fight for France, would stick it out. The war will probably be over this fall; then no doubt, I will go back and work and lead a quiet, uneventful life for a year or so, and then see some other fool stunt to do.

I thank you very much for your wishes for me and your offer to send me anything I want. We are well fed and have plenty of clothes. I often think of American cigarettes and tobacco, but doubt if they would ever reach me even if you sent them, so let it go at that and wait and buy me a drink and a good all-Havana cigar at the M.&M. Club the first day I am back in Atlanta. I thank you for the introduction to the Dr. in Paris, and will make use of it when I return there. Regards to all.

Sincerely yours
(Signed) K. Y. ROCKWELL

Kiffin's leg wound gnawed and pained, and although French authorities must have realized that he was no longer capable of long marches with full infantry pack, sent him back to the trenches. Around that time the first hints of a possible American flying squadron were heard, and through Bill Thaw Kiffin put in for a transfer to the French Aviation. By September 2, when he had been back at the front for about a month, the transfer came through and he received the training routine at Avord and Pau. He gained his wings on an old Maurice Farman, a prehistoric biplane that was powered with a 75-hp Renault engine. He was one of the original members of the Escadrille Américaine formed on April 20, 1916. What he did between October 22, 1915, when he was brevetted, and the following April seems to have been lost in the dusty pages of history, but probably he put in the time training on various pursuit planes.

The honor of gaining the Escadrille's first victory on May 18 came as the result of the typical conditions of the period. Kiffin decided to do a lone-wolf show and shortly after crossing the enemy lines his engine began to miss and splutter, so he turned back hoping to make some carburetor adjustment and get going again. Before he could complete any of this he spotted a German aircraft about two thousand feet below that was flying up and down just inside the French lines. He "reduced his motor" as he said later, and nosed down. He then realized that he had taken on a German two-seater and the gunner was wasting no time in shooting at him. The enemy's first burst caught Rockwell's Nieuport clean and the plane rattled with the fusillade. Kiffin did not turn away, but kept straight on until he was about seventy-five feet from the two-seater. He pulled the trigger cord and his gun fired four bullets. By that time he had to swerve sharply to avoid a collision and as he passed by he could see the gunner had fallen away from his machine gun; the weapon had been abandoned and hung with its barrel pointing straight up into the air. The pilot too seemed to have folded up and was draped over the coaming of his cockpit.

The two-seater fell off helplessly and then turned for the German lines. Smoke began to pour from under the engine cowling and she nosed down into a sharp dive as more smoke and some flame appeared. As Sergeant Rockwell circled to make sure of the location, the doomed airplane surged toward its own area again and piled up amid the wire, shell-holes, and debris of the enemy line, where it crashed and burned, assuring Kiffin of a clean confirmation.

It was Rockwell's first combat, the first time he had seen an enemy plane, and the first time he had fired his machine gun. The squadron armorer verified the story later, as only four rounds had been fired from the drum that was still attached to Kiffin's Lewis gun. An observation post telephoned the news of the crashed plane to the squadron before his return, and his comrades gave him a great welcome.

Whether or not they were ready for real action the Escadrille was next ordered to the Verdun front. All of them were sorry to leave the comparative calm—at that time—of

Luxeuil, but most of them were anxious to serve in this very active and dangerous battle area. The night before their departure the Germans gave them a real farewell by sending over several night bombers that destroyed four transport trucks and killed several mechanics. It was impossible to go aloft and chase these night raiders, but the volunteers promised restitution when they reached the Verdun sector.

The airplanes were flown to the new field, and all other equipment went by truck or tractor. The flight took a little more than an hour and on arrival their machines were sheltered in three Besseneau hangars and the pilots went into Bar-le-Duc where a commodious villa was turned over to them for sleeping accommodation. The comforts here were as generous as those at Luxeuil.

By this time the American personnel included Bill Thaw, now a lieutenant, Adjutants Norman Prince, Bert Hall, Raoul Lufbery, and Didier Masson. Kiffin Rockwell, Dudley Hill, Paul Pavelka, Charles C. Johnson, and Laurence Rumsey were sergeants. The rank of adjutant in the French service was to some extent comparable to that of a regimental sergeant major, or a warrant officer in the United States Navy. It was the highest noncommissioned rank in the French Army with only a very narrow line separating it from a lieutenancy. The adjutant rank was marked by a narrow gold strip similar to that worn by the second lieutenant, but a thin scarlet thread was woven through it pointing out the almost-but-not-quite commissioned officer. Adjutants were saluted, and generally were devils where military discipline was concerned. The true difference between the adjutant and the second lieutenant was in the pay; the commissioned officer had much the better of the deal.

The Verdun sector was a beehive of aviation activity. There were dozens of flying fields within a twenty-mile area, and the Escadrille Américaine was placed on schedule with other front-area units, and given specified flying hours, a plan of rotation to assure that there always were aircraft over the line in the sector to fight for air control. A field wireless station was also used to keep track of all movements of the aircraft, particularly to warn of activities of enemy planes.

At this point an interesting aside comes up. Second Lieutenant Charles Nungesser, a youthful and most impulsive French airman, who achieved a score of forty-three victories by the end of the war, became interested in the American volunteers while he was recuperating from a war wound. Unknown to his squadron commander and members of the hospital staff, he made an unofficial visit to the Escadrille Américaine on the Verdun front. Naturally, he was queried as to his manner of operating, and asked to explain some of his tricks and give any advice that might aid the newcomers.

Nungesser was delighted and made a very enlightening lecture to which he added, "But why so much talk? Let's go out and see how it is done!"

Captain Thénault furnished a plane, and as many Americans as could went up to the lines, led by the convalescent French ace. His lecture was then illustrated in actual combat when he attacked a two-seater in the accepted manner by going in from behind and under the tail, a position in which he was safe from the rear gunner's fire. The German two-seater went spinning down and the Americans had seen how it was done by an expert.

After celebrating that exciting incident, Lieutenant Nungesser returned to his hospital bed, and it was weeks before the exploit was mentioned in official circles.

The Nieuport aircraft furnished the Escadrille was still the same model, and all necessary instruments and machine guns had to be fitted and adjusted on the field before they could be flown on active combat. Naturally, everyone was anxious to get time and figures in his logbook, and made every effort to have his machine available. They had scarcely settled down, however, before Bert Hall brought down a German aircraft, the second to be credited to the Americans.

This Hall—not to be confused with James Norman Hall— was the "character" of the organization, typical soldier of fortune and at times a mystery. He would make a statement one day and contradict it the next. When he was in one mood he admitted that he had been born in Kentucky around 1880. On other occasions he called Higginsville, Missouri, his birthplace. At his best he could tell amazing stories of how he had fought on one side or the other—as an airman, of course— during the Turkish-Bulgarian War of 1912. Later on he wound up in England and may have served in Lord Kitchener's Army. When next he reported in we find Bert a Legionaire credited with front-line service between August and December of 1914. How he compressed all this in is a mystery, but most of the time he was a lovable old rogue, and no one would have questioned him had he declared that he had guided Dr. Frederick A. Cook to the North Pole in 1908.

Following in the footsteps of Bill Thaw and others, Bert soon made his way out of the trenches and was accepted by the French Aviation where, despite his "glorious air battles for the Turks—or the Bulgarians," he showed no evidence of having encountered an airplane before. But he went through Pau, Avord, and Buc until he was brevetted on August 19, 1915, and was assigned to MS.38, a Morane-Saulnier squadron, where he carried out routine observation missions through the late summer and autumn of that year. From all accounts he held up his end, for he was accepted eagerly for the new Escadrille Américaine in April 1916.

Once in the company of his own countrymen, Bert, for some unexplained reason, came under the suspicion of espionage. Previously, while he was in training at Avord he was under surveillance by the French Secret Service. Two Army intelligence men, posing as student pilots, occupied beds on either side of Bert's, and he was seldom out of their sight, but from all accounts, he never proved to be anything but a happy-go-lucky, garrulous, ne'er-do-well adventurer. He had few manners, and his American companions found him overly shrewd in card playing, dice rolling, or signing mess chits. Although he had downed three enemy aircraft and had been awarded the Médaille Militaire and the Croix de Guerre, he in time was formally "invited" to leave the squadron.

With rare dignity, Bert requested a transfer in November 1916 and was posted to a French Nieuport *chasse* squadron, N.103, where he served for about a month, and received a special citation that declared him to be "A clever, energetic, and courageous pilot, full of spirit, daily attacking enemy planes at very short range." Why he left N.103 has not been explained, but in January 1917 he was granted permission to accompany a French aviation mission to Rumania, although some reports have it that Bert went to Russia. Shortly after this assignment Hall requested and received permission to return to the United States, ostensibly to join the United States Aviation Service. He failed to turn up at any American enlistment bureau, and to this day is still listed as a deserter in French military records.

Bert next turned out to be an author and in a short time mystified readers with his *One Man's War* and *En l'Air*, two volumes that prove how one man can be in several places at the same time.

With the coming of peace in 1918, Bert, like so many other soldiers of fortune, found it difficult to get back into action, but by scanning the newspapers carefully he decided that Nationalist China might be a fertile field. Once there he promoted a contract to train Chinese airmen. To teach anyone to fly one had to have an airplane or two, so Bert next induced the Chinese authorities to entrust him with $34,000 for a consignment, which, oddly enough, never arrived on any Chinese field. This brought him under the eye of United States consular officials, and for the first time Bert Hall was unable to wriggle out, and wound up in the federal penitentiary at McNeil Island, Washington, where he spent the next two and one half years. On December 6, 1948, Hall was killed in an automobile accident while driving between Chicago and Castalia, Ohio.

Following his death, his tangled domestic life was revealed. A Hollywood syndicate with which the author was associated,

planned to film a complete documentary of the Lafayette
Escadrille, and to do this the producers had first to obtain
full clearances from all concerned. In coming up against
Hall's background—and one or two others who also served in
that organization—it was obvious that it would be impossible
to "clear" most of Bert's adventures, since in one form or
another they had been parceled out to survivors of his several
marital affairs to atone for his alimony commitments. This is
one of the chief reasons why no motion picture producer has
been able to present a complete and full history of the
Lafayette Escadrille: too many survivors with delusions of
importance concerning their rights in the presentation of such
a history.

Few Boswells of the Lafayette Escadrille have given Bert
Hall much space in their chronicles, which is unfortunate,
for he must have been an intriguing character.

Chapter IV

THE ROAD OF THE PATRIOTS

The third victory for N.124 was scored by the guns of
Bill Thaw. Although he had spent time with other French
squadrons, it was Bill's first "kill," and came on a day, May
24, when he was prowling about on his own well beyond the
security of the French lines.

Bill always said, jocularly, that he had gone out with a
formation but somehow had lost track of his pals and was
flitting up and down the Meuse River hoping to find the rest
of them when he came upon a lone German plane a few
hundred feet below him. He started to attack, but caution
prevailed, and he turned away to make a wiser inspection to

make sure that this was not "Hun bait," flown there to draw in novice fliers for the eagle packs to finish.

Bill moved into the sun, and, after ascertaining that there were no hostile aircraft above, saw that his "chicken" was a fixed-gun Fokker, a type about which he had heard a good deal in the preceding months. While he was pondering on this problem, the Fokker pilot wheeled over and took a wild potshot at Bill, an act that greatly annoyed the man from Pittsburgh. He threw his Nieuport around until he had the Fokker in his sights. A series of short telling bursts soon had the enemy in trouble. He tried to wriggle out and reply in kind, but Bill was determined not to lose this rare opportunity. While these maneuvers were taking place both planes were moving toward the French lines, and Bill saw his chance. Picking away, driving in, and herding the unfortunate Fokker pilot deeper into Allied territory, Bill finally changed to a new drum of ammunition and poured the full magazine into his foe. The Fokker, with a dead pilot at the stick, piled up inside the French lines near Douaumont.

This most satisfying victory charged Bill like heady wine. He believed that at last he had discovered the knack, the touch, the trick, and markmanship to score again and again. He was so enamored with this idea that he went out once more that afternoon, determined to add to his score and give the French good reason to be satisfied with their new Escadrille Américaine.

This time he found not one Fokker, but three! He had not counted on such odds, but once committed, he made the best of it. The encounter was at thirteen thousand feet, and for a few minutes Bill was uncertain what to do in this situation. At first the Fokker pilots showed little interest in the lone Nieuport and maintained a tight formation as they cruised up and down inside their own lines. Bill watched the threesome for several minutes and then worked out a plan of attack that might reward him with not one, but three Fokkers.

This came to be known as the Thaw concept of confusion. Pulling up for a little extra altitude and making for the

sun, Bill suddenly went down, firing wildly. The Fokker pilots
had lost him in the glare and for a minute or so had no idea
how many Nieuports were attacking. Bill was spraying every
inch of the sky with tracers and hissing ammunition and for a
short time was in his element. He wasn't causing any particular damage, but he was driving the enemy threesome down
toward their own trenches.

By this time the Fokker pilots decided that they had to do
something or be forced into the mud, and when they realized
that all this furor was being put on by a lone Nieuport, they
suddenly pulled back in climbing turns. Bill hadn't figured
on this, and when the enemy began to pick chunks out of his
wings and fuselage, he decided to bow out gracefully, but
unfortunately with every turn he made he found himself
floundering into another cone of Fokker fire.

The novice American was soon in real trouble, and although
he fought well with what he had he was plainly outnumbered.
Bill flew as he never had before, but no matter where he
moved he was in a cross fire. He darted in and out, fighting
to get near his own lines, but there was small hope of overcoming this lineup, and while in a tight turn trying to avoid a
long burst of fire, he received a bullet wound in the left arm.
With that he nosed down with engine full on, risked plum-
meting out of his wings, and escaped with the enemy still
drilling long-range shots at him.

There was little left of the Nieuport's controls, and once he
had eased her out of her wild dive, Bill sensed it would be
wise to get down as fast as possible. He found a small stretch
of open ground near the French third line and dabbed the
plane in, thankful that she held together that long. He was so
exhausted he could not move for a time, and it was not until
a couple of poilus crept out of a communication trench and
lifted him clear that he was able to crawl away to a first-aid
dressing station where he was cared for and then driven back
to his squadron.

Thaw was advised to go to a hospital where he would receive proper care, and someone suggested the American Hos-

pital in Paris. Why not? Bill put up only token resistance and
went off to the City of Light where surgeons and doctors
examined his wound, took proper measures and assured him
that it was just a painful puncture that would soon heal if he
took proper care of himself.

Bill did. Once the bandages were adjusted and a sling provided, he moved out of the hospital, found some friends, told
the story several times, and after a couple of days of that
medication, returned to Bar-le-Duc to make certain no one
had rubbed his name off the Escadrille roll. A short time later
Lieutenant William Thaw was awarded the Legion of Honor
for his varied exploits of May 24, and needless to state the
wording of the citation was a trifle more classical than Bill's
explanation of his front-line activities. When both the Legion
of Honor and Croix de Guerre came through, Bill modestly
covered them up with the generous-sized sling in which he
cradled his wounded arm. He seldom, if ever, clanked about
with war medals on his active-service jacket, for he knew the
proper procedure for military decorations. Only at actual
award ceremonies was he photographed wearing his medals;
the representative ribbons were all that were necessary for
Bill Thaw. He was that sort of volunteer.

The names Bill Thaw and Lafayette Escadrille are synony-
mous to many people, but although Bill had not been too
enthused with Norman Prince's original idea, he came in
time to appreciate its over-all worth and worked incessantly
for its fulfillment. He was the only American to be with the
Escadrille from its inception till the day it passed into history.
As is known, N.124 was eventually transferred to the United
States Air Service and became the 103rd Pursuit Squadron.
Bill went through the whole affair, starting out as a common
poilu when the war bugles blew, gaining the American rank of
lieutenant colonel, and covering himself with glory and Allied
decorations.

Bill Thaw did not strike one as such a man. He was big,
bulky, overly affectionate, hardly the slick, dress-dagger type

of hero. He looked fine in clean uniforms, smart belt and polished field boots, but war is not a theatrical performance in that neat sense. He also sported a walrus-like mustache which, when waxed and trim, would bestow a true military expression, but more often this face fungus was allowed to get scraggy and droop, and in this guise he looked like "Old Bill," Bruce Bairnsfather's cartoon character of the British trenches. When Bill could get his batman Percy, a West Indian Negro, who had served with him in the Foreign Legion, to buff and polish his gear, he could outsmart any French general, but most of the time Bill was more interested in flying. He was said to be twenty-four years of age at the time, but the walrus mustache made him look more like forty.

Bill Thaw was born in Pittsburgh, Pennsylvania, and seldom had to worry about where the next ten-spot was coming from. He went to Yale where he spent much of his spare time learning to fly a Curtiss flying boat off the waters of Long Island Sound where his family had a summer home. One day he decided to attempt a flight to Atlantic City, and suddenly encountered the Williamsburg Bridge. Bill's aircraft wasn't too good on altitude and when the big structure loomed ahead, he knew that he had no chance of leapfrogging it—so he nosed down and flew under it, thereby setting a new style for aviation and possibly a new record for early aerobatics. "I always fly under bridges," Bill explained to his passenger. "You meet a better class of people. The yachting crowd, and all that."

When the war began, Bill was in France where he had been gracing the race tracks, theaters, and the social salons of Paris. The crisis was a shock to many people since it burst amid the summer holidays, halting the gaiety of the tourists and casting a dull cloud on the beautiful weather. Americans rushed to the ticket offices to rearrange their return plans. Nearly everyone wished to get home as soon as possible. Some made urgent appeals to the United States consular office, others lined up outside the American Express Company to change their French francs into American dollars. But, on the

strength of his Curtiss hydroplane license, Bill immediately
offered his services to the French Aviation. As explained before, France had plenty of pilots but few aircraft, and to be
frank few people in August 1914 had any idea that aircraft
would play an important part in the war. Bill, who had fluttered through some hair-raising personal flights, willingly accepted the proposition that he volunteer for the Foreign Legion, and was soon fully equipped and sent to the front where
the fighting was thick and heavy. When the summer and
autumn had passed, months that saw Germany victorious on
practically all sectors until General Joffre defeated Von Kluck
along the bloodstained Marne in mid-September, Second
Class *Soldat* William Thaw realized there was no future in
the mud, cold, vermin, and sudden death of the trenches.

It has been explained how Bill appealed to Lieutenant
Brocard of D.6 Squadron in an effort to be relieved of this
dreary trench warfare, and how Brocard arranged to have
Bill transferred as a *mitrailleur*—aerial gunner—and how in
the course of events he became a corporal pilot. But flying
80-hp Deperdussins as observation machines was not especially rewarding, so Bill next applied for a transfer to a Caudron
two-seater group. The Caudron C-III of Escadrille C.42 was
a single-engined biplane in which the crew's nacelle was
mounted between the upper and lower wings. There was no
armament to speak of, but in some instances a light automatic rifle could be mounted for the observer-gunner. However, since the tail assembly was attached by a weird skeletal
structure of tail booms, braces, and wires, the gunner had a
very limited field of fire.

Later on Bill was entrusted with a Caudron C-IV, a twin-
engined biplane, and given a series of long-range observation
missions to carry out. The engines on this aircraft were 80-hp
Le Rhone rotaries, and when both were running well, the
C-IV could attain a speed of 82 miles per hour, and might
climb to 10,000 feet in 33 minutes.

These sorties were not joy rides although C.42 was operating
in a fairly quiet sector. On one occasion, while carrying a

Lieutenant Felix on an observation mission "in depth," Bill had one of his many exciting experiences. On spotting this impudent aircraft well inside their own lines, the enemy turned on every ack-ack battery and splashed the sky with thick smoke and screaming shrapnel. This flight took more than two hours to accomplish, but Thaw and Felix boldly carried on although their Caudron was being systematically taken apart minute by minute. First the wings were peppered, leaving long strips of torn linen trailing behind, and the flimsy tail assembly was little more than a splintered framework by the time they had their information and were turning back. For the rest of the trip the Germans seemed to concentrate on the gleaming engine cowlings which were plugged time and time again, but the Le Rhones continued to churn like coffee grinders. Interplane struts were shot away and wing spars began to sag, but amazingly, neither Thaw nor Felix was touched.

At this point Lieutenant Felix decided he had missed a couple of items for his report, so Bill turned around and went back to give the area another look-see. Then, according to Bill, Providence took over and they somehow floundered back to their own lines, found their field and put down the hulk before it completely fell apart. In truth the Caudron hardly held together long enough to make the landing; it was so badly shot up it had to be junked.

For this exploit Sergeant Pilot Thaw was given a citation, a piece of paper, duly signed by someone in authority, that stated he was a brave man and France was proud of him. Bill collected several of these testimonials before the end of 1915, but no medals. After one year of service with C.42 he was promoted to *sous lieutenant*—second lieutenant—the first of the American volunteers to be so rewarded.

When N.124 was formed in April 1916 Bill was released from C.42, and he went to Luxeuil where he had to learn to fly a Nieuport *chasse* plane, for up to this time he had not been allowed to fly alone, except on a school plane.

Once he had joined his countrymen Bill Thaw relaxed and

enjoyed life. He was no longer selling himself to the French and proving that Americans could be gentlemen of culture and good manners. All that was behind him, and with a few kindred spirits, notably Raoul Lufbery, Bill relived some of his more boisterous hours, such as he had known on Long Island.

Bill was the ranking American in the Escadrille Américaine, but he never made any attempt to lord it over his comrades. He never ordered anyone to fly a mission that he himself would not undertake. He was often in trouble with his French superiors for his disciplinary let-downs and his knack of turning his head to miss some minor infraction of the rules. Bill had seen enough of war to know that he could lead a man just so far. He also analyzed every flying man in the squadron and quickly sensed how he should be handled. He seldom made a mistake.

In the air Bill Thaw was as good a leader as any. He soon picked up the tricks of the *chasse* pilot, and as fast as new volunteers came in, gave them many hours of his time and much valuable advice. Once flying duties were over, he organized all types of let-down activities; one among them was the concoction of the famous Lafayette Cocktail, a murderous potion devised by him and Lufbery in which equal parts of brandy and champagne were mixed. All those who partook of it remember that it went down smoothly, and then concluded its course with the kick of a mule. A round of these to open the ceremonies was all that was needed to break down the most surly guest. The present-day variation of this potion is known as the Luxury Cocktail, made up of three ounces of brandy, three ounces of chilled champagne, laced together with two dashes of orange bitters.

With funds from home, his outgoing comradeship, and wealth of personality, Bill soon became one of the legendary figures at the front. Because of his early service with the Foreign Legion, and later with two French observation squadrons, he could always pick up a new group for whom to stage a party. He was more than welcome in all the small towns and villages nearby. The Escadrille never ran short of feminine guests, and on his many countryside rambles, Bill could usually promote a visit to a nearby château, particularly if it boasted a good wine cellar.

The complete individualist, it was Thaw who first conceived the idea of a special aircraft insignia for the Escadrille. This idea was not original with the Americans, for the pilots of the French *chasse* squadrons in the Verdun sector already had developed a series of small markers for their Nieuports that at first took the form of birds' wings, heraldic crests, simple pennants, and designs representing legendary talons or dragons. They generally were done with some artistic restraint in subdued colors.

No such modesty for Bill. Since the Indians were the original Americans, all Escadrille Américaine planes should carry the head of a screeching Indian, complete with war bonnet of gay feathers. There are a dozen variations concerning the origination of this design, the best of which is that the squadron artist copied an Indian head from a Savage Arms ammunition box. At any rate such a design was drawn and accepted, and to the amazement of the French officers commanding the squadron, the garish insignia was plastered on the side of the Nieuports, at least twice the size of their national *cocardes*. No question, an Escadrille Américaine plane could be spotted a mile away, and if the enemy made the most of this gaudy identification, well . . . ?

But this was not the end. Once the Indian head had been accepted, Bill next decided that every N.124 pilot had the right to fly under his own personal insignia, a design that showed his own artistic taste or peculiar superstition. This resulted in some weird and sometimes brazen decorations. Didier Masson adopted an Indian swastika, possibly the first such design flown into battle; Bill Thaw was satisfied with a large letter T that was painted in scarlet on his upper and lower wings; Bert Hall had BERT in tremendous block letters along the sides of his fuselage; Jim McConnell's looked like a massive white footprint, said to be a fraternity emblem;

Clyde Balsley, the Texan, preferred a plain white lone star; and Charles C. Johnson, to indicate his gambling instincts, had a large white dice showing the one-spot, on his fuselage. Someone else painted a pair of dice with the reassuring 7 showing.

Bill Thaw was the accepted leader of the American volunteers, but two French officers were in charge of the squadron and, in addition to leading patrols, maintained liaison with French headquarters.

Captain Georges Thénault had been in French Aviation since the outbreak of the war and his experience was of great value to the American novitiates. He served early at the front as a pilot with Escadrille C.11 until December 1914. He spent some time as an instructor at Avord but in March 1915 was posted to another Caudron squadron, C.34, and flew continually until July 31, 1915, when he was made commanding officer of C.42. It was here he met Bill Thaw and so strong a friendship was cemented between these two that Thénault was selected to command the proposed Escadrille Américaino. He was promoted to captain, and led the American unit until January 1918 when the pilots were transferred to the United States Air Service.

All who remember Captain Thénault praise his leadership. His association with the pilots, who regarded him as a fine friend, always was intimate and cordial. He carried out his duties with kindliness, sympathetic understanding, and tact, usually delegating much of his authority to his French assistants, Lieutenants de Laage de Meux, de Maison-Rouge, and Verdier-Fauvety. He also insisted that both Thaw and Lufbery assume some of the executive responsibility. At first Captain Thénault took his regular turn at leading patrols when formations were required, but as the American pilots grew more experienced, he permitted them to take lead positions so that they might broaden their experience. Since this was an American squadron, he felt that Americans should run it as far as possible.

When the Escadrille was transferred to the American forces, Captain Thénault was sent to command the School of Acrobacy and Combat at Pau where he remained until the Armistice. He was awarded the Legion of Honor and the Croix de Guerre with four palms.

After the war Captain Thénault was posted as air attaché to the French Embassy in Washington and while in that service married an American girl, Sarah Spencer. They had two children, Catherine and George. Today the son is serving in the United States Air Force.

In 1936 Thénault was recalled to France to take command of an aviation group. After the fall of his country to the Germans in World War II, he engaged in valuable underground activity until France was liberated. He died December 17, 1948, and was buried in the Lafayette Escadrille Memorial near Paris.

Lieutenant Alfred de Laage de Meux, second-in-command of the Escadrille Américaine, was a professional farmer in peacetime, but had served his conscript time as a second lieutenant in the 14th Regiment of Dragoons. After being called up on the outbreak of the war, he was in many of the opening skirmishes, and on August 31, 1914, while out on a scouting patrol he met a force of the enemy and had his horse shot from under him, and received a bullet in his leg. His orderly, a private named Jean Dressy, carried him back on his own horse, thus enabling the young officer to report directly to his superiors. Dressy followed de Laage into the aviation forces and served with him until the French officer's death. Dressy later became an aerial gunner.

Since it was obvious that cavalry would not have an important part in trench warfare, Lieutenant de Laage, after a short convalescence, was given the opportunity to transfer to the flying service. He first flew as an observer with C.30, and although he performed his tasks brilliantly, he yearned to become a pilot which he did by learning to fly while serving as a gunner-observer. He picked up the skill by watching his pilot and taking over the dual controls of their Caudron whenever possible. He never went to a flying school.

He was next transferred to a Farman squadron and scored his first victory from one of these old planes. By now de Laage had gained a reputation for unusual courage and contempt for danger. On two occasions his gunner was killed in the air while in conflict with the enemy, and many times he returned from patrol with his aircraft totally riddled and ready for the "unserviceable" pile.

Lieutenant de Laage next served with a *chasse* squadron, and again distinguished himself during the first battle of Verdun when he fought a series of mid-air combats that were talked about from one end of the front to the other.

It was during this 1916 period that Captain Thénault first met de Laage, and after a short talk decided that this impetuous Frenchman was just the type of airman the equally impulsive Americans would admire and follow willingly. Lieutenant de Laage joined the squadron on the day of its original muster at Luxeuil where his personal magnetism and leadership endeared him to all. It was he who took them out in small groups, or singly, teaching them the wiles of the enemy and the tricks of the victor. The Americans were most respectful of his spirit of patriotism. This was a fighting man they could follow and esteem.

On one occasion while flying with Lieutenant de Laage, Kiffin Rockwell found an enemy airplane over Etain, and, without examining the rest of the sky, went down to attack. Just as he was about to open fire he came under the attention of two other Germans whom he had not noticed. It looked like a bad day for Kiffin, but Lieutenant de Laage, who was in trouble himself trying to clear a gun stoppage, went instantly to Kiffin's aid. His attack was so savage and determined, although he had no gun to use, the German airmen were driven off.

The brave Lieutenant de Laage deserved a better end, but even the best make grave mistakes. He was killed May 23, 1917, when the squadron was at Ham on the Somme in an accident that never should have happened. On this day he was testing out a new Spad and, as he gained take-off speed, he suddenly pulled up into a tight climbing turn. At a critical period the Hispano-Suiza engine cut out and there was not room to regain control; the Spad spun in and de Laage was killed instantly. The British ace Major James McCudden died in the same manner a few months later.

De Laage was succeeded by Lieutenant Arnoux de Maison-Rouge, another former cavalry officer turned airman. Maison-Rouge transferred to aviation in 1915 after several engagements with the cavalry. He gained his brevet aboard a Maurice Farman on November 6, 1915, and soon became a *chasse* pilot assigned to a Nieuport squadron, N.67, with which he served from September 22, 1916, until May 27, 1917. On May 28 of that year he was transferred to the Lafayette Escadrille when the Americans were at Ham on the Somme. A tougher assignment could not be conceived, for the Americans had taken their second-in-command completely to their hearts; anyone following him might be considered a usurper.

But Maison-Rouge sensed the situation and used great tact so quietly that any resentment was quickly dispelled. He was a first-class pilot and leader and soon distinguished himself over Verdun by skilled airmanship and rare courage. He had consideration for the men under his command and never led them into situations too difficult for their abilities; he never set up a patrol that he would not take part in himself.

Maison-Rouge was not a strong man and his continual drive often exhausted his strength. Late in 1917 he was taken very ill and had to have an enforced rest. After this layoff he was assigned to the French Spad squadron, S.78, and during the heavy fighting in May 1918 was shot down in a terrific dogfight while battling against great odds far behind the enemy lines.

A third ex-cavalryman took over the second-in-command spot of the Lafayette when Lieutenant Louis Verdier-Fauvety was detached from Spad S.65 Squadron on October 6, 1917. He had served with this French force from November 18, 1916, to October 1, 1917—almost a year of stiff front-line fighting. He had been wounded on October 12, 1914, while serving with the 8th Hussars, a setback that put him in the hospital for several months. On his release he took flight training from February 26, 1916, until November 16 of the same year when he received his brevet at Juvisy.

S.65 was one of the most famous of the French Spad squadrons and Verdier-Fauvety was an excellent example of the type of pilot that made up that noted organization. He had a remarkable escape from death in August 1917 when during an air fight his plane collided with that of a comrade. They were then at twelve thousand feet and Verdier-Fauvety saw that his stablizer—tail plane—and one of his elevators had been torn away. He fell out of control all the way to the ground, but, fortunately, most of the way down he was in a series of flat spins and "falling-leafs," and finally crashed into some tree tops of a small wood and escaped with superficial injuries.

Verdier-Fauvety was accepted immediately when he was assigned to the Lafayette Escadrille for he soon showed his superb skill and coolness in action. He usually insisted on leading the more dangerous missions, particularly those requiring low flying against ground concentrations, or escort chores that took them well over the line. He inspired every man under him.

After the Lafayette Escadrille pilots were taken over by the American forces, Lieutenant Verdier-Fauvety was made commanding officer of a new Spad squadron, S.124. Later he was assigned to S.163, and, finally, given command of his old Spad squadron, S.65. Then, after nearly four years of service, he was killed during a night bombardment of his field—not in air action as he would have wished, but in the rubble and wreckage of his hangar. The French Air Service lost one of its finest pilots, and the Americans a true friend.

James R. McConnell, born in Carthage, North Carolina, was perhaps the most representative American to join the original Escadrille Américaine. His attitude and viewpoint epitomized the changing point of view of the more mature American who volunteered to help France long before his country showed any national concern. Jim McConnell was not dramatic, nor flamboyant, or one who deluded himself with high romance or a spirit of adventure. He was a clever man, perfectly balanced, with appealing human attributes. He was most observant, and his letters, essays, and in particular, his little book *Flying for France*, have afforded historians much valuable material on the volunteer service.

At first McConnell believed that the war would not last very long, and he did not sign up as an ambulance driver with the American Field Service until January 1915. During that spring and summer he served through the heavy fighting around Pont-à-Mousson and the Bois-le-Pretre where he saw war at its ugliest. Several of his letters were published in *Outlook* magazine the following September, stimulating American interest in the war, and particularly in the activities of the American Field Service. It was these tragic experiences, evacuating wounded and dead, that inspired Jim to seek a more active (?) part. He enlisted in the French Aviation October 1, 1915, and was brevetted from the G.D.E. school February 6, 1916. His first squadron assignment was with the newly formed Escadrille Américaine on April 20, 1916.

Jim McConnell was a big man in every sense of the word. He was a good pilot and had plenty of courage. At first he made no outstanding contribution, but he was always ready and available for any mission. During August 1916 while the squadron was at Bar-le-Duc, McConnell was out on patrol with Kiffin Rockwell and Norman Prince. There was heavy ground fighting between Fleury and Thiamount, and their mission was to intercept any German aircraft that was bent on observation work. This patrol was held in the air as long as there was light so that when they turned for home darkness had caught up with them; in fact the stars were shining as they began their glide for their turfed landing field. Prince and Rockwell got in safely, but Jim's engine conked out at a critical moment, and he attempted a dead-stick landing. All might have gone well, but in the final approach he misjudged his distance and since he had no power to pull out and go around again, he slammed through two trees and ended up in the bank of a sunken road. His engine took most of the shock and his belt held firm, which may have saved his face, but his back was wrenched severely, an injury that plagued him for weeks. He had to go to a hospital for treatment and did not rejoin the squadron until they had moved on to the Somme front.

Elliott Cowdin, one of the original seven of the Escadrille Américaine, was another volunteer from the American Field Service. It was while serving in that activity that he met Norman Prince who was trying to promote the idea of an American flying group. Cowdin, who was from New York City, made the first contact with Colonel Barrés, then Chief of Military Aeronautics, and won his backing and eventual support that encouraged Prince and Dr. Gros to go ahead with the plan.

A hard-riding polo player of a well-known sporting family, Cowdin had an equally active time in the French Aviation. From all accounts he seems to have been one of the more boisterous characters of the volunteer group and did not stay with any squadron for very long, shuttling in and out of four different French escadrilles before joining the Escadrille Américaine. Cowdin was an aggressive man and seemed always to be in trouble and his companions found it hard to get along with him. According to one or two members of the old group, "Cowdin was a barracks-room and mess-hall fighter." But there is no question as to his flying skill and determination, for he served long and well, but his history was somewhat marred by his propensity for causing trouble.

In all fairness it should be understood that Elliott earned his keep as a wartime airman. In some records he is credited with destroying one enemy aircraft, and on one occasion almost went to glory when he "ambushed" the famous Oswald

Boelcke. This happened on July 4, 1916, and resulted in a long, drawn-out battle with the German ace. This encounter has been claimed on the strength of an extract from the German flier's diary, which, to many historians, scarcely satisfies close investigation.

An examination of the details of this fight makes interesting reading. During the time when the squadron was operating in the Verdun sector, Elliott found and attacked a German two-seater, and was in turn pounced on by a German airman *believed* to be Oswald Boelcke. According to one version of the fight Boelcke, who was flying a new Albatros, discovered six Nieuports, and later wrote in his diary: "I distinctly saw the flag on the machine!" At any rate, he nosed down, cut out one of the Nieuport pack and began shooting. His gun failed after firing seventy rounds, "and the imprudent American escaped." By this time Cowdin's companions turned and went to his aid and drove off the German Albatros.

How true the Oswald Boelcke statement is, is doubtful. In the first place, no Nieuport of N.124 carried an American-flag insignia, or any that might be mistaken for an American flag. There is no question that Cowdin first attacked a two-seater, and was himself under heavy fire, but the inference that the famed Boelcke was his adversary has long been questioned, and by the same token the Cowdin-Boelcke battle continues to be written by each new crop of aviation writers.

By August 1916, when the squadron was up on the hazardous Somme front, Elliott's many months of active-service flying began to take their toll. His health broke down, and he had to spend six weeks in a military hospital. On being released he was attached for a time to the British aviation headquarters in Paris, presumably in a liaison post. In January 1917 he was formally released from the French service and returned to the United States. In June of that year he was commissioned a major in the U. S. Air Service and attached to the Lockhart Special Mission, Board of Aircraft Production, with which he served until the end of the war.

Chapter V

CHAMPAGNE AND ORANGES

Victor Chapman, a native New Yorker, was studying architecture at the Ecole des Beaux-Arts in Paris during the spring of 1914. He had graduated from Harvard the previous year, and when the war broke out was touring through England with his family. He hurriedly left them and returned to France and enlisted in the Foreign Legion. Like Kiffin Rockwell, Chapman had a distinguished background. His great-great-grandfather was John Jay, a member of the Continental Congress and a diplomatic companion of Benjamin Franklin in Paris in 1782, which perhaps accounted for his sympathy for France when the call rang out. His father, John Jay Chapman, also a graduate of Harvard, had been admitted to the bar in 1888, but after ten years of practice, abandoned the law for literature, and became a pertinent and fiery observer of his times, and in his later years was considered one of the finest writers of the English language in the United States. A prefatory note to the book *The War Letters of Edmond Genet* is a stirring example of his prose in which he so clearly defined the spirit of the American volunteers when he explained that they represented the idealism of the youth of America.

"Mere romanticism and the desire for adventure would not have brought them together; and the more we find out about these boys the more we see that in each of them there was a soul's history that led up to this especial consummation. They are national characters—symbols of America. In life and death they express the relation of America to the war."

Victor was assigned to the Third Marching Regiment of the Foreign Legion and received his early training at the Reuilly Caserne, Paris. He mastered the machine gun, and for a time was a close companion of George Preston Ames, a volunteer from Paraguay whose father was an American dentist practicing in South America. These two friends managed to be in every exciting incident that the regiment encountered. On one occasion another volunteer, Eugene Jacob, was buried alive in a shallow dugout that had been caved in by the concussion of a trench mortar. Chapman and Ames ignored enemy fire from all sides and dug and dug until Jacob could be hauled to safety. After that experience Jacob designed a bombproof shelter that was adopted and used throughout the war by most French infantry regiments. Jacob was also one of the prize scroungers of the time and his platoon seldom went hungry; on the contrary his companions more often dined lavishly on the savory portions of pigs, milch cows, and poultry that had "wandered" into Eugene's "area of observation."

Victor Chapman was in the front line where action was thick and fast for more than three months. Once, when a patrol took him deep into enemy territory, he received a bullet through the muscles of his lower arm, but after a first-aid man had applied a temporary bandage, Victor "forgot" to report his wound to his company commander. When it was disclosed, he refused to withdraw for more professional attention.

Some of the other volunteers were not so lucky, or so durable; several had to be relieved and removed to a hospital because of wounds, trench fever, or pneumonia. Their places were taken by Henry Weston Farnsworth of Boston, Edmond Charles Clinton Genet of Ossining, New York, Joseph Lydon of Salem, Massachusetts, and David E. Wheeler of Buffalo, New York. By this time many noted American college fraternities were well represented in the trenches; members of Alpha Delta Phi, Alpha Tau Omega, Sigma Phi Epsilon, Psi Upsilon, Delta Kappa Epsilon, Kappa Alpha, and several of the well-known clubs of Yale and Harvard were on the roll of the Foreign Legion.

As did many others, Chapman learned of Norman Prince's attempt to form an American group of fliers, and after several letters to his father in New York, he put in for a transfer to the French Aviation. He wrote later, however, "I shall regret it sincerely if my recall comes now—July 21, 1915—before we have another attack. The regiment, as I told you before, did incredible things at Arras . . . I now predict that my heavenly prospects are just going to miss each other by hairbreadths—I shall be transferred to the Aviation just before this company goes into action and makes a brilliant attack. And the war will end just before I get my license and go to the front."

Chapman actually hated to leave his friends in the Foreign Legion. He had collected a most amazing group. There was Heredia, a Spaniard from Málaga who had translated Mark Twain into Spanish, and was working as a newspaper reporter in London when the war started; there was Nedim Bey, a Turk who had been sent by the Turkish government to Paris to study business methods, and had volunteered and enlisted in August 1914. Cluny was an ex-sea captain from Portuguese West Africa who could entertain them for hours with his amazing tales of sailing vessels of many kinds all over the world. José Garcia Calderon, the son of a former president of Peru, was a gifted writer and painter. When Chapman left the front line for his transfer, his place was taken by S. L. V. Sukuna, a Fiji Island prince whose father was king of one of the larger islands in the Fiji group; his maternal grandfather, King Thakombau, the last great ruler of the Fijis, had ceded the islands to the British Crown in 1874. Of such men was the new Foreign Legion composed.

Chapman's transfer came through by August 1, 1915, and he was officially entered on the rolls of the Aviation, but not as a student pilot; he was too good a machine gunner to be wasted. He was assigned to V.B.108 (Voisin bombers) as a *mitrailleur* (machine gunner), a post he somewhat resented, but after thirty days of flying day and night with this long-distance Voisin outfit, during which time he acquitted himself well, he was released for pilot training at Avord.

Victor soon made friends with Kiffin Rockwell after his arrival at the primary training school and wrote to his father:

"I find a compatriot I am proud to own here. His name is Rockwell. He transferred about a month ago from the Legion after being wounded on May 9. This Rockwell has the knack of telling exactly what war is like. I think I shall like this man very much."

On that same day Rockwell wrote, "An American named Chapman from the Third Marching Regiment arrived here this morning and seems to be a very fine fellow indeed."

And on that meeting was based one of the finest comradeships of the war.

Training planes were scarce and tuition time sparse, and Chapman did not qualify for his wings until January 9, 1916, but he had plenty of time, for the progress of the proposed Escadrille Américaine was very sluggish. To keep their hands in and to earn their rations, both Chapman and Rockwell were sent to Paris to fly with the Air Guard, a temporary organization assembled to defend the city from enemy air raids. On the face of it, the duty promised glory and medals aplenty for anyone fortunate enough to destroy an enemy Zeppelin while the populace of Paris cheered, but to carry out this important duty, the pilots were given ancient Voisins, a front-seat gunner—and one machine gun! It was desultory and tiresome work since not many German airmen risked flights that far. The Eiffel Tower was probably their greatest menace, and what thrills they experienced were during night operations when the pilots, flying these slovenly pusher biplanes without proper night-flying equipment or ground facilities, performed tasks under difficulties that were unmatched by any aircraft at the front.

These gaunt-looking machines were kept in squadron service until well into 1917. A bomber version was used on daylight and night raids. One night-bomber squadron, V.B.101, commanded by a Captain Laurens, dropped a record number of bombs in the early months of 1917. During two consecutive days in June of that year they delivered a total weight of 21,750 pounds of high explosive, and in the previous April had dropped 25½ tons of bombs during a series of one hundred raids. The Voisin also was equipped for trench strafing and for attacks on enemy pillboxes, and for this work were fitted with either 37- or 47-mm *avion canon,* heavy-caliber weapons that more than paid for the space they occupied.

By the time the Escadrille Américaine became a reality both Rockwell and Chapman were sent back and joined the first small group of Americans in the new organization. As soon as their Nieuports had been fitted with guns and a few primary instruments, these two men started flying and never stopped until enemy bullets ended their sterling careers. Victor Chapman in particular flew incessantly. He would take off, do a two-hour patrol, return, and as soon as his plane was refueled and checked, would go off again on any pretext and scout the enemy lines for two more hours. He was the first off the ground in the morning and the last one in at night. He munched his meals as he walked up and down the tarmac, awaiting maintenance. What citations and decorations came his way, he dismissed as unimportant. Although he was glad that such credits went to the squadron, he seldom wore his ribbons or mentioned that he had received any awards.

On May 24 he was cited for the Croix de Guerre with Palm for a courageous attack on three enemy aircraft, a scrap in which he soon discovered that he had taken on more than he could manage. He threw the frail Nieuport about the sky amid a hail of enemy fire, hoping to come out in position to draw a bead on one of them, but the opposition was too much, for no matter how Victor twisted and turned trying to get his gunsight on an Iron Cross insignia, there always was another in the same position drawing a bead on him. His aircraft was perforated from engine cowling to rudder. A number of bullets clipped or pierced his coverall and one drew a hot searing slug along his forearm and made him wince. It was soon obvious that this was not his day, and at the first opportunity Victor pulled out, nosed down, and escaped into a muffin of cloud.

He continued on in this manner over the next three weeks and his squadron mates realized that this six-foot man with

the thick black hair was completely without emotion in all his
activities. He put in more hours of flying than any other volunteer, and looking back over his record and considering his
lack of experience, it is a mystery that he lived as long as he
did. He continually attacked against overwhelming odds
simply because he had nothing but contempt for the Germans.
He fought like a man charged with some wild quest, but on
the ground he was the consumate gentleman. He ignored all
the horror of war. His artistic soul rejected the blood and
tragedy and took in only the beauty of the day, the scene, the
environment. The shell-torn landscape, the battered villages,
the stark ruin of the battle-burned forests blended into classic
pictures, for he overlooked the unpleasant, and accepted his
many companions on the same optimistic terms.

On June 17 Victor had a very narrow escape from death.
He was, as usual, flying alone when he came across a formation of five enemy planes; two Aviatik C-1s, almost replicas
of the contemporary Albatros C-3, were moving to cross the
French lines with the idea of taking photographs. They were
being escorted by three Fokkers, and the antiaircraft puffs
that blossomed about the enemy planes attracted Victor. He
went headlong into the fray, but noting the three-ship escort
above, he eased off and began to circle to find an opening.

Secure in their strength, since they did not expect a lone
Nieuport to interfere with them, the intruders ignored him.
When the Aviatiks split up to cover their assigned areas where
each would photograph his particular strip of ground, Victor
saw a faint chance to make a strike, and swooping like a hawk
he went down. His Lewis gun chattered, and a photography
pilot intent on holding his course, was startled to feel his
plane being stitched with short snarling bursts. He immediately changed course and hurried to a position below his
Fokker escort. Determined not to let the two-seater escape,
Victor kept after him and pounded the full drum of bullets
into the broad-tailed biplane. Every burst had gone home
clean. The Aviatik whirled and then staggered, and the pilot,
with half a dozen bullets in his shoulders, fell forward on the

stick. The enemy gunner had been killed before he could crawl back from the camera mounted in the floor, and the Aviatik fell away and plunged to earth in long flame-streaked sweeps.

The Fokker pilots, with revenge in their hearts, bore down on the impudent Nieuport, and Spandau-Maxim guns returned the bullet tattoo. When Victor turned he saw that his attackers were members of the famous Oswald Boelcke circus, no neophytes. Boelcke usually hand-picked his pilots by selecting the best and boldest from all other staffels on his front. They poured down on Chapman from three tight angles and again Victor must have realized his indiscretion.

He had to employ all his skill, daring, and chance-taking as he darted, twisted, and turned and tried to maintain some altitude. He then realized that he had used all the ammunition in the drum on his Lewis and had to replace it somehow before he could defend himself; there was no alternative but to grip the stick between his knees, haul the gun down from its impractical mounting and try to get a new pan of ammunition affixed and the loading sequence run through once more.

During all this frantic activity the Fokker pilots used him as a practice target. They could see his brave efforts to replace the gun drum and knew how handicapped he was—there would never be a better chance to get in some foolproof target practice. Bullets screamed all around Chapman's head, slug after slug crashed into the machine and pierced the instrument panel, indicating how close they came to his skull. They hissed and ripped off long sections of wing fabric that dragged in streamers from the trailing edges.

Finally a telling shot was scored by one bullet that caught the metal aileron bracket protruding from the upper wing; the bracket was severed, and the slug ricocheted, tore through Victor's helmet, and hacked out a gash four inches long across his scalp. With practically no aileron control, the plane started to spin, and with his vision obscured by blood streaming down his face, Victor hauled the broken sections of the bracket together and held them with his gloved hand. This at least produced neutral aileron effect and he reverted to wriggling and darting to evade his tormentors. Finally, he allowed the Nieuport to fall off, giving the impression that he finally had been sent down, but once he was clear, he eased the Nieuport out, and still clutching the jagged ends of the aileron bracket landed at a French field located at Froids.

Victor was given emergency medical care and a meal while mechanics repaired the aileron control. Later that afternoon he flew back to his own squadron, and, although his head was swathed in bandages, he laughed off the situation and refused to go to a nearby hospital for full medical attention.

"I'm quite all right," he insisted. "You know how scalp wounds are. They bleed a lot, but unless you suffer some concussion or skull damage, there is no real danger. I tell you, I am fine."

Bill Thaw suggested that Victor go to Paris for a brief visit. "You could visit Ken Weeks' mother. She'd love to have you for a few days. It would ease her loss a bit to have some other American boy to mother."

Kenneth Weeks, another American volunteer, had been killed a week or so before while fighting with the Foreign Legion. His mother had taken a house in Paris, and her door was always open to any of the volunteers when they were on leave.

"I don't think this is the time," Victor countered.

"Well, you're not flying for a few days," Thaw said flatly. "There is no plane for you. Take it easy."

"Sure. I'll sit around and grow whiskers until I have a new machine."

"You must have a large headache," Bill continued sympathetically.

"It's no bother. I feel fine."

"Well, try to get some sleep."

Two days later, June 18, Clyde Balsley was shot down near Verdun and was moved to the Vadelaincourt hospital as his condition was considered to be critical. As soon as Victor heard of Clyde's misfortune he went over to see him.

H. Clyde Balsley was a native of San Antonio, Texas, but he in no way resembled the typical Texan. He was sleek, aristocratic, wore his hair perfectly groomed, and sported a smart military mustache. In fact he looked more the part of the accepted version of a British airman, but Clyde was one of the most respected pilots in the Escadrille Américaine.

Desirous of aiding the cause, Clyde had joined the American Field Service as an ambulance driver at the start of the war. He had no particular aspirations regarding any form of active service, but once he had driven a few tours of duty at the front, he realized that he was the type who could contribute more, and on one of his trips into Paris heard the rumor that a number of Americans were trying to form an aviation squadron to serve with the French. Careful inquiry revealed that Dr. Gros, who had been a guiding light in the ambulance service, was a member of the committee attempting to organize such a venture.

Balsley was accepted by the French Aviation on September 16, 1915, was enrolled at the Pau aviation school by October 1, and won his wings on January 2, 1916. At first he was attached to Escadrille V.97 and flew with the Paris Air Guard with Charles Chouteau Johnson until May 26, 1916, and then went to the front with the Escadrille Américaine on May 29.

Clyde Balsley arrived at the same time as Raoul Lufbery and they were both assigned to a little cottage near the field that was owned and occupied by a French couple. The patroness explained that she had one large airy room with a feather bed, and a smaller, rather dank cell with a cheerless cot. As the senior airman who spoke French fluently, Raoul elected to do most of the talking. Now and then Clyde chipped in with his atrocious patois. The French owner became suspicious of Lufbery; she couldn't reconcile the idea of an American who spoke such good French. To her way of thinking, Balsley was honest, sincere, and probably needed mothering. That man Lufbery, he was too slick.

Corporal Balsley was given the luxurious front room and Adjutant Lufbery banished to the back room; the innocent *pilote* with no ribbons on his chest was rewarded with the feather bed, and the *adjudant* ordered to the cell-like bunk. Madame was not having any of that smart French talk hoodwink her. Clyde did his best to explain that the *adjudant* was a very important man and because of his elevated rank was entitled to the better room. At that madame went into a screaming tirade.

"O.K.! O.K.!" Lufbery said to pacify her. "Just as you say, Madame. I'll take the back room," and he picked up his duffle and quickly disappeared.

"That was one of my luckiest breaks," Clyde said later. "I got the best room, but I certainly learned a lot from Luf. I wish I could have put it to better use."

V The aristocratic Texan was the Escadrille's first serious casualty when he was shot down and wounded on June 18, 1916, in one of the closest escapes experienced by any aviator in the war. He had seen little service, and was soon forgotten, but in his role of the first American flier to be badly wounded in action he was for a short time a brave figure who made America's friendship for the French people clear and unmistakable.

During the first few days he was on the front Clyde had had one or two inconsequential engagements with enemy aircraft, but his setback came in his first real combat, one of the so-called dogfights. The Americans of that period were lucky to have survived their first weeks as well as they did, considering that at this time the enemy was better equipped, better armed, and more experienced in formation or "circus" flying.

On this particular Sunday morning Captain Thénault had been ordered to lead a dawn patrol and he selected Norman Prince, Kiffin Rockwell, and Clyde Balsley as his flight. Lufbery had also been selected, but at the last minute his Nieuport was found to be unserviceable. McConnell and Victor Chapman were held at alert on the field, a tour of duty that came to all pilots in routine order.

Thénault's task was to furnish protection for a couple of French artillery aircraft, an assignment that took them well over the enemy lines at an altitude of about ten thousand feet. As they were cruising up and down over the "spotter" planes, they were intercepted by a large German formation and a small-sized dogfight ensued. According to Balsley's report the Americans were in no particular formation, but were flying fairly close together over an area between Saint-Mihiel and Verdun.

"When over Hill 305, well within the German lines, I spotted a German plane. Deeper inside the area I saw several more, although they were indistinct because of the clouds and haze. Rockwell and Prince were flying together off to my right and since I felt no one had noticed the Boche, I moved up close to Thénault and waggled my wings and made sure he had spotted the enemy.

"I was somewhat concerned and watched the single enemy plane carefully and then saw him separate from the others. It looked like a good chance to pick off the straggler and I turned to look at Thénault with the idea of getting permission, but the captain had started to dive. I figured he was going after one of the other Germans, so I nosed down too, but swung to the left to get the man I had selected. Down, down, down I went.

"As I moved in closer, I realized I was taking on a two-seater, quite possibly an Aviatik, and I presumed he would be as fast as I was if he went into a dive. I considered all this for a second or two and then decided to take him on.

"I nosed down steeper and was certain the gunner had not seen me, so I moved in even closer, deciding to give them my first burst from close quarters, and then come up from below for a second. I held a straight course and gradually he came into my sights and by now the gunner was certainly alert. I fired one burst, then a second . . . the last shots I was to fire in that war. My machine gun jammed, but the observer had not fired in return. I hoped I had got him, and then pulled away, the stick between my knees, and started to swing the weapon down to remedy the stoppage.

"At that instant a gun opened up against me from the left. Bap-bap-bap, and another opened up on my right. I was surrounded and there was no time to replace that drum. It seemed now that there were enemy aircraft all around me and since they had seen me trying to remedy a gun stoppage, they must have known they had a sitting duck. The others were far over the line and I was too far over to risk diving for the ground. I had to hold what altitude I had until I could maneuver my way back into more friendly territory.

"I guess I began to fly like a wild man. I zoomed, turned, did falling-leafs, and darted about trying to evade the continual gunfire. I felt bursts zipping through every portion of my plane and then saw a small cloud into which I darted with streams of lead in hot pursuit. Inside the cover I sideslipped and actually got over on my back and in that time took a quick inspection of my plane. There were great holes and lines of perforation everywhere. Fabric was ripped and wide swaths of it streamed back from the upper wing. As I worked to come out of my inverted position something hit me like the kick of a mule. The blow struck somewhere in my leg and I actually stuck my hand down to make sure it was still there. I could have sworn it had been blown away.

"I was thankful for my safety belt, for I was positive at the time that the impact would have tossed me out of the cockpit. My legs were paralyzed and since my feet were in leather loops of the rudder bar, I found myself doing all sorts of crazy tricks over which I had no control. In this position all controls were reversed, of course; the rudder was acting as the elevator and the elevator had become the rudder. Unable to control my rudder I soon found myself in a tight spin. Around and around I went, and in seconds I knew it would soon be over. I knew I would hit the ground with a dreadful smack. I had seen aircraft crash and had lost so many friends in this manner. I remembered the first man I had ever pulled out of a crash, and I knew I would end up looking exactly like that. I particularly remembered a Captain Jolain, and that I a grown man had cried at what I had seen. Now it was my turn. I wondered if anyone would cry for me.

"Around and around, down, down I went, and as the features of the landscape became more definite I wondered if this was the end. There was an emotion of ecstasy and I wondered if I was giving up. I sensed no terror, no dread, no mental fuzziness. My mind was unusually clear and then suddenly I resolved that Death could not be like this, and another flash taunted me with the fact that I was giving up without a struggle. I could still be useful to France. I was shouting: 'Do something! You're not dead. Don't quit. There *is* a chance.' In that second came my redemption.

"My mind cleared and I tried to push my right leg. It took all my strength, but since my feet were in the loops of the rudder I managed to straighten out the glide. The spinning eased off and then I drew back carefully on the stick and the spin came to an end. Now where was I? I kept my hand on my knee to make sure I'd keep that rudder neutral. As I finally leveled off I was shocked to hear machine guns again. Zing! Zing! Zing!

"I had forgotten about the Boche, but there was one still on my tail. But what could I do about it? I had no gun, my legs were paralyzed and I was in no condition to stage any evasive maneuvers. I did what anyone else would have done. I nosed down so steep I should have pulled my wings off. Instead, only a machine-gun drum slipped out of its rack and smacked me on the upper arm. I thought I had been hit again, but soon realized what was going on. The rest of the drums fell out and the tachometer needle had crawled up to the red segment of the dial. My engine was roaring away at 1500 revs, but while it was risky, it was better than staying in front of those Hun guns. Besides, I now realized that friendly territory was just below and ahead. I could see shellholes, trenches, and men in blue helmets. France!

"I held her steady, keeping the rudder neutral by controlling the bar with my hand on my knees. I pulled out of the dive carefully and was thankful when the wings stayed on. I was beginning to feel faint, for I must have been bleeding badly, but ahead were green fields and I risked working my rudder and broke my speed with a sideslip. It looked like a field at first, but when it was too late I realized it was crisscrossed with old swaths of barbed wire, so I tried to pancake in.

"I did fairly well, considering, but my wheels became entangled with the wire and the Nieuport tripped, turned over and crashed. Upside down, hanging in my belt and rudder loops, I hung there for some time, hardly able to realize what had happened. Then gasoline began to trickle down and soak me and the odor of it acted like a restorative. I flipped my belt buckle and dropped out on my head. I tried to get to my hands and knees but my legs were still paralyzed and I was helpless. Still, I realized that fire could break out at any minute, so I tried crawling, dragging myself along with clumps of weeds. I was struggling along like a dog with a broken back, and managed to cover about ten yards. No more.

"Exhausted, I lay there and somehow realized that loud explosions were going on nearby. I tried to figure it out, but I was deaf as the result of the terrific dive, but my war experience told me that those explosions were shells and in all probability the Boche were trying to hit my plane.

"I felt no particular pain and by now I figured I was not badly wounded. Oh, I'd be hauled off for hospital and then get a short leave in Paris, but in a short time I'd be back on the front. I ignored the 'seventy-sevens' that were dropping all around me, although one was a direct hit on the Nieuport. In a little while it all subsided and four French soldiers came out of a dugout and, crawling along under the wire, dragged me to safety. I didn't know it then, but I had made my last flight for France."

Clyde Balsley had been hit by an "explosive" bullet and his wound, instead of being minor as he had hoped, was very severe. He was held at an evacuation hospital at Vadelaincourt where his life hung in the balance for some time. During the course of the next twelve months he was operated on six times as surgeons removed the bullet splinters that seemed to fill his body. In the autumn of 1917, nearly eighteen months after his big fight, Clyde was well enough to return to the United States where he overcame his crippled condition and joined the U. S. Air Service and served in an executive position in the Pursuit Division at Washington.

Swathed in bandages himself as the result of his encounter with three Fokkers two days before, Victor Chapman hurried over to see Clyde and to learn if there was something he could do to make his stay more comfortable. Men in the hospital under such circumstances could use their toilet gear, and were glad to receive any mail that had arrived, or better still any packages of food that might have been sent from home.

Victor aroused Balsley: "Hello, old boy. I just brought your toothbrush. How goes it?"

Clyde, who was deep in despond and as thirsty as a man alone on the desert, was overjoyed to hear words in English.

"Victor! I'm so glad to see you. Can you get me out of here? I'm not too bad, am I? It's just that I'm so thirsty all the time, and all they let me have is an old wet bandage to suck."

Chapman did not dare tell Clyde how serious his wound was, but cheered him with, "Think nothing of it. Tomorrow I'll be back again with some oranges. They'll let you suck on an orange."

"That will be wonderful. How's everything?"

"Everything's fine. Now take it easy. I'll be back tomorrow."

"You won't forget the oranges, Victor?"

"Leave it to me. And I'll get champagne when the doctors let you have real liquid."

Clyde dropped off to sleep convinced that he would be well taken care of.

The next morning Captain Thénault appeared at his bedside along with a major and a colonel.

"Ah ha, my little one," Thénault began. "I have a little present for you."

"Oranges?" gasped Balsley.

"Oranges? *Mon Dieu, non!*"

The colonel stepped forward and began, "In the name of the Republic," he took a large box from his pocket, "I confer on you the le Médaille Militaire and la Croix de Guerre."

"For me? Whatever for?"

The colonel almost choked. "*Pourquoi?* You are the first American aviator to be severely wounded . . . for France. Suffering greatly as you must have suffered, you flew far, far over German ground to bring your machine back safe to . . . France. There is sometimes a braver thing than overcoming an enemy. It is overcoming yourself. You, my son, have done this . . . for a country not your own."

In the solemn hush a cork popped. Madame, head of the women nurses, had produced some champagne and was pouring a little into the glass of every man in the room.

"*Vive le petit Américain!*" she proposed.

Clyde was impressed and honored but he remembered that only the day before he had seen two other men so decorated, and both had died within the hour.

"*Merci,*" he finally said in a low scared voice, "but I am not going to die!"

When the officers had gone, and the other wounded men had settled back in their beds, Clyde held the two decorations in his warm hands and in his feverish desire muttered, "If they were only oranges."

Victor Chapman made some concession to his head wound by sleeping a little later than usual, but by June 21 a new Nieuport was flown in and he busied himself adjusting the compass and the machine gun. The weather was not too good, so he satisfied himself by flying the new aircraft around the field to work out a few control bugs. Late that afternoon some Germans were reported over the French lines and Victor joined the others in the search, but the whole thing turned out to be a false alarm.

Despite continued warnings and appeals, Victor refused to ease up or take a short leave. He flew without a helmet since his head was so swathed in bandages it would not fit. The morning of June 23 was fine and Victor insisted on flying a regular patrol, taking his turn with the rest. Fortunately, there were no enemy planes in the air and the patrol was uneventful. After lunch Victor gathered a basket of oranges intended for Balsley, but when he went out to the hangars he found Thénault, Prince, and Lufbery were warming up their machines to go on a flight.

"Look," Victor explained to them, "I'll put the package behind my seat. I'll go up to the lines with you and if there is nothing important going on, I'll break off and drop down and see Clyde. He's dying for some juicy fruit."

"Go deliver your oranges," Thénault ordered. "You've flown enough for today."

"Take it easy, Victor," Lufbery pleaded.

Their engines were turning over, and on a signal from Thénault, all three rumbled away for the take-off. Annoyed, Chapman called a mechanic, had his prop swung, and was soon haring after them. Thénault's group quickly found two enemy planes on which they dived, and while they were engaged with them three more dropped out of the clouds above and the Escadrille planes prudently withdrew, and carried out a routine patrol up and down the lines without encountering Chapman. On their return to their field, they presumed that he had flown to the hospital to see Clyde.

Still believing that Victor had gone to deliver the oranges, the other pilots of the Escadrille felt no concern for him until late that afternoon when the pilot of a Farman plane that had been up in the same area reported that he had seen three Nieuports in a combat with five German planes, and that in the middle of the engagement he had noticed a fourth Nieuport diving in full speed to join the fight. The Farman pilot was positive that this plane, for no apparent reason, had gone down with its engine full on.

There is another version to this story. The German planes concerned were two L.V.G. observation machines, and as soon as Captain Thénault signaled for an attack, he found that, as usual, the two-seaters were covered by three Fokker fighters. Realizing that they were too far over to engage this many, Thénault pulled out and got back to his own lines. In the meantime, Chapman who had followed them, nosed down to give what aid he could. No one in the Nieuport formation saw him and he was left to fight his way out of the tangle. Whether any of the Germans raked his plane is not known. What is believed is that after his first attack, seeing that he was all alone, Chapman began a series of wild maneuvers to get away, and, harried and outnumbered, he may have overdone the violence of his tactics and wrenched off the wings of his plane. A German report had it that Victor was shot through the head, and this seems to be what may have happened. The French Farman pilot insisted, however, that Chapman simply went into a full-power dive from which he never recovered. He went into the ground with the power on, and must have been killed instantly.

A typical wartime misunderstanding occurred when Chapman's body was pulled out of the wreckage. Besides the package of oranges, Victor had a couple of letters addressed to Clyde Balsley in his pocket, which he intended to deliver to Clyde with the fruit. When these letters were found it was presumed that the dead pilot was Clyde Balsley and the information was given to the International Red Cross. Clyde Balsley who was recovering from a wound in a French hospital was reported officially to have been shot down and killed in German territory.

Escadrille Américaine lost one of its finest characters when Victor Chapman went down, perhaps the victim of his own strong determination. Kiffin Rockwell wrote to Victor's mother; "I find it almost impossible to write in full justice to Victor or to really express my sympathy with you. Everything I would try to say seemed so weak. So I finally said, 'I will just go ahead and work hard, do my best, then if I have accomplished a lot or have been killed in accomplishing it, they will know I have not forgotten Victor, and that some of his strength of character still lived.'"

These were some of the men who had volunteered to fight for France and the freedom of all men.

Chapter VI

PETS AND PRACTICAL JOKES

Although this small band of volunteers had been in action but ten weeks, it had booked a commendable number of combat-flying hours. Bill Thaw and Clyde Balsley had been wounded; Jim McConnell was still hospitalized with a wrenched back, and Victor Chapman had been killed. It is true, as pointed out by some historians, that their activities were blown up far beyond their actual importance by American correspondents; in several instances the pilots of N.124 were outraged by ridiculous accounts of their exploits that appeared in American newspapers and magazines. Up till now they were not a complete squadron, but every man had worked so hard to justify the organization's being that French officials realized they were due for a rest and change of scene.

Norman Prince and Bert Hall had been made adjutants, and all corporals on the list were promoted to sergeants. At a special decorations parade held on June 26, 1916, Rockwell and Hall received both the Médaille Militaire and the Croix de Guerre. Bill Thaw, now a full lieutenant, was awarded the Legion of Honor and an additional Palm to his Croix de Guerre with which he had been honored previously. Victor

Chapman was awarded the Médaille Militaire and the Croix de Guerre posthumously.

Early in September N.124 was relieved of duty, and the pilots turned over their old Nieuports to a replacement unit. Everyone was ordered to report to Le Bourget, the aviation center outside Paris. The mechanics and administration personnel were to make the trip in squadron trucks, but the pilots were furnished transportation aboard the Paris express which stopped at Bar-le-Duc. Naturally there was considerable enthusiasm, particularly when they learned they were to have a week's leave in Paris; the airmen capered about like boardingschool boys heading home for the holidays. All sorts of rumors were rife as they awaited their train, and it was agreed generally that on their return to the front they would be operating along the Somme where the new von Richthofen staffels were fighting to the death with the boys of the Royal Flying Corps. But, as usual, rumor was well awry, for they were destined to return to Luxeuil to take part in the famous bomb raid against the German Mauser factory.

At the time the Escadrille Américaine was composed of Norman Prince, Bert Hall, Raoul Lufbery, Didier Masson, Kiffin Rockwell, Dudley Hill, Paul Pavelka, Charles Chouteau Johnson, and Laurence Rumsey.

Jim McConnell was in a Paris hospital and Thaw was "off strength" with his wounded arm, so, although the average British fighter squadron was composed of three flights of six pilots for a total of eighteen airmen, and the French *chasse* force had at least twelve, N.124 had to make the best of it with nine Americans, backed up by two French officers, Captain Georges Thénault and Lieutenant Alfred de Laage de Meux. They actually operated as a flight and also maintained a two-pilot *alerte* during the daylight hours with what men and machines were available.

All the way to Paris the conversation was kept at high pitch by the report that they were to be equipped with the new Nieuport-27, a fifteen-meter fighter that had a slightly larger and flatter wing surface. Power was supplied by a 110-hp Le

Rhone rotary that gave an extra ten or fifteen miles per hour. The Nieuport-27 was a fast climber and much more maneuverable than the model they had just relinquished, and had a ceiling of nearly eighteen thousand feet. This plane was to carry a Vickers machine gun that was synchronized to fire through the blades of the propeller by using the British Constantinesco gear. This arrangement put the fixed gun down low where it could be serviced in case of stoppages, and since the Vickers was belt-fed, it was not necessary to change ammunition drums. However, the earlier Lewis gun was also included in the armament, but by now this weapon was mounted on the Cooper-Foster sliding bracket, which improved its handling in the air.

These aircraft were being assembled at Le Bourget, a task that usually required several days, and demanded much activity at the firing butts, and on the compass-swinging platforms where the navigation instruments were checked and compensated. During this time the American pilots were ranging far and wide in the Battle of Paris with skirmishes through the hotels, theatres, boulevards, night clubs, and bars. Well in the van was a small lion cub, now the squadron's official mascot.

Who bought this animal, or how the idea of such an unusual pet originated is one of the Lafayette's prize legends. One version is that, on an earlier trip to Paris, Bill Thaw had seen an advertisement in a newspaper that a dentist in Brazil—of all places—had a lion cub for sale. This seemed like a great idea, and at the time a syndicate was formed of Dudley Hill, Norman Prince, Kiffin Rockwell, and Bill Thaw to raise five hundred francs to complete the deal. How long all this took, or how soon after the purchase was made the animal was delivered, has not been fully explained, but this is the best version that anyone can remember. A variation on this story is that the cub had been born on a French ship during a voyage from Africa; at any rate it was a cuddlesome pet that tried to roar to prove he was a lion, but more often was content to be held and suck a human thumb.

He was everyone's pet and was whisked all over the city, becoming a wonderful conversation factor for the American airmen. One or two chorus girls who were at first frightened of the young lion suggested that when he grew up he would have to be put behind bars.

"Bars!" protested Jim McConnell, who was mobile although still convalescent with a lame back. "Why put him behind bars? He'll see all he'll ever need traveling with this mob." By now the cub had been named Whiskey.

Choteau Johnson wrote home about Whiskey.

"I must tell you about our new mascot. You will never guess what it is so I will tell you right off the bat; it's a four-month-old lion cub. Four of us bought him in Paris. He's a great little fellow and plays like a kitten, except when he eats; and then look out for his claws. Whenever he goes out we have the whole population following, just to look at him.

"I had a funny experience returning to our field. We came up by train since we were to take delivery of our new machines at the airdrome. I had 'Whiskey' (that's his name) in my arms, standing in the corridor of the car. When the guard came up he said: 'You can't bring that wild beast in here. Dogs or cats, yes, but not a lion.'

"Whiskey was asleep and I said: 'Don't be a fool; he's just as gentle as a kitten,' and I was getting away with it O.K. when a woman tried to go by and sort of pushed me and woke up Whiskey. He let out a young roar and made a pass at her, showing a full set of ferocious teeth and a paw bristling with large-sized claws. The dame in question let out a scream, *Mon Dieu.*

"That ended it and I got the bounce out of the train at the next station and had to get a special box made for Whiskey. That meant I had to stay overnight and take another train the next day. Poor Whiskey had to ride in the baggage car.

"On the field here he is quite happy and runs around playing or sleeping in a stable where it is warm."

Whiskey joined the usual menagerie of pets that were to be found on any wartime airfield. N.124 had dogs of all breeds, mangy cats, birds, including parrots, and even a goat or two, but Whiskey was king of them all.

At one time Didier Masson unwisely invested in a small red fox that had been offered by two cash-hungry poilus. The unfriendly little beast was fitted with a dog collar and leash and given the full treatment in the hope that Reynard would become a rival to Whiskey, but the fox took a dislike to Masson and bit him several times. Captain Thénault's pedigreed Alsatian, Fram, had an instinctive antipathy for the fox, and, apparently knowing what was best for him, the animal slipped out of his collar and left camp. Two days later the same two poilus returned the fox, claiming a reward. Fram was so outraged at the course of events that he wasted no time in finishing Reynard. The rest of the fable has it that Didier gave the pelt to his mechanic who had it made up into a neckpiece for his sweetheart.

Another pet at N.124 that will be long remembered was purchased by Bill Thaw and Ted Parsons, who in a mellow moment bought what was offered as a civet cat. This was a sleek-looking animal that bore suspicious black and white stripes and Parsons had an idea that the pussy might be related to the American skunk. But the villager who was offering the animal for sale declared that Esther, as she was known, was a perfect lady, fully housebroken, and had had all objectionable organs removed.

All went well at the Escadrille field for almost twenty-four hours, and then Esther asserted herself. To add insult to fragrance, Esther turned out to be a male animal with none of his offensive capabilities impaired and "she" soon had the premises uninhabitable. This might be considered "Fifth Column" operations in World War I, but fortunately Sampson, the squadron chef, took umbrage at the indignity and laid about with a broom handle until "Esther" was no more.

Meanwhile Whiskey remained the favorite of the squadron, and his chief companion was another pet of Didier Masson's, a white hound of questionable parentage by the name of Carranza. Carranza did his best to bring up Whiskey like a gentleman, but although he almost made him believe he was a dog, Whiskey gradually displayed some of his jungle background, and chewed up anything he could get his teeth into. Spare uniforms, kepis, blankets, and personal garments were ripped to shreds, until one day one of the pilots discovered that Whiskey had destroyed a brand-new hat. He was so enraged with the young lion that he picked up a chunk of stove wood and hit the cub a sharp blow over the head. It was meant only as a reasonable penalty for the damage, but the blow must have injured an optic nerve for in a short time a white film spread over one eye, and Whiskey lost his sight on that side.

When Whiskey reached the end of his first year the Escadrille pilots decided that he should have the company of a wife and after some investigation and search a female cub was purchased and, of course, named Soda. Whiskey was entranced with his new friend and the two animals got along famously, but being a lady Soda was not as free with her affection for humans as was Whiskey. She had cold dignity and reserve and although she did her best to live up to Whiskey's standards and learn the tricks he had been taught, she knew she was a lion. Instead of playing she would claw and scratch and would not submit to human petting. Only Whiskey enjoyed her good behavior.

Raoul Lufbery held a fascinating charm over Whiskey. They would romp and roughhouse together for hours at a time, and it was said that Whiskey was the only one on the field who really understood the mysterious Luf. He had but to cry, "Whiskey Man!" in a certain tone and the big lion would tear the squadron apart to get to him.

The two used to perpetrate a somewhat cruel act that was long remembered from one end of the front to the other. No matter where the Americans were located they always drew large numbers of visitors from nearby towns or military rest camps. Wounded soldiers, in particular, enjoyed walking around the hangars to inspect the Nieuports at close hand and ponder on the significance of the Indian head insignia.

Whenever there was a good-sized crowd on the field Luf and Whiskey would stage their so-called joke. The lion was usually hidden in a dim corner of a hangar, and on signal, just as a convalescent poilu was limping past where Whiskey was snoozing, Lufbery would give a special call at which the lion would let out a roar, leap from his shelter, stand up on his hind legs and clamp his front paws on the shoulders of the victim. Amazed to be confronted by an actual lion, the unfortunate visitor would in most cases collapse with fright, whereupon Whiskey, carrying out the game to the limit, would spread himself out on the prostrate victim, and once in command, would throw back his head, open his mouth wide and let out what sounded like a maniacal laugh.

With that bellow of triumph and on a second signal from Luf, Whiskey would withdraw and curl up in his master's lap like a huge affectionate dog. Only then was the frightened soldier helped to his feet and reassured that Whiskey was a very tame lion.

This was the sort of joke that Raoul Lufbery enjoyed. Most of us would fail to see any humor in it, but Luf was an unusual man, and it might be well to look into his background to see what influences accounted for his distorted sense of humor.

Raoul Lufbery was not a native American, having been born in France on March 14, 1885, and was somewhat older than the average airman of World War 1. His mother died one year after his birth and he was placed temporarily with a family living in the Auvergne Mountains. It is rugged country and the people there reflect their environment, being volcanic and moody with distinctive touches of the early Celts. In 1890 Raoul's father, an American citizen, remarried, and the next year took his new wife to the United States, leaving Raoul and two other sons with their grandmother until he knew what his position would be in the New World. In 1901 the second wife died and Raoul's father was left with five children, the youngest of whom was nine months old. In

the meantime young Raoul found a job in a chocolate factory
at Blois and sent his father most of his earnings for nearly
three years, thereby helping M. Lufbery to establish a comfortable home in Wallingford, Connecticut.

In 1904 when Raoul was nineteen he decided to see the
world. He was employed in a factory at Clermont-Ferrand
at the time, and he went from there across the Mediterranean
to Algiers, Tunis, and Egypt, and continued on to Con-
stantinople—now Istanbul—and worked for a short time as a
waiter in a restaurant. He traveled in this nomadic way to
every exotic city he could think of. From Turkey he moved
through the Balkans into Germany, and in Hamburg signed
on as a seaman with the Waerman Line. The vessels of this
company plied between Hamburg and German Southwest
Africa. Raoul finally reached America in 1906 after years of
globe-trotting and picking up a dozen trades and almost as
many languages. He made his way to Wallingford where he
hoped to rejoin his father, but unfortunately, Lufbery senior
had left Connecticut to go abroad on business; he was now a
dealer in stamps and wished to fill out his stock and pick up
a few unusual items. Since father and son had not corre-
sponded regularly, neither knew the plans of the other. As a
matter of fact Raoul had arrived in New York City on the
very day that his father had sailed from the same port for
Europe. They were never to meet again.

Raoul stayed in Wallingford for some time where he no
doubt improved his English, but he was not geared for set-
tling down, and next moved on to Cuba. From there he returned to the United States and tried his luck in a bakery in
New Orleans. San Francisco next saw him, where he was a
waiter in a hotel, but when times became sluggish following
the financial panic in the fall of 1907, Lufbery joined the U. S.
Army and was sent to the Philippines. It was this military
service that enabled him to claim American citizenship years
later. When his two-year hitch in the Army expired, he took
his savings and headed for Japan and China.

All this wandering had developed a bold sense of independence in Luf. He was completely individual, charged with restlessness and a sincere belief in his own abilities and had little concern for the opinions of others. He was a good worker but would drop his tools at any presumed slight or an imperious order from a superior. His two years of soldiering had instilled little discipline or developed an orderly pattern of behavior. A job with the Chinese customs service lasted only long enough for Lufbery to cause trouble and be fired.

He next became a railroad ticket agent in Bombay, India, where he again received his walking papers for beating up a passenger who complained of his incivility. It was unfortunate that the aggrieved patron was a heavy stockholder in the railroad.

In 1912 Raoul wandered into Calcutta where he made the acquaintance of Marc Pourpe, a noted French aviator who was making a series of exhibition flights with a Blériot monoplane. Lufbery had followed a crowd of people to the flying field and noted that the French pilot was having trouble with a gang of coolie laborers who were supposed to put up a tent to shelter the airplane, so Raoul volunteered to take over. He bossed the job so well he was signed on as a regular. There are many legendary sides to this era of Lufbery's service with Pourpe, but the most rational one is that after handling the heavy work and becoming Pourpe's gang foreman, he gradually picked up some of the tricks of the aviation mechanic and in time was able to fill in when Pourpe's chief mechanic fell ill. Then Pourpe's flying partner, an unnamed airman, was killed while they were performing in India, and with that Pourpe decided to return to France to obtain a more improved airplane. He took Lufbery with him.

Now complete comrades in every respect, these two men barnstormed around Europe and Africa during 1913 and added to aviation's growing records and epics. Pourpe attempted a flight from Cairo Egypt to Khartoum in the Sudan and return, a feat that would have been impossible without Lufbery's superhuman efforts to keep his pilot supplied with fuel, spares, and mechanical service. He preceded or followed

Pourpe on every stage of the trip, moving his tools, tanks, and equipment on river steamers, donkeys, camels, on foot, and wherever possible, by train. Marc Pourpe became one of the outstanding airmen of the period after this successful flight.

He and Lufbery were bound by unbreakable ties of friendship, and at times their association had the warp and weft of a classic comradeship and it is believed that neither had had any particular ambition in life until the day they met. From then on Pourpe wished to be the greatest airman in the world, and who knows how far he might have gone had not his wings been burned by the flame of war.

Lufbery had been a nobody, a professional vagabond, but from his first encounter with Marc Pourpe he seemed to take on a new viewpoint, a new ambition; his every move and thought were based on what Marc wanted or might desire. Neither one remembered or cared what had happened to the other before they met.

In the early summer of 1914 they returned to France to purchase a Morane Parasol monoplane with the idea of going back to the Far East for another exhibition tour, but just as all details had been completed, war broke out and Pourpe offered his services. He was accepted immediately by the French Aviation.

Contrary to popular belief Lufbery did not join up with his companion, but accepted the breaks of fortune, bid Marc good-by, and was among the first American volunteers to gather at the Hôtel des Invalides in Paris. He joined the Foreign Legion as an infantryman on August 24. Whether Pourpe pulled wires, or whether Raoul's mechanical skill had anything to do with it, Luf was transferred to Pourpe's squadron as an aviation mechanic by the end of August. Three months later Marc was killed in action, leaving Luf desolate and morose. He stayed on servicing other planes, but over the next few weeks perceptive French officers sensed what a spirit of devotion had existed between the two totally unalike men. Pourpe had been an artist in every sense of the word, a

talented officer and, socially, many brackets higher than Lufbery. Lufbery may have felt that he had lost his guide and
master, and that his future was bleak. He knew that he was
a hard-bitten adventurer with no basic roots, no family ties,
little formal education, a man who had been a hard drinker
and took his fun where he found it.

After Pourpe's death, Raoul was given the opportunity to
become a pilot, an offer that he accepted gratefully with no
dramatic resolutions or theatrical declarations of revenge. He
was not capable of such histrionics; he just picked up his
gear, took one long look to the east where Marc Pourpe had
last flown, and strode out of camp.

He received his early training at Chartres and won his
wings on a Maurice Farman. Later he had bomber training
on a Voisin, and his first war flying was with VB.106 (Voisin)
Squadron where he proved to be a workmanlike performer,
carrying out his duties in a creditable manner.

It will be interesting to see Lufbery through an article he
wrote giving an account of his first combat. While not a highly
educated man he had a keen sense of storytelling and when
he expressed himself in his native tongue, he could produce
a thrilling tale. The following was written by Lufbery when
he first served with a French squadron:

"In January 1916 I was a pilot of a 140-hp, which formed
a part of the bombarding escadrille, No. 102.

"One fine day, at about 1 P.M. we received orders to hold
ourselves in readiness to depart on a bombing expedition. As
is usual under the circumstances, our objective was not indicated, but judging from the amount of gasoline we were told
to carry, and the direction of the wind, we concluded it was
to be the Metz-Sablons station. Every available aeroplane was
to participate in the raid. In all there were about forty machines, half of which belonged to my group, the balance to
Group 101, under the command of the intrepid Commandant
Roisin.

"At the extreme end of the field the machines were drawn

up in line, facing the wind. The mechanics gave a last look at their motors, the gunners tested their guns and laid in their stock of bombs. There were bombs of 10 kilos each which, we were told, wrought as much havoc as the ordinary 155s. I took six; some of my comrades took eight, others nine, or even ten, the number varying according to the capacity of one's machine.

"We were all ready. We waited for our final orders. At length these came. Cards were distributed among us, indicating our itinerary. We regulated our watches according to that of our chief. Fifty minutes after the departure of the first aeroplane we were all to meet over Saint Nicholas du Port at a maximum altitude of 2000 meters. Then, according to the signals of our commandant, we were to go over the lines or return to the aviation camp—defective groupings or bad weather might compel us to do the latter.

"The throb of a motor sounded at the left end of the line. An aeroplane rose, circled around for a few seconds, then climbed into the air. This was followed by a second, then a third. I was number seven. My turn was near. I turned to Sergeant Allard, my observer, and inquired if he was ready. On his reply in the affirmative I opened my motor, circled around like my comrades, then began my ascent.

"Before we started Allard had told me that he would try to rest as I mounted, claiming that he would thus be better able to study the map on the other side of the lines. I saw no objection to his doing this as he could not help me to rise. As I mounted I turned several times to look at him. His eyes were closed. Was he really asleep, I wondered. Anyway, he did right to rest, for shortly he would need all his energy and sangfroid.

"At 2:20 P.M. I was at my rendezvous with the majority of my comrades. Suddenly, from the signal-aeroplane, distinguishable by the red pennons flying from its planes, I saw several rockets shoot out as a sign for us to depart. All that I had to do was to follow my group.

"As we passed the lines, the swifter machines executed

several spirals in order to give the slower aeroplanes time to come up. When our group was complete we continued to advance, here and there greeted with shrapnel. No one was affected by the fire. It was a matter of luck. For a shell fragment to be dangerous it must hit the pilot, or a vital part of the machine. One or even several bullets through the canvas of the planes is of no importance.

"I gazed at the landscape as it unfolded itself beneath me. To the right was the Seille River, barely recognizable at this time of the year. With its curves broken by the rains it looked like one long link of swamps. To the left lay the Moselle with its canal forming two narrow silvery lines, one of which extended to the north where it lost itself in a veil of mist. That which I had taken for a dense fog, I found was the smoke from the factory chimneys at Metz.

"As I drew nearer I could distinguish, through the smoke, groups of houses, churches, long buildings covered with red tiles, probably barracks, encircled by small green, geometrically formed squares. These were the famous forts. From up above they seemed inoffensive.

"A few minutes later I found myself over the spacious station of Metz. This was our objective. The machine in front of me executed a semi-circle in order to give the slower aeroplanes time to come up. Handicapped by my 140-hp, I took no part in this maneuver, but flew straight to the point where I was the first to arrive.

"Our coming must have been announced as several enemy planes came from every direction to meet us. One of them advanced toward me. Quickly, I turned my head to see if my observer was on his guard. His machine gun was pointed at the enemy, his finger was on the trigger. At an altitude of one hundred fifty meters the enemy made a brusk movement to get beyond our range, turning to enable its gunner to fire at us. But this maneuver was useless, for the greater number of bi-place machines have two guns, one stationary which fires from the front, the other mounted on a turret in the rear.

"I kept my eye on my adversary. I could clearly see the

black-painted cross on his fuselage and helm. The fight began. We exchanged a shower of bullets. The Boche *piqued,* apparently having had enough. I did not think it worth my while to follow him, as there was nothing now to obstruct our way, and I had an important mission to fulfill.

"Through the windshield I could distinguish railroad tracks, trains, stationary and on the move, stores of goods, hangars, etc. My observer tapped me on the shoulder and signed me to go ahead. Another tap informed me that the bombs had been dropped. Our mission was accomplished. All that remained for us to do now was to get back to the camp as soon as possible. The Boche were hurrying up in numbers. We had to keep a watch on all sides. We were surprised by a monoplane Fokker which hurled a shower of bullets at us and departed before we had time to respond. Two or three short, sharp, familiar sounds, informed me that my machine was hit, but my motor continued its regular throb and my observer reported that the gasoline tank was untouched.

"The wind blowing from the north facilitated our return. In a short time we were over our lines. Then I laughed, without knowing why. I looked at my observer, and he too laughed. We were both feeling good. Now that we were out of danger we wanted to compare notes, but the noise of the motor hindered all conversation. We would have to be patient and wait until we had landed.

"Slowing down the motor in our descent we glided smoothly over the valley of the Meurthe, and so on home. My comrade lighted a cigarette and passed it on for me to take a puff. How I enjoyed it!

"Gradually the scene beneath us grew normal. The smooth carpet of green moss slowly developed into forests, the long and narrow black ribbons became railroads, the white ribbons, roads. That which in the distance I had taken for a large factory partly hidden in a cloud of smoke, now assumed gigantic proportions, and I recognized the city of Nancy. I was at an altitude of 200 meters over the plateau of Malzeville which served us as an aviation field. One last spiral and I landed near the hangars of my escadrille. My first care was to examine my machine. I found that the planes were pierced in several parts by bullets. I had made no mistake as to the nature of the short, sharp sounds I had heard during the Fokker's attack.

"With those of my comrades who had returned I discussed our expedition. Some of our group were still missing. It was expected that several would not answer the roll call. A number of the men claimed that they had seen some Voisin machines fall. From time to time a white silhouette appeared. 'That must be the one I saw behind me,' announced one. 'More likely it is the one I met on my return,' declared another. Meanwhile the silhouette drew nearer and we were able to make out the distinctive mark of the Escadrille No. 106, a black ermine on a white field.

"Finally, all had returned and our captain no longer looked uneasy. He expressed his satisfaction at seeing his escadrille complete.

"Unfortunately, this was not the case with the other formations participating in the raid. Though it was still too soon to make sure, we feared that some of our comrades would be the guests of the enemy that night."

This was typical of an early bombing raid and beyond his ability to relate in some interesting detail what actually happened, Lufbery made no outstanding contribution and after a reasonable number of hours of war flying and anxious patrols over the line he applied for *chasse* training. Since experienced bomber pilots were at a premium, his commander tried to dissuade him, but when that failed, he pulled many wires to retain this strange, but reliable airman. However, Lufbery was rewarded eventually and sent to Plessis-Belleville for transition training for the Nieuport. He showed no particular skill and for a time appeared so heavy-handed and clumsy, his instructors feared he would have to be sent back to the bomber squadron. But Luf persisted until he

gained some proficiency and on May 24, 1916, was able to
join the Escadrille Américaine. It is difficult to understand
why he yearned for American companionship, for, except for
the two years in the United States, and his short hitch with
the U. S. Army, his background and associations were completely French. If any of his companions had any explanation,
they have never revealed it. His actions too, in seeking to join
this American squadron would seem to be a reproof to the
continued claim that Lufbery became a pilot only to avenge
Marc Pourpe's death, and to pay his debt to his homeland.

When Lufbery turned up at Luxeuil he was a veritable unknown, a small chunky man, not much over five feet tall, with
broad shoulders, primitive speech, and with apparently no
emotions of any kind. He seldom laughed, but when he did he
exploded with a hearty cavalier's roar and his eyes would
sparkle like newly cut gems. Most of the time he was morose,
uncommunicative, and made few friends. He was inscrutable,
and men like Ted Parsons who lived, flew, slept, and shared
leaves with him, admit they never really knew him. He seldom
spoke and when he did his English was a polyglot of every
patois he had picked up; certainly he did not speak like a New
Englander. He had no fears and no outstanding personal qualities, but none of these factors reflects on his skill, daring, and
courage as a flying man. Lufbery had the making of a great
"ace," and had he been more fortunate he might have ended
as the outstanding airman of that campaign. He was in the
same class as Mickey Mannock, another hero who came up
from the dregs of poverty. A Hun-hater to the end, Raoul
fought his foe with unreasoning passion, a man who contributed so much to the cause and yet lost his own individuality
and identity.

Few people today have any idea who Raoul Lufbery was
or where he came from. There is no marker on his birthplace,
no flying field has been named for him. An ancient defensive
maneuver, known as the Lufbery Circle, bears his name, but
it is doubtful that Lufbery originated it any more than Max
Immelmann was the first to perform the "Immelmann" turn.

1. Norman Prince, the American who first conceived the idea of an All-American air squadron to serve with the French. He bought his own flight training and worked for months to sell the idea to the head of the French Aviation. Later, he was to be killed in an accident after returning from a patrol. *(National Archives)*

2. Most candidates for the Lafayette Escadrille had had previous service in the American Field Service or the Foreign Legion. Here, left, is seen James McConnell when he was an ambulance driver, with Paul A. Rockwell who wears his Foreign Legion uniform. Rockwell was to be seriously wounded and invalided out of the service and he finished out the war as official historian of the Lafayette, while performing public relations duty for the French Government. *(Paul A. Rockwell)*

3. Bleriot "Penguin" airplane, the school plane all French airmen used to begin thei
training. It was underpowered and was not intended to fly: merely to give the studen
the feel of flying and handling a propellered vehicle on the ground. *(National Archives*

4. Caudron G. III trainer-reconnaissance biplane, widely used in French flying schoo
for completion of primary training. Powered with either an Anzani or Le Rhone rotar
engine, it served many purposes through the early years of the war. It was easy to f
and made a valuable school machine. *(National Archives)*

Four immortals of the Lafayette Escadrille. With Captain Georges Thènault (center) e seen, left to right: James McConnell, Kiffin Rockwell, Norman Prince and Victor hapman. This photograph was taken early in April 1916. Only Captain Thènault rvived the war. *(Paul A. Rockwell)*

Early Nieuports carried this extemporized Lewis gun mounting as well as one fixed ckers gun. It will be seen that the pilot would have a difficult time changing the ammu- tion drum or remedying stoppages, but it helped solve the fixed gun problem. The ot shown is Dudley Hill. *(Charles H. Dolan II)*

7. The rocket plane of 1916. Here is Charles Chouteau Johnson. Born in St. Louis of French parents, he rushed to France early in the war and eventually wound up in the Lafayette Escadrille. His plane carried not only two guns but eight anti-balloon rockets specially devised for that type of work. They were fired electrically from the cockpit. *(Paul A. Rockwell)*

8. Kiffin Yates Rockwell, the most beloved American in the Lafayette Escadrille. He was probably the first citizen of the U.S. to offer his services to the Allied cause, volunteering with French authorities in the U.S. immediately after the outbreak of war, August 1, 1914. He was killed in September 1916. *(Paul A. Rockwell)*

9. Victor Chapman, the first American to die in an air battle on the western front. He is shown here with his Nieuport in which he had been shot up on June 17, 1916. He suffered a severe scalp wound and was ordered to take a rest. He ignored the advice of his comrades and continued to fly and eventually was trapped over the lines by five Fokker pilots and killed. *(Paul A. Rockwell)*

10. Willis B. Haviland of St. Paul, Minnesota, with a Nieuport-17, which had discarded the top-wing Lewis gun armament. Willis had been a volunteer ambulance driver before joining the Lafayette and when the U.S. entered the war he transferred to the U. S. Navy and ended the conflict heading a naval air station at Porto Corsini, Italy. *(Paul A. Rockwell)*

11. Adjutant Raoul Lufbery, adventurer and naturalized American who was to become leading ace in the Lafayette Escadrille. Credited with destroying seventeen enemy aircraft, he was the inspiration for all Americans who were to follow the original group of volunteers into the French Aviation. Soon after transferring to the U. S. Air Service, Lufbery was killed when he jumped from a burning plane. (*U. S. Air Force*)

12. William Thaw, shown on leave in the U.S. in 1916 when he had to wear civilian clothing to comply with America's neutrality. Thaw was the only volunteer to see the history of the Lafayette Escadrille from start to finish. Later he flew with the U. S. Army forces and took command of the Third Pursuit Group. (*National Archives*)

On the Aisne sector in 1917. Left to right: Robert Soubiran, Courtney Campbell, ...eth Marr, Bill Thaw, French mechanic, and David Peterson. *(Paul A. Rockwell)*

...he Lafayette at Behonne in July 1916. Left to right: Lieutenant deLaage (French ...r), Chouteau Johnson, Laurence Rumsey, James McConnell, Bill Thaw, Raoul ...ery, Kiffin Rockwell, Didier Masson, Norman Prince and Bert Hall. *...A. Rockwell)*

15. Robert L. Rockwell of Cincinnati, a distant cousin of Kiffin Rockwell who was i
terning at the Anglo-American Hospital in France at the outbreak of the war. He join
the French Aviation early in 1916 and continued to fly war patrols until the Armistic
Here with his Spad of the 103rd Pursuit Squadron, he is shown with another variati
of the Indian Head insignia so popular with American fliers. *(National Archives)*

16. On the Somme front. A typical group of American volunteers gather when N. 1
was at Hamm on the Somme. Left to right: Bob Soubiran, Chouteau Johnson, Rona
Hoskier, Bill Thaw, Frederick Prince, Stephen Bigelow, Ted Parsons, Edmond Ge
and Thènault's dog "Fram." *(U. S. Air Force)*

The trick of a number of planes getting on each other's tail and flying in a tight circle to prevent an enemy from moving into that dangerous position had a different name on every front. Planes on both sides of the line had adopted that maneuver long before Raoul Lufbery had flown an airplane.

This polyglot American was always shrouded in legend, and the subject of many contradictory situations by the time he joined the small group of men who were to build America's first war squadron. He had few social graces and no cultural background, but again, as in his association with Marc Pourpe, he responded to the enthusiasm and spirit of the young American patriots with whom he found himself, and most certainly contributed more than his share to the glory of what was to be known universally as the Lafayette Escadrille.

Although Luf joined N.124 on May 24 he did not score a victory until July 30 when, singlehanded he knocked down an enemy plane east of Etain in the Verdun sector. This victory triggered his gallant war-air career and he told it in the following manner for the *Guerre Aerienne,* a military magazine of the period.

"It was north of Verdun in the environs of Douaumont and Vaux that one morning, with my flying comrade, McConnell, I departed on patrol.

"We left the aviation camp at Bar-le-Duc at eleven o'clock. The weather was superb and the atmosphere so clear it was easy for us to distinguish the shellholes and mines, and here and there the fragments of a trench. By consulting one's map and examining the ground below one can get an idea of the location of the forts whose massive walls form geometrical designs in the midst of this chaos. The villages that were here have ceased to exist; an entanglement of lines, straight, crooked, and broken, is the last vestige of what were once streets.

"Absorbed by this vision of a great battlefield I lost sight of my friend, Mac. He too, doubtless was fascinated by the scene. Finding myself alone, I realized that I must be on my guard in order not to be taken unawares. I cruised around, changing my course from right to left, the better to scan the horizon. My altimeter pointed to three miles. I reduced the speed of my motor, as I was then at my favorite height. Suddenly my attention was caught by a camouflaged machine, about a thousand yards below me, headed for our lines. I could not distinguish its mark, but its silhouette raised my doubts. It was too big, far too big for a Nieuport, the only French aeroplane at that time that bore resemblance to a Boche machine. Now there is the Spad and others, but these did not exist at Verdun.

"There was not a minute to lose; it was a great opportunity. Yet, as a matter of prudence, I looked around me to make sure the machine had no protectors. It would be stupid to fall into a trap, especially now that I knew the enemy's favorite ruse, having several times been a victim of it.

"Evidently the occupants of the suspicious-looking machine had not seen me. I must make the most of the occasion. I stopped my motor and *piqued* towards it. As I drew nearer I saw the Boche's black crosses showing through the camouflage. I placed myself about thirty yards in the rear of its fuselage, just a little above, so that its fixed plane and helm would serve me as a shield. Finally my adversary saw me, but it was then too late. Vainly the pilot sought to turn his machine in order to enable his gunner to fire. It was no use. Their lack of vigilance was to cost them their lives. I pressed the trigger of my gun. Pan! Pan! Pan! In a few seconds forty-seven bullets were fired. We were now so close together I was forced to dive to my left to avoid a collision. I righted my machine and looked down for my adversary. He was still there, but now to my surprise, his machine was white. I removed my glasses (goggles) the better to examine it. To my great satisfaction I found it was upside down; I could see its chassis and wheels. It remained thus as it continued to fall. Black smoke and fire spurted from it. Its descent grew more rapid as the fire became more intense. Finally, in a mass of flames, it fell in a ravine only a few yards from our trenches.

"Pleased and proud of myself, I turned my machine in the

direction of my camp. As I flew homeward I thought of the brave poilus beneath me who doubtless had witnessed the aerial combat, encouraging me and applauding the bird that bore the Tricolor cockade."

That afternoon Lufbery returned to the same area and racked up his second. Some historians claim that this "double" was the first ever scored by any pilot on the French front, but such a statement must be questioned in the light of the records of many French aces of this period.

Raoul became a remorseless stalker from this time on, prowling the sky hour after hour, never returning until his fuel was exhausted, or there was no ammunition in his guns. He evinced no elation over any success or frustration over any failures. At first, he was not a skilled duelist for he often returned to his field with his aircraft a veritable sieve from bullets and antiaircraft shrapnel. He is said, on one occasion, to have encountered the redoubtable Major Oswald Boelcke when these two pilots engaged in a long desperate struggle as they twisted and turned, each striving for a full shot, working back into position hopeful of a chance to pack home a full burst, flying and hanging on for dear life minute by minute. Only those airmen who have engaged in such battles can appreciate this kind of physical strain. Opportunities are lost and won, and when at last the enemy is brought into the sight, some other influence usually takes over.

Perhaps the guns refuse to fire, or you suddenly wonder whether the hydraulic interrupter-gear has been set for action; if not, the gun will fire "late," and you can shoot your own propeller to matchwood. All these problems, and more, arise. You wonder what your speed is, but dare not take your eyes off your opponent. When you have the wild idea that at last you have him where you want him, you suddenly realize he may be "bait," that at any minute someone else will be pouring a deadly stream of lead into your back.

While you make other plans, you next realize that you began this brawl well inside the enemy lines. You have been in a series of crazy circuits for some time. How far inside have these battle gyrations taken you? What was the wind like when you took off? How long has this business been going on? If you risk a glance at the typography below, you might miss your great chance. Nine times out of ten you have absolutely no idea what the area below represents. You are positive you have not seen it before—and where the hell are the five other pilots who started out with you?

It was just such a situation as this that must have confronted Raoul Lufbery in his fight with Boelcke. Round and round they went, taking grave chances with their aircraft structure, and firing wild, erratic bursts whenever a wing tip came into view. Time mattered not. The tight circuits took their toll and both planes were down low where the antiaircraft of either side could give them a bad time. Both must have been exhausted with the physical and mental strain. Both opponents had fired every round they had and then realized that neither one had anything left. So, according to the legend, they accepted the situation, exchanged formal salutes and returned home. Both had received dozens of bullets, but apparently none in critical parts. Lufbery's boots had two bullet holes and another had flicked through the folds of his coverall. The legend also asserts that his plane was so riddled that it collapsed all around him when he landed back at his field, and possibly there is some substance to the statement, but these dramatic returns have been related on so many occasions, they lose some of their impact.

I served many months on the Western Front and engaged in many an air contest, but in all that time I never saw a plane fly back from an air battle—and then collapse dramatically on arrival on its field. I do not deny that it could have happened; it probably did, but not as often as the "yammering-gun" type of writer would have us believe.

Lufbery kept up this work all through August, putting in numberless hours over the line. On August 8 he met an ancient Aviatik near Fort Douaumont and shot it down in flames. Another Aviatik fell before his guns on October 12 during the famous bomb attack on the Mauser works. This was Luf's fifth, which made him officially an ace.

With these successes, Lufbery began to show a new side. As the first American ace he naturally won great popularity both in France and in the United States. His story was told again and again until even Luf wondered how much of it was true; he was among the first to argue that success in the air was largely luck. He was the toast of the boulevards, and noted airmen such as Guynemer, Fonck, and Nungesser greeted him as an equal, and since he could respond to their cheery cries in fluent French, he was accepted instantly and told how great he was.

Now a new simplicity marked Lufbery. He no longer put on garish acts on his return from a patrol. He realized that damage that was unseen or unnoticed might have taken place during action, and he never risked hair-raising displays to show off or announce a new success. He came in well throttled back, making careful turns, so that no undue strain was put on bullet-pocked wings. He knew now that too many exuberant young airmen had killed themselves in these unnecessary displays of triumph.

This was the Lufbery the men of the Escadrille Américaine best remember, the Lufbery who went with them to Le Bourget to pick up their new two-gun Nieuports, the Lufbery who was to be their fighting mainstay until at last America entered the war and reclaimed her flying sons, and placed Raoul Lufbery once more in the numbing position of uncertainty.

Two figures who entered this history early in the war are entitled to some accountancy. Frazier Curtis, who, with Norman Prince, worked hard to organize the American force, was not among the fortunate ones when his opportunity for training came. Although Frazier had had some hydroplane flying in the United States, he could not keep pace with his friends, since he experienced two severe crashes at Avord, one of which put him in the hospital. Following that, he was granted forty-five days' leave during which time he continued to work

with Dr. Gros enticing young Americans into this new service. He finally was released from the French Aviation in
August 1915.

Paul Ayres Rockwell, the brother whose services Kiffin had
offered early in the war, had been working on the Atlanta
Constitution but gave up his post and joined Kiffin in the
Foreign Legion. Paul was wounded in December of 1914 and
from that time on was unfit for full infantry duty. On the
strength of his newspaper training he was attached to the
Section d'Information of the French Army as a combat
correspondent, and later was listed as an official war correspondent.

He never went into World War I aviation, but when the
Escadrille Américaine was first organized, the pilots named
Paul their official historian and public relations counsel, an
assignment he holds to this day. It was intended originally
that Paul would write the first official history of the Escadrille at the close of hostilities, but he went down with a serious bout with the flu that was raging at the time. Knowing the
interest in the Escadrille and the importance of getting the
vital statistics organized as soon as possible, he turned all the
available material over to James Norman Hall, who with
Charles Nordhoff, produced the renowned—and now out of
print—two-volume history titled *The Lafayette Flying Corps*.

It is interesting to note here that Paul Rockwell was made a
reserve officer in the Foreign Legion following World War I,
and when the Rif War in Morocco broke out in 1925, he was
made a captain in the Escadrille de la Garde Cherffienne,
a new unit of American volunteers, and while in this service
flew thirty-seven missions as an observer-bomber.

Paul eventually turned to free-lance writing, contributing
regularly to American, French, and British Empire newspapers and magazines. At the outbreak of World War II Paul,
along with Edwin C. Parsons and Harold B. Willis, once
more offered his services to France and began to recruit
young Americans to volunteer with the idea of reorganizing
the old Lafayette Escadrille. At this point officials in Wash-

ington frowned on the plan since America was still neutral. Rockwell and Willis then went to France and tried to repeat in full the 1914–15 plans that had resulted in the original organization. But it was not to be, for France fell before much progress had been made, so Paul returned to the United States and joined the U. S. Army Air Force in May 1942, and served as a liaison officer with the Free French forces in the Tunisian campaign, in Italy, in Corsica, and was then chief of the French Advisory Division of the First Tactical Air Force. Later on Paul was made chief of the GI education program in France, and did not return to his homeland until June 1946. For all this service he was honored with the Legion of Honor, the Croix de Guerre, Croix des Blesses, the Bronze Star, and several others of lesser importance. He is now retired and living in Asheville, North Carolina.

Chapter VII

THE TWO ROCKWELLS

In due course the Parisian holiday drew to its close, and the bistro-weary pilots of N.124 were rounded up for their return to the wars. Another Rockwell had joined them before they gathered at the Gare de l'Est. He was Robert Lockerbie Rockwell, a volunteer from Cincinnati, Ohio, a distant relative to Kiffin who was more fortunate than his Asheville namesake, for he lived to hear the triumphal peal of the Armistice by which time he had racked up a distinctive record.

As a medical student, Robert Rockwell had offered to serve as an interne at the Anglo-American Hospital at Saint-Valéry-en-Caux where he stayed from February 29, 1915, until February 3, 1916, when he transferred to the French Aviation. He was brevetted on a Blériot on May 20, 1916, and assigned to the Escadrille Américaine by September 17 where he served with considerable luck until February 18, 1918. He then joined the United States Air Service, was elevated from a French adjutant to a U.S. captain and eventually commanded the 103rd Pursuit Squadron. During his many months of service he was awarded the Legion of Honor and the Croix de Guerre.

To regress: on his transfer from the Anglo-American Hospital Robert Rockwell was given a flattering letter of introduction, in which the person who penned it was either a master of the art or had sinister intentions of getting rid of this young American, but it carried Robert well on his way. It was explained in this laudatory masterpiece that M. Rockwell was a skilled automobile mechanic and was fully trained as a *pilote aviateur*. Actually, Robert Lockerbie wasn't even keen about country-fair roller coasters.

Notwithstanding, on his first interview this Rockwell modestly admitted to the glowing qualifications, but fortunately for him, Dr. Gros was aware of the artful games played by some of his medical associates in the various areas. He quickly quashed some of the superlatives, and, although he allowed Robert to bask in this specious background, he quietly advised his instructors to ignore the introduction. Robert received exactly the same training as any other American candidate.

He may not have been very successful on the front, but he was most fortunate. Week after week he took terrific beatings from the enemy but he carried on manfully. On one occasion while on a lone patrol he ran into a formation of seven enemy aircraft, and decided that since he was well up-sun from them he could take a long chance on a rear-rank straggler. But the Germans evidently allowed him to move in and once he was where they wanted him turned on him savagely. Rockwell received such a beating that it was a miracle he escaped and returned to his field. He brought in his plane with both tires punctured, the undercarriage braces shot away, his aileron control damaged, and the wings pierced in many panels, but the *avion* held together all the way to the hangar.

Another time his engine played a dirty trick on him when he was well over the enemy line. He had spotted a formation of single-seaters, and once more moved boldly into an up-sun position to attack. However, the enemy planes quickly reversed their course and prepared to shoot him down. At this point Rockwell pulled the unexpected; instead of climbing away and heading for home, he nosed down and dived straight through the enemy formation. Just as he was about to spray anything that appeared in front of him, his oil radiator burst, sending thick hot lubricant in all directions, and for some minutes he was blinded and completely at the mercy of his enemies. He just sat there, stirring the stick and kicking the rudder which induced an amazing series of maneuvers. The enemy leader must have presumed that a dying man was at the controls—the final reflexes of a tortured body—and he kept his formation aloft to await the crash. Instead, Rockwell wiped off his goggles, noted that he was down to about one thousand feet, and automatically turned on his engine. By some freak chance the Le Rhone began to function again, and he was able to contour-chase all the way back to his field.

This was the sort of life that Robert L. Rockwell endured for more than two years, but he had a rare sense of humor and took it all in such good spirits, he was popular everywhere. Like so many other heroes in the Escadrille he was the recipient of many letters from adoring girls in America, and since this long-range adulation came under the hazards of war Robert took it in his stride. He had a Parisian photographer fake a particularly flattering portrait of himself, copies of which he shipped off by the dozen, and then ignored his admirers, allowing them to believe they had been wantonly deserted by one of the most attractive young men in the world.

When the Escadrille pilots arrived back at Luxeuil they were pleased to learn that they were to share the airfield with a special force of the British Royal Naval Air Service, numbering more than fifty pilots and about one thousand mechanics and other personnel. This group had been deployed to this area, equipped with Sopwith two-seaters and special armament intended for a planned attack on the German Mauser factory at Oberndorf. The two English-speaking groups got on well together, and many new and lasting friendships were made over the next few weeks.

In the meantime the improved Nieuports with their twin guns and greater speed and maneuverability, although apparently available in job lots at Le Bourget, did not arrive at Luxeuil in great numbers—only five had been ferried in and those still required much attention before they could be flown on service patrols. So there was little to do but await the routine work of the French mechanics, and much of this time was spent loafing around the town hotel where the American pilots were quartered. Raoul Lufbery, who was very fond of mushrooms, roamed the nearby pastures gathering his favorite fungi and had them served on the slightest pretext. His companions were afraid to eat these hand-picked specimens and fully expected to find Raoul flat on his back after a meal in which these delicacies were served. But Luf knew every species and did not have to rely on those produced commercially and purchased in expensive specialty shops.

Bill Thaw, the inveterate sportsman, whipped the nearby trout streams and did very well despite his lame arm. Thus, for some days the routine orders of N.124 offered only details of the length and weight of Thaw's fish, or the number of basketfuls of "ptomaine" Adjutant Lufbery had delivered to the camp kitchen.

Many of the Americans spent considerable time visiting the English-speaking pilots of the Royal Naval Air Service, learning how the other half carried out its aerial duties. These friendly intercourses added pleasure to their dull lives when most of them were kept on the ground owing to the lack of flying equipment.

Finally two Nieuports were equipped and ready for service flying and Kiffin Rockwell and Raoul Lufbery took them over. This was September 23, and these two prepared for the first patrol that was made since the outfit had arrived back at Luxeuil. There was some jovial rivalry as to who would get back into action first, but when Rockwell and Lufbery decided that this was their honor, there was not much objection. Kiffin's plane was serviced first and he was about to take off on a lone patrol, when Luf yelled, "Take it easy. This one is about ready, I'll go along with you."

Kiffin waited in his new cockpit, allowing the Le Rhone to warm up slowly in order to break it in correctly. Luf was overanxious and probably rushed his take-off, for they were hardly off the ground when his engine acted badly, and he turned back. Kiffin went on by himself, but considering that this front was becoming lively, and that the Germans were suspicious of the combined French-American-British concentration there, it probably was foolhardy for him to cross the line alone, particularly with a machine he had not flown before. Oddly enough, he headed for enemy territory in the exact same area that had given him his first victory. The circumstances were strangely reminiscent of that event.

A short time before Kiffin reached the lines he identified a German two-seater observation plane that was moving into the French area. He probably hoped he could bring down this enemy well within the Allied area. In some of his previous combats his victims had retreated well inside their own line. Here was a chance to get one and have it available for personal inspection; he might even hack off an Iron Cross insignia to send back home as a war souvenir.

Vibrant with excitement, Kiffin nosed down like a winged javelin. The enemy gunner started hosing a stream of machine-gun fire the instant he spotted the oncoming Nieuport. Rockwell ignored the threat and continued on until it seemed that he must collide with the two-seater. Observers below heard

the Nieuport's guns begin their staccato rage, and saw the
German plane appear to fall away. Then, as they watched for
the "kill," Rockwell's Nieuport seemed to falter. It turned its
nose down steeply, and the wings on one side flipped away
from the fuselage. The main portion of the French scout began to spin. The wings that had been ripped away, fluttered in
the sunshine, their clean doped surfaces reflecting glints of
light until at last they parted and threw away the gleaming
vee-strut that slithered across the sky like a boomerang. Meanwhile the rest of the Nieuport tightened its spin and augered
down at terrific speed until it crashed with an unearthly roar
in a field of late summer flowers. The French trenches were
only a few hundred yards away.

A short time before Kiffin had stated idly that if he were
shot down and killed, he wished to be buried where he fell,
but in this case his wish could not be granted; the field of
flowers was too close to the front. German artillerymen were
already laying down a box-barrage to make sure the downed
Nieuport would not fly again. French gunners from a nearby
battery raced out and pulled Rockwell's body clear. He was
dead from a dreadful wound in his chest that had been inflicted by what in those days was termed an "explosive" bullet,
but more likely was an incendiary intended for use against
observation balloons. When a surgeon examined the body
later, he stated that if it had been an ordinary bullet, Kiffin
would have had better than an even chance of recovering.
The special ammunition usually reserved for kite balloons
must have inflicted a wicked wound, for it would have spread
on impact, just as would a dumdum bullet, and the incendiary load probably caused a severe internal burn.

Real explosive bullets were for more specialized targets and
were fitted with a percussion cap on the front end, and carried
a charge of powder in a small cavity. They were used generally
against caissons and magazines. It is doubtful that any true
explosive bullet was used at this time by the German pilots
or gunners. Ammunition, carelessly termed "explosive," usually took the form of the "tracer" round, a bullet that bore a

packing of magnesium and barium peroxide. Later the British produced the S.P.K. Mark 7-T, generally referred to as the "sparklet," or "tracer," and was in accepted use by all the Allies. Further experiments were made with flat-nosed envelopes containing phosphorous intended to ignite kite balloons, and were known as the Buckingham round. While fairly effective against the hydrogen-inflated bags, the blunt shape left much to be desired as far as accuracy was concerned.

The nearest thing to an "explosive" bullet in 1916–17 was the British Pomeroy, or P.S.A. missile, also devised for use against Zeppelins or kite balloons. This had a very sensitive nose and would expand and break up simply by striking fine fabric, but even this was not truly effective against hydrogen-filled airships. It was not until late in 1918 that a combined incendiary-explosive bullet was made available, but it was used only in very special situations or against particular targets. This proved to be effective against Zeppelins that raided Great Britain; so much so in fact that the R.T.S. round, as it was known, was finally furnished squadrons in France by September 1918. There is no reliable record of explosive bullets in the air armament of the Germans during 1914–18.

News of Rockwell's death was telephoned to his squadron, and in the excitement someone added that the sky in the area was alive with enemy planes. Raoul Lufbery was so enraged at Rockwell's loss that he took off again and raced for the area, but there were no planes of any kind anywhere. He even ranged deep into the German lines as far as Habsheim where a well-known enemy airfield was located, but no one took off to accept his challenge.

This was the most severe blow suffered so far by the Escadrille Américaine and when the N.124 pilots gathered in the hotel lobby that evening, Captain Thénault said, "We are all saddened. When Rockwell was in the air, no German passed. The best and bravest of us is no more."

The British boys of the Royal Naval Air Service practically took over the funeral. The pilots, wearing black arm bands, formed an honor guard, eight hundred mechanics were in the

procession, and behind them came a regiment of French Ter-
ritorials, a battalion of Colonials, and hundreds of French
pilots and mechanics to fill out a most impressive cortege.

Kiffin's brother Paul, by now a civilian, was permitted to
attend the funeral. Airplanes circled the procession, and
mourners, civilian and military, from the nearby areas banked
the grave with flowers. Captain Thénault prepared and read
the following tribute:

"Here, by this tomb so recently closed, we meet today to
pay our final tribute to our comrade.

"Sergeant Kiffin Rockwell was a descendant of an ancient
family of soldiers, among whom was one of Washington's
officers who distinguished himself in the War of Independence. Later the family provided several officers who also distinguished themselves during the War of Secession. Kiffin received a thorough military training, which gave him the
imprint that characterized his life.

"Learning of the cowardly aggression of which our country
was the object, and loving France as a second motherland, he,
with his brother, here present, hastened to France to enlist in
the Foreign Legion. He took part in the combats of Artois
in May 1915, and after a valiant charge of four kilometers,
fell, wounded in the thigh, near Nouville-Saint-Vaast, of
glorious memory. Immediately on his recovery he joined the
Aviation Corps, where he obtained his brevet in an exceptionally short space of time. On the formation of the American
Escadrille, he came with it to Luxeuil. Here he at once attracted attention. On May 18 of this year he was the first at
Hartmannsweilerkopf to engage in battle, in which he was
victorious. Shortly afterward, for his services, he was awarded
the Médaille Militaire. Ordered to Verdun, he took part in
every expedition against the enemy. He was happy in the
midst of danger; the greater the strength or the number of the
enemy, the more anxious he was to attack. Never did Rockwell consider that he had done enough.

"His courage was sublime and when the flights prescribed

by the commandant were accomplished, he would set out again on his 'Baby,' barely allowing his mechanic time to refill his tanks.

"Indefatigable, he would fly over Vaux and Douaumont, above the crash of the enemy's guns. Where Rockwell was the German could not pass, but was forced rapidly to take shelter on the ground. Daily he compelled enemy airships to descend on their own territory, far behind their lines, his own machine returning with glorious marks of these encounters.

"One day an explosive bullet struck him in the face. He would take no rest despite the advice of his chiefs, but returned to the combat and brought down one more enemy machine within our lines.

"He was a great soldier with a high sense of duty. This he accomplished simply and valiantly, without boasting and without ambition. 'I am paying my part of our debt to Lafayette and Rochambeau,' he would say. He gave himself to France and for France he sacrificed himself.

"On September 23, immediately on his return to Luxeuil, he burned with a desire to fly over the fields of Alsace. He flew over them, and not far from the spot where he had fought his first glorious battle, he attacked the enemy. But here cruel fate willed it that he, Rockwell, who for four months fought at Verdun; who, singlehanded, attacked ten enemy machines, should fall with a bullet in his chest as he advanced to meet his adversary.

"Glory be to him who fell valiantly in the pursuit of his dream of love and justice. He met the glorious death he so much desired. On the night of his death, when we were gathered together, I said to his comrades, 'The best and bravest of us is no longer here,' and never was commendation more merited.

"Glory be to his noble family and to his brother, whom a serious wound has forced to leave the field. We share in their great sorrow.

"And to thee, our best friend, in the name of France I bid thee a last farewell. In the name of thy comrades, who have so often proved that they know how to keep their promises, I salute thee reverently. And with the memory of those who have already fallen, and whom we invoke, we swear faithfully to guard thy memory and to avenge it."

Another poignant tribute to Kiffin Rockwell was penned by Charles Chouteau Johnson in a letter to his mother:

> September 24, 1916.
> Luxeuil-les-Bains.

Dearest Mother:

When I wrote you in Paris I was very much pressed for time and couldn't write a decently long letter. So here goes for a lengthy earache. As I said, we left the Verdun sector and when I was in Paris we didn't know what sector we were sure of going to. However it was quickly decided, the result being here (Luxeuil-les-Bains). It is way back from the lines and takes us about 30 to 45 minutes to get there. As far as infantry and artillery action goes, it is exceptionally quiet and the war in this sector seems to be confined to aerial activity. We are here for two reasons, i.e. to protect this and another town, (the Germans often come over both at night), and to do *chasse* over the lines and accompany bombardments; that is, protect the bombing (slow machines) from the Germans.

Yesterday we were bereaved of one of our comrades and best pilots, Kiffin Rockwell. While flying over the lines he attacked a German plane and was brought down. Fortunately he was killed outright in the air and didn't have to suffer that long agonizing chute to the ground badly wounded and conscious of the fact that he had no control over the machine. He had a great hole in his chest, caused by an explosive bullet. I am awfully upset about it as he was one of my best friends in the Escadrille and we went around a lot together.

There isn't space to tell you what a man he was. A man all the way through, hard to know at first but once your friend he would stick all the way through. Brave to the core, never flinching.

Kiffin engaged August 21, 1914, in the Foreign Legion, was wounded in the big attack in Champagne 9th May 1915, went back to the Legion and then was transferred to the Flying Corps where he won the admiration of officers and his comrades through

his daring and bravery. Last April he brought down a German in
our present sector and then, in front of Verdun he was wounded
in the face by an explosive bullet. A week later he brought another
Hun plane down. He then got the Médaille Militaire, the highest
honor France can give, (he already had the War Cross). The day
before we left Bar-le-Duc, he brought another Hun plane to earth
which fell on the trenches. Then this last deal which ended so
disastrously and cast us all in a gloom. You can rest assured that
the Huns will have an account to pay and I think they will realize
the Escadrille is seeing red and some of them are going to catch
hell.

You may wonder why I write at such length about a fellow you
don't know from Adam. Simply to let you and everyone know the
type of Americans giving their all for a cause which is for the
freedom of the world over a greedy, foul enemy who carries on
warfare in a way the savage would be ashamed of. There are some
of us who aren't too proud to fight! *Vive* the time when the Hun
is thoroughly crushed and permanent peace is restored. Rest assured that until he is thoroughly crushed or ground to pieces we
will keep right on. There's no half-way this trip.

                                                    Chouteau

Instead of draping a curtain of gloom, Kiffin Rockwell's
death taunted the rest of the Escadrille into greater determination, and as fast as their new machines were fitted for
fighting service they zoomed into the sky. Norman Prince
scored his first victory, a success for which he had strived so
long. Luck had been dead-set against the man who had done
so much to bring this volunteer organization into being, for
no matter what he did, how many times a day he flew or
how many engagements came his way, no enemy plane had
fallen before his guns. Norman fought savagely, never giving
an inch. He took them on singly or in groups, but all he ever
received for his efforts were bullet holes, damaged engines,
battered wings or nerve-racking frustration. Plane after plane
flown by Prince was rendered unserviceable, but he never
could report anything worth while to show for his activities,
except flying time jotted down in his logbook.

The day Norman broke the ice was one of the most memorable in the history of the Escadrille. Actually it was the same day that saw the end of Kiffin Rockwell, for like Lufbery, Prince had taken off in a spirit of revenge. When well over the enemy line he encountered a two-seater Aviatik that seemed to be acting suspiciously like a "bait" plane. Norman wanted to roar in for an immediate attack, but decided to wait and avoid being drawn into a trap. Once he was certain that there was no tight formation of single-seaters above, he pounced suddenly and struck. His first bullet killed the observer, and the German pilot in the machine found himself at the mercy of the man in this maniacally flown Nieuport with a screaming Seminole's head daubed on the side of the fuselage. It was a hopeless task for the blundering Aviatik to outmaneuver the gnatlike Nieuport; the two-seater lost Norman for a few seconds, and then the pilot saw the Nieuport standing on her tail somewhere below and pouring short bursts up at him. Tipping the Aviatik over on its wing tip, the German tried to make a diving getaway, but Prince was after him like an enraged hornet.

Then came a display, the like of which had never been reported before. The frantic German pilot flipped his belt, stood up in his cockpit, and raised his gloved hands above his head in a token of surrender. For a minute Prince was incredulous, but quickly realized that here was the opportunity of a lifetime. For weeks the boys of the Escadrille had hoped to down a German plane in Allied territory, if only to see what it was made of, but chiefly to prove to the cynics that an American had shot down an enemy aircraft. This was even better—if the situation was real and not some strange midair phantasy. It seemed unbelievable, but there was the possibility that this frightened pilot might be induced to land his plane practically undamaged on the Escadrille's field; they might even kid the poor devil to relate his side of the "fight" from start to finish. Lady Luck might be smiling at last . . . but then Prince remembered Kiffin and silent revenge billowed up in a crimson surge. Why should this man be allowed to surrender so easily? For a minute Prince considered finishing his opponent then and there, but he remembered that previous fighting action had taken them to within ten kilometers of the front line. Amazing! There was a chance of accomplishing the unbelievable trick.

Norman leaned out of his cockpit and pointed toward the French lines. The German pilot nodded his helmeted head and then slid back into his seat. Prince gave a quick glance above and behind to make sure he was not being drawn into a trap, and then moved to a position behind the "captured" Aviatik and herded it home. Each time the enemy pilot seemed to be easing off course, Norman drilled a burst of sparkling tracer bullets past the wing tip of the Aviatik. That put him in the proper mood and they both finally arrived safely over Luxeuil. The enemy plane was put down with no damage, the pilot was taken prisoner, and the Allies had a serviceable Aviatik to inspect and check out.

Norman's victory also brought promotion; he was made adjutant, the final step up the military ladder before he would be commissioned.

Later, on this same day, Raoul Lufbery took on another load of fuel and ammunition and sallied forth for the third time, and when he was a short distance over the line encountered a Fokker that he recognized by its markings. He had engaged this plane before, but he had no idea whether it was flown by the same pilot. After some tricky maneuvering neither pilot was in a position to fire a shot, and by then Raoul noticed a number of white antiaircraft bursts, evidently French, that were indicating to all friendly airmen in the area that an enemy plane was over French territory.

This was much more important and Luf broke off with the Fokker and raced back to his own line and almost suffered the same fate that had befallen Kiffin. He nosed down on a snooping two-seater, hoping to score his fifth victory and be listed in French records as an "ace," but in his anxiety to get at the intruder he completely missed another enemy who came down from above and surprised him. Three bullets dam-

aged his engine and another ripped through the fleece of a
flying boot. His elevator controls were also damaged and he
knew he was in a tough spot, but he flew so masterfully his
adversaries gave up. He scrambled back to Luxeuil and
landed safely, though the new Nieuport was unfit for even a
major repair, and had to be junked.

Didier Masson was one of the more substantial pilots in
the Escadrille, and should be introduced at this point since
he was one of the four airmen of N.124 to take part in the
famous raid on the Mauser arms works at Oberndorf. He was
born in Los Angeles, the son of French parents. Always the
adventurer, he had learned to fly in France and was brevetted
on an old Antoinette monoplane. He was nicknamed "Rubber
Man," because he had recovered from numberless crashes
and accidents. Between 1911 and 1913 Didier did considerable exhibition flying in California, but this soon became tame
and he volunteered to build an air service for General Alvaro
Obregón who in 1913 was trying to establish some definite
rule in Mexico. General Victoriano Huerta was his chief opponent, who at the time held command. This guerrilla warfare was not important internationally; there were few massed
battles, neither side had much in the way of artillery, rifles,
or modern equipment, and international gun-runners were
furnishing both factions with anything that would make a
noise.

Someone suggested to General Obregón that a modern military airplane in the right hands could play an important part,
and Didier Masson was approached and engaged through
devious channels. With an almost obsolete Curtiss biplane, a
British soldier of fortune, Tommy Dean, as a mechanic, and
a Mexican major's commission, Didier set up a Mexican Air
Force. This was the only plane in Mexico and Masson was
the only pilot south of the border. To smuggle the airplane
across the border in bits and pieces was a feat in itself, but
eventually plane, pilot, and the comic-opera mechanic arrived and reported for duty.

The sea lanes were Obregón's big trouble, for General Huerta's "navy" was having things all its own way, running guns in from all points along the Gulf of Mexico and the islands of the Caribbean. His navy was composed of a slab-sided gunboat that was powered by a wheezy engine, capable of almost four knots, and manned by a crew of beachcombers and sailors of fortune, all claiming to be admirals.

Didier was ordered to break up this "freedom of the seas" in any manner he saw fit, and since his pay depended on his performance, something exemplary had to be accomplished. For this Tommy Dean devised a number of aerial bombs that were actually empty syrup cans filled with explosive, rusty bolts, big nails, screws, and even discarded razor blades— Tommy was all for mass destruction.

These missiles were first tried out against opposing troops whenever they were found in the open. The "bombs" were rigged with wire handles that in turn were hooked to a primitive bomb rack with a release mechanism controlled from the pilot's cockpit.

All would have gone well, but at the last minute both Masson and Dean realized that these dangling projectiles might be swept off by the scraggy bush that infested their airfield. After some consideration Didier suggested that since Dean had initiated the idea in the first place, it was his duty to make certain all would go well. Tommy was persuaded to perch on the lower wing, clinging to an interplane strut and sitting so that he could peer below and see whether the bombs were well clear of the brush and cactus as the pilot taxied the plane slowly.

The reader will have to envision much of what took place, as the story has been told so many times and from different points of view. Dean had never flown before and was not keen about risking his neck in that manner, but he made this ground test willingly without considering what would have happened had one of the bombs been knocked off while he was so mounted.

Once it was fairly evident that they would have no trouble,

Didier turned around, rolled back to their starting point, and then, instead of allowing poor Tommy to crawl down, he quickly opened the throttle and roared away with the astounded Englishman still clutching at the interplane strut. In a few seconds they were aloft to carry out what was probably the world's first ground-strafing patrol. Unfortunately, official records seem to ignore this hair-raising exhibition.

In time Tommy's courage—and sense of the ridiculous—was restored, and as they roared out across a desert which was said to be infested with enemy troops they saw an adobe shack that might be sheltering a platoon or two enjoying their siesta. So, with Tommy still hanging on for dear life, Masson nosed down, swept over the enemy concentration and released the bombs. Two made direct hits and bellowed out with a roar that rolled across the hot sands. Tommy might not have liked flying but he made up for that with his devastating formula for ground operations; there was a great puff of white smoke, and after the initial roar, chunks of structure, furniture, window frames and slabs of adobe twirled through the blast.

So far, so good. The attack had been most successful, but just when their cup of joy was brimming, Tommy looked down and spotted a bomb that still clung to the do-it-yourself bomb rack. Of course it was the one that was mounted farthest away. This was the one Tommy had devised for a special occasion, and it was jammed with sticks of dynamite. He tried to signal to Masson and explain the situation, but Didier was too satisfied with his attack, and Tommy's antics had little effect on him. The Englishman, who had made the racks as well as the bombs, knew that there was a hundred-to-one possibility that the hung-up bomb would topple off the instant their wheels touched back on their own field. That was all it would need—the rampaging Curtiss would provide its own grave and ceremonial firing party.

Tommy had no choice. He had to leave his hazardous position on the leading edge of the wing, and forsake his grip on the interplane strut. As Masson turned his head he saw his mechanic trying a wing-walking act, inching along the main spar, clutching at cross-bracing wires and stays until at last he was where he could lie flat on the wing and reach out to the recalcitrant bomb. At that particular instant Masson's ancient engine decided it had done its bit and began to splutter. Tommy fumbled at the rack, trying to dislodge the bomb, but it was well hooked. Wild-eyed from the slipstream and the dread of the ground that was coming up fast, Tommy made one final effort and managed to untangle the wire-and-hook device, and the bomb fell free just as the wheels of the plane touched at the top fronds of the desert vegetation. The Curtiss surged on and received a terrific "nudge" from the explosion, but they got down safely. Tommy was half-frozen with cold and fright, and Didier tried to laugh, but the effort was not convincing.

After a few days, when the engine had been rebuilt and Tommy had assembled a few more bombs, General Obregón requested that an attack be made on Huerta's navy. This was a more orthodox operation with Masson chasing the floundering gunboat all around a tropical lagoon. He found it just as the freebooters were trying to unload a new shipment of Mausers and blunderbusses. The enemy seamen, it is said, had never seen an airplane, and on its first approach they shoveled on fuel and attempted to make for the open sea. But Masson charged down, pulling his bomb releases whenever he flew through the gunboat's funnel smoke. He scored several direct hits, but, sad to relate, the bombs refused to explode, and the only effect registered was a crew of badly scared beachcombers.

Things went on like this for almost a year, but when affairs became too one-sided, Didier switched allegiance and flew for Venustiano Carranza against Francisco "Pancho" Villa. There now were several airplanes in the Mexican conflict, one of which was flown by Edwin Parsons, who had signed on with the opposition. By a stroke of fate these two men never met in the air. Later on both gave up this hopeless campaign and volunteered to fly for France, and worked together on many occasions on the Western Front.

After Masson relinquished his Mexican commission and hurried over to Paris at the outbreak of the European war, he served with the 129th and 36th Infantry Regiments between August and October of 1914. He transferred to the French Aviation late in October and was sent to Pau, and despite his time aboard the old Curtiss did not get his French "wings" until May 10, 1915, although at the time he enjoyed the unusual distinction of holding two brevets, one issued by the Aero Club of America and one by the Aero Club of California. He served for a time as a bomber pilot with C.18, flying Caudrons, but later he requested and received *chasse* pilot training which took him to N.68, a Nieuport squadron that was one of the first to be equipped with this airplane. Following that he was transferred to the Escadrille Américaine, where we shall pick him up again during the raid on the Mauser plant.

Chapter VIII

THE DEATH OF NORMAN PRINCE

The Allied air attack on the German Mauser arms plant at Oberndorf gave the pilots of the Escadrille Américaine their first opportunity to work on a combined offensive. They sensed that this was recognition at last since they were to assume the role of fighter escorts in a fully integrated mission. The assignment brightened their prospects and they were grateful to be accepted, for until now they felt themselves to be a group of amateurs playing in a field of hardened professionals.

This raid, one of the first with a true strategic concept, had been planned for some time; the date selected was October 12, 1916, and some eighty bombers were allotted to the mission. The main force was provided by the Royal Naval Air Service which flew Sopwith 1½-Strutters. (This name indicated the splayed center-section struts that appeared to be composed of one and one half struts, the inner short and the outer long.) It is interesting to note that these two-seaters, probably the first aircraft fitted with trailing-edge flaps, were flown solo so that four one-hundred-pound bombs could be carried. The French squadrons that were included in the mission used their Breguets and Farmans.

The available fighting scouts of that period could stay in the air for about two hours, and could not accompany the bombers all the way to the target some one hundred fifty miles away. So, as was the general rule, they did the next best thing; they covered them as far as possible, turned back at the last moment, and refueled on an emergency field at Corcieux in the Vosges. Then, timing their take-offs so that they could pick up the returning bombers as soon as possible, they furnished escort cover over the rest of the journey home. Needless to state, this sort of co-operation demanded courage, devotion to the cause, and accurate timing if it was to be executed successfully.

N.124 could provide only four Nieuports and pilots, so the four most experienced airmen were selected: Lieutenant de Laage, Raoul Lufbery, Didier Masson, and Norman Prince. The raid itself proved to be much more successful than had been hoped, as the Germans were caught completely unaware, and considerable damage was inflicted on the important arms factory.

No real opposition was met in the air on the way out, and all fighters returned to the refueling fields. The bombers found their various targets with no trouble and a good pattern was delivered. In order to evade any enemy aircraft sent up to intercept them, they took a circuitous route home and were a long time in making contact with the escort planes. It seemed hours before the Nieuport pilots could find the bombers, and when they did they arrived just in time to face a formation of determined Fokkers that were bent on beating down the raiders. It will be remembered that the Nieuports had no rear gunners for defense, the light was fading fast and it was difficult to distinguish friend from foe, but in one of these melees, Norman Prince shot down a Fokker.

Once the bombers were escorted across their own lines, the four N.124 pilots broke off and made for the same emergency field that had given them the additional fuel and ammunition. Prince must have become confused in the uncertain light and the unfamiliar surroundings for as he spiraled down and S-turned to approach his glide-in position that began near a small patch of woods, he failed to see a high-tension cable that stretched just over the tree tops. The wheels of his landing gear caught this trip wire and the Nieuport was snubbed so that it nosed down suddenly and hit hard. The aircraft rolled itself into a ball, and the safety belt that might have saved Norman, broke as the plane hit, and he was somersaulted from the cockpit.

The shock of the double hazard multiplied Norman's pile-up; he had both legs broken and suffered serious internal injuries. But in spite of his condition and pain he made a brave effort to make sure that no one else made the same mistake. When ground crewmen rushed up to help him, he waved them away and gasped, "Light some gasoline and make some sort of a flare. We don't want anyone else to hit that cable."

Lufbery who had landed a few minutes before, hurried over to console his friend. "Don't worry, Norman. You're going to be all right," he said cheerfully. "We'll get you to a hospital fast. A good night's rest . . ."

All the way in to the nearby town of Gerardmer, Luf attempted to keep up Norman's spirits by croaking wartime ditties, telling jokes in his amusing accent, and whistling the popular tunes they had cranked out on the squadron phonograph. He had no idea how badly Prince was hurt, but when he went to visit him the next day he found his friend had sunk into a coma. The best available skill and care were provided, and every effort was made to revive and encourage him. A Captain Happe, accompanied by a number of Escadrille Américaine officers, promoted Prince to a second lieutenant as he lay there on his bed. Later, Norman was awarded the Legion of Honor, but he knew little of this, for he died on October 15, 1916, and his body was returned to Luxeuil where a very impressive burial was arranged in his honor. In May 1937 the remains of Norman Prince were brought back to America and entombed in a memorial chapel in the National Cathedral at Washington, D.C.

For a few weeks formal funerals seemed to be the routine order in the Escadrille Américaine, and the volunteers quickly realized that war-front flying was not all glamour, glory, hilarious furloughs, and fancy uniforms. This was the Big League, the area of truth, and one had to be very brave, or lucky to survive.

Although the true father of the Escadrille had passed on, the name continued on the rolls, as Frederick H. Prince, Jr., Norman's brother, was posted to N.124 soon after. This member of the family proved to be a worthy successor to carry the laurel, and still living he is a respected representative of that gallant band.

Frederick enlisted direct into the French Aviation on January 29, 1916, and trained at Pau, Buc, and Cazaux until he was formally graduated on a Caudron on May 21, 1916. He joined the Escadrille at Luxeuil shortly after Norman died, and served with devotion and determination until February 15, 1917, when he was returned to Pau as an instructor. Following that assignment he was ordered to join the French Military Mission in Washington and did not return to France until late in September 1917. After filling several such posts, Frederick was released. He tried to join the United States Air Service, but, despite his months of war flying, his instructing ability, and varied experience, he failed to pass the presumptuous standards insisted upon by the Washington experts of that day. He was even refused the request to serve in some executive capacity, so, determined to still do his bit, Frederick accepted a lieutenant's commission in the Quartermaster Corps and probably wound up his war signing indents for cavalry spurs—handy items to help paunchy Top Brass keep their heels on their desks.

A few days after Norman Prince's death two incidents were recorded that add considerable interest to the Escadrille Américaine story. First, now that the Mauser factory had been properly assaulted, it was decided that N.124 was quite capable of contributing to important assignments in another critical area; this time the Somme, where anything was likely to happen.

Once more the ground equipment was packed up, the hangars stripped, and all the non-flying material hauled away in trucks. The planes were flown to Cachy-sur-Somme and their field was to be known as Cachy Wood. But of course such an upheaval could not be carried out without a short stopover in Paris. Next, two more new pilots were assigned to the squadron, Willis B. Haviland of Chicago and Robert Soubiran of New York. Frederick Prince had also been assigned, but he did not actually join N.124 until the vanguard reached Paris.

Willis Haviland had been driving an ambulance for the American Field Service since 1915, and had transferred to the French Aviation on January 26, 1916. He was brevetted on a Caudron by May 20 and signed on with the Escadrille by October 22. Haviland served with some distinction until September 18, 1917, when he was assigned to a French escadrille, Spad 102, where he put in two arduous months. He was then transferred to U. S. Naval Aviation and raised from a French adjutant to a full lieutenant and became the chief pilot of the U. S. Naval Air Station located at Dunkirk. After several weeks at this post, he was attached to Number 13 Squadron, Royal Naval Air Service. He was next sent to Italy where he was the commanding officer U. S. Naval Air Station at Porto

Corsini until the Armistice. All told Willis Haviland served long and well.

Robert Soubiran was an expert mechanic and a competent driver of racing cars, and among the first handful of Americans to volunteer at the outbreak of war. He was of French descent and spoke the language fluently. After some limited training Robert was assigned to the Foreign Legion and fought as an infantryman from August 28, 1914, until February 25, 1916. At one period French soldiers were called on to harvest the crop of winter wheat, and Soubiran, who was skilled with tools and understood intricate mechanisms, ran a threshing machine.

After being wounded in the knee Robert spent four months in a hospital before he was again ready for active duty, and it was during his convalescence that he heard of the formation of the Escadrille Américaine, and because of his mechanical ability was soon taken into the French Aviation.

Soubiran was unlike any of the other Americans. He had spent so much time with French infantrymen that he had taken on many of their active service characteristics and manners. He could have passed for a native-born Frenchman. He hacked at his bread with a scimitar-sharp jackknife, and on switching to the wine *bidon* would plunge his blade deep into the top of the deal table and grin with Gallic satisfaction. Most of the villagers were astonished to learn that their favorite *estaminet* patron was an American.

But this New Yorker became one of the most valued assets of the organization. He was a camera bug, and might have become a professional, had not the war intruded into his gay life. He seemed to be on hand whenever the squadron moved. He turned up at every crash or amusing accident, and recorded every ceremonial in which his pilot pals had any part. Had it not been for Bob, much of the pictorial history of the Lafayette Escadrille would not have been made. Today, his many photographs are priceless.

Soubiran endured an unusual length of service, and his career reflects a complete log of the Great War. He put in about eighteen months as an infantryman, next he flew almost daily for nearly two years with some unit of the French Aviation, after which he was transferred to the U. S. Aviation and served with it from January 26, 1918, until the Armistice. This entailed another nine months of war flying with the 103rd Pursuit Squadron, the American unit that was built from the Lafayette Escadrille.

As commanding officer of the 103rd Pursuit Squadron, Captain Robert Soubiran served meritoriously during the Saint-Mihiel and Meuse-Argonne offensives. Long after the Armistice he was still carrying out important executive duties in France. He was one of the first Americans to take part in the war, and one of the last to leave. He had been away from home for nearly five years.

Before the organization settled down at Cachy, a bleak, wind-swept field within the sound of the front-line guns, a new emergency arose that caused considerable displeasure and grumbling until a most fortunate solution was found.

All through the autumn of 1916 the activities of the Escadrille Américaine had been made known both in Europe and the United States; their victories and defeats were featured, often beyond their actual value. These stories did just what the French had hoped—aroused great interest and enlisted American sympathy for France—but German diplomatic officials in Washington complained and pointed out that America was behaving in a manner unlike a true neutral. As a result, Colonel Barrés, chief of French Aviation at General Headquarters, informed Dr. Gros on November 16 that the organization of American volunteers no longer could be known as the Escadrille Américaine. In future their front-line activities were to be credited to N.124 Squadron.

Dr. Gros, on making inquiry, was told that the German ambassador at Washington, Count Johann Heinrich von Bernstorff, had brought to the attention of the United States Government the fact that a number of Americans were fighting with the French. (A number of Americans were also fighting with the British, but since they were not flaunting their nationality or flag, no mention was made of them.) Von Bernstorff had pointed out too that French communiqués often contained mention of an American escadrille and he felt it necessary to protest in the name of his government.

To keep peace Washington sent a dispatch to the French Ministry of War which in turn resulted in the following letter from French General Headquarters:

The Commander-in-Chief,
To the General Commanding the Armies in the North.
Villers-Breteonneux.
By decision Number 9763D the Ministry of War has decided for diplomatic reasons, the Escadrille N.124 should be called the *Escadrille des Volontaires,* and that the name *Escadrille Américaine* in use at present, must be given up. Will you be kind enough to communicate this decision to the commanding officer of the 13th Combat Group, and to give orders that only the name *Escadrille des Volontaires* be used?

POINDRON.

This was most unsatisfactory from the American volunteers' point of view since the new name in no way proclaimed that N.124 was originated by and composed of Americans who had offered their services to France. The suggested name would indicate that the squadron was made up of volunteers from any nation. It might even include renegade Germans; there were a number of Germans fighting with the Foreign Legion.

After consulting with the embittered Americans, Dr. Gros returned to Paris and went into the Ministry of War to ask for an interview and further explanation. Captain Bertaud pointed out that the new designation was being considered; nothing was final. Whereupon Dr. Gros had a joyful inspiration: "Why not call it the Lafayette Escadrille? Such a name would reflect the boys' recognition of the debt owed by America to France, and with such a designation it could only be an American volunteer squadron. Even the Germans could find no fault with that."

This substitution satisfied everyone, and from that day on N.124 was known as the Lafayette Escadrille, and remained under that designation until the organization was absorbed into the American Air Service.

The Somme area, that but a few weeks before had seen the famous Blood Bath carnage, a massacre never before equalled in modern warfare, proved to be a grim reminder of war's unrelenting toll and travail. Victory had been an illusion, but it had buoyed up both the British and French. Fort Douaumont had been recaptured, and the enemy forced back a few miles. It was the conflict in which for the first time armored tanks had taken a part. Perhaps the most important factor of the Somme Blood Bath was that it marked the turning point of the war in the air, and the enemy knew it, and put on a final-ditch stand over the following year.

The new Lafayette Escadrille was tossed into this arena of savage retaliation to give welcome relief to the front-line squadrons that had fought to a standstill. It was still short-handed and inexperienced, but if the American volunteers could give a few hours of support or relief in any sector, they would more than pay their way. At best the Lafayette could launch only a flight of planes and pilots, but even such a small formation could prove heaven-sent, if it could be put into the critical skies at the right time.

Before its arrival on the Somme, the organization usually had been accommodated in small, pleasant towns; areas that could furnish a few creature comforts for the flying men. They had lived in village hotels, or commandeered villas with the comparative luxury of civilian beds and sanitary facilities. Cachy was a rude awakening. The de luxe war was over, and it came as a shock to the volunteer airmen. Here their quarters were set up in a number of portable barracks that had been recently erected in a slimy acreage of mud; the nearest town was nine miles away.

The Americans had never been grouped with so many combat squadrons, nor located so close to the front. The war was brought home to them in many new ways. They could lie in bed at night and hear the dull rumble of the big guns, as the great chorus of Mars rang out hour by hour. In the daytime they saw the line of kite balloons and above them small formations of fighting planes that darted like chimney swifts, daring the shrapnel bursts, and playing with the puffballs of antiaircraft fire. On nearby aprons were heard the uneven roar of aircraft engines being tested, and the chatter of machine guns at test butts, all adding their percussion notes to the giant symphony of war's grim carnival.

Their particular living area had once been a farm, and their barracks were set amid a tangle of battered barns, steaming manure heaps, and piles of decayed vegetation. A few mongrel dogs skulked about, and mangy cats whimpered from the wreckage of dairy sheds or old cellar holes. Their Besseneau huts leaked and bitter winter winds whistled through the badly fitted panels. Whatever relief time they had was spent in varied attempts to keep warm and dry. Most of the pilots slept in their flying gear since there were no blankets at first, but even worse there were no cooking facilities and the Americans had to rely on the generosity of nearby French escadrilles for food.

N.124 was now part of the French 13th Group which included N.15, N.65, N.84, and N.88 that joined this fighter force soon after. The Americans obviously were competing with professionals, and all of them knew that the wraps were off, that they were no longer to be eased along on soft fronts, or given the opportunity to feel their way around, gaining experience in small palatable doses. They were front-line fighters.

But they had no cause to complain for their record showed that in spite of the few hours they had flown, and the small formations they had been able to put into the air, they had made a very commendable effort.

Their squadron record could be seen on their operations-room wall, listing their victories—seventeen in all, including one by Charles Nungesser who had attached himself to N.124

for a few days when he was supposed to be recuperating from
his latest wound, and one by Lieutenant de Laage de Meux,
one of their French flight leaders. The scores were entered as
follows:

1	May	18, 1916	Kiffin Rockwell
2	May	23, 1916	Bert Hall
3	May	24, 1916	William Thaw
4	July	21, 1916	Charles Nungesser
5	July	23, 1916	Bert Hall
6	July	27, 1916	Lt. de Laage de Meux
7	July	31, 1916	Raoul Lufbery
8	Aug.	4, 1916	Raoul Lufbery
9	Aug.	4, 1916	Raoul Lufbery
10	Aug.	8, 1916	Raoul Lufbery
11	Aug.	28, 1916	Bert Hall
12	Sep.	9, 1916	Norman Prince
13	Sep.	9, 1916	Kiffin Rockwell
14	Oct.	10, 1916	Norman Prince
15	Oct.	12, 1916	Norman Prince
16	Oct.	12, 1916	Raoul Lufbery
17	Oct.	12, 1916	Didier Masson

Why the enemy plane usually credited to Elliott Cowdin, that
he shot down during his first week with the squadron, has not
been included in this list has never been explained.

Although they could hold up their heads with the best of
France's fighting men, the squadron had little pride in what
they could offer in mess conveniences, and the impossibility
of returning these social favors rankled. Bill Thaw and Didier
Masson, who had a few extra francs between them, obtained
permission to go to Paris with a light truck, and in a few hours
returned with a complete kitchen—stove, utensils, and crock-
ery. The main barrack building was partitioned off into small
rooms and one end was refurnished as a dining room. A
stove was set up, and the squadron scroungers were sent off
on the prowl. Eventually, the dining room with its warmth
attracted everyone from pilots to lion cubs. The mechanics
were accommodated in nearby Besseneau huts, and within a

short time the spirit of the original Escadrille had been recaptured. Next, a bathhouse was erected, and someone "borrowed" a mobile power truck which generated current for a string of electric lights to illuminate the huts, hangars, and tents. Of course, the most popular shelter was the community bar where pilots of the whole group congregated. The profits of this daily ceremony were usually forwarded on to the French Red Cross.

The quarters established by the men of the Lafayette eventually became the social center of the whole area. Didier Masson was made mess president, and with his background and cultural tastes soon had a character named Sampson transformed from an ex-sauce cook at the Ritz in New York to a front-line chef of amazing ability. And since theirs was the only general mess where officer and noncom pilots ate together it was the rallying point for all active-service airmen, a point the British could have adopted, but never did in World War I. According to Edwin Parsons, who should know since he was with the Lafayette from this period on, practically every meal from breakfast to dinner included at least a dozen guests from gold-braided generals to corporal air gunners, and at times Masson and Sampson were well put to it to cope.

The base was soon discovered by newspaper reporters, American ambulance drivers, visiting Congressmen, and junketing sightseers of all categories. All were greeted cheerfully and suitably embalmed with Lafayette cocktails.

One may wonder how all these miracles were subsidized by men who were presumed to be operating on French service pay. None of it could have been done without some outside help. By this time the Lafayette Escadrille Committee in Paris, thanks to the untiring efforts of Dr. Gros and Mr. Vanderbilt, was well financed and all of the American volunteers were being paid a hundred francs a month, and given an extra hundred francs whenever they went on leave in Paris. In addition, funds were made available for them to purchase their own somewhat swanky uniforms, and there were added funds to cover their mess bills. There was a time, too, when each pilot was rewarded with five hundred francs for every enemy aircraft shot down. The franc in those days was worth considerably more than it rates today (about four to the American dollar).

Later on when the squadron victories threatened to plunge Mr. Vanderbilt into bankruptcy, the French airplane and machine-gun manufacturers chipped in and offered all French pilots considerable sums of money if a victory was scored while flying their particular equipment or using machine guns that had been assembled in their plants. It may seem sordid today, but in the heat of action, there was little time to consider the ethics or morals of war. Few men thought of the financial reward while engaging a Fokker or Albatros, but by the same token there is no record of anyone's refusing to accept the money on moral grounds.

The Lafayette Escadrille remained at Cachy from October 19, 1916, to January 26, 1917, when it was shifted to Saint-Just on the Oise-Aisne sectors. From May 1916 until March 1917 the Lafayette could boast of only twelve pilots, but imbued with the spirit of Norman Prince and Kiffin Rockwell, they slogged away and carried on.

It was at Cachy that Paul Pavelka first distinguished himself as a volunteer airman. This colorful person was born in Madison, Connecticut, and had had an amazing pre-aviation career before he met the men of the Lafayette. He had been brought up on a farm, and left home at the age of fourteen after differences of opinion with his stepmother. During his teen-age years he worked as a cook in a sheep camp, a cowboy, a male nurse in a San Francisco hospital, and finally became a seaman going to ports of call all over the world. When the war broke out Paul was living at a seaman's home in New York City from where he made an effort to join one of the Allied armies, and accepted the offer of an English recruiter who took a number of British volunteers up to Halifax, Nova Scotia, from where, it was pointed out, they might work their way over to England by feeding and watering some eight hundred horses intended for the British Army.

I can vouch for this arrangement, for I was one of those who also "worked" his way over, possibly on the same vessel, the R.M.S. *Etonian* out of Halifax, Nova Scotia, in early October of 1914. I enlisted in the British Army and eventually transferred to the Royal Flying Corps. Paul, instead, appears to have joined one of the most mystifying organizations to emerge from that conflict. It was known as the Army of the South American Republic of Counani, a fictitious government that was contrived in order to transfer a number of these volunteers, Paul Pavelka included, across to France. Paul enlisted in the Foreign Legion at La Rochelle on November 28, 1914, and served with rare distinction until October 10, 1915, when he was wounded during an attack on German positions north of Arras. It was Paul who had given Kiffin Rockwell first aid when he had been wounded five weeks before. Paul's wound was received during a bayonet attack at Givenchy-en-Gohelle.

Still limping from his bayonet wound, he applied for the French Aviation and was accepted October 18, 1915, and was brevetted by February 23, 1916, after a routine training period at Pau, Cazaux, and the G.D.E. His timing was perfect, for after some *chasse* flying he was sent to N.124 on August 11, 1916, when it was located at Verdun. Shortly after his arrival Paul had an experience that would have dismayed many a stouthearted man, but he ignored it and continued to fly. On this particular occasion his engine caught fire, and since he had no parachute he had to sit tight, or find a way out. Paul kept his head and performed a series of falling-leaf sideslips to keep the flames away from himself, and the gasoline tank. He managed to keep the aircraft together and finally pancaked unhurt into a swamp.

Pavelka evidently had "cat's eyes," for he showed amazing skill as a night flier, and never refused to take off after dark whenever the enemy bombers came over in the shelter of night. On the evening of December 9, 1916, German aircraft sneaked over and dropped eight bombs on the Cachy field, and one of these scored a direct hit on a hangar of N.3 Squadron, the famous Stork outfit then headed by the French ace Georges Guynemer. Since there was plenty of gasoline about the bomb created considerable damage and the flimsy linen-covered aircraft went up like dry tinder.

The enemy planes continued to circle the area, making the most of the illumination created by the burning hangar, and during all the excitement Pavelka got his Nieuport away and into the air. Previously he had made two night flights, but then his plane had been equipped with navigation lights and extra instrument-board illumination. This time one of these connections was broken on take-off and "Skipper," as he was known then, found himself airborne with no lights of any kind. His first thought was to turn back and land, but on considering the condition of the field, the activity overhead, and the uncertain light from the blazing hangar, that seemed too risky, so he continued on.

Paul was truly flying blind and by instinct, since he could not see what few instruments he had—a compass, an altimeter, a tachometer to indicate engine revolutions, an oil pulsator to show that oil was flowing through the lubrication system, and a small clock. He had no contact with the ground, and the bewildering roar of enemy planes above made matters even more perplexing. The ground guns were firing at him as well as at the raiders since he had no system of identification, and a couple of searchlights were set up, adding to the confusion.

Boring his way upward, he evaded the layer of explosion and shrapnel and looked for the enemy bombers. They were up there somewhere but the antiaircraft fire and the criss-crossing searchlight blades created the impression that he was flying through a maze of theatrical lighting, holiday rockets, and the roar of hundreds of guns. Whenever he thought that he had seen something, a scissors of searchlight clipped the view away, or a garish splash of explosive flame eradicated the object.

Skipper realized that this was a hopeless quest, and decided to head for Amiens on the presumption that some of the enemy force might be raiding there—possibly on the Allied hospitals which seemed to be prime targets for enemy bombers in those days. But the defense authorities at Amiens thought Paul was an enemy and quickly doused all lights in the area. It was a black enough night, but with the elimination of all artificial light there was nothing to identify any section or area. There he was in a plane with no lights of any kind and a topography below that showed no marker for identification.

The Nieuport carried fuel for about two hours of normal flight, and dawn was some time away. As his night vision improved, Paul decided to ease down to look for a level area where he might risk a landing, but every time he dropped below two thousand feet "friendly" machine guns opened up from all sides. The gunners could not identify the outline of the plane, but they could hear its engine and spot the jagged flame that was emitted from its exhaust. Tracer bullets raced up from the ground, and as they burned to ill-formed slugs they went berserk and danced about all over the sky until their phosphorous content was consumed. This was one of the peculiarities of tracer bullets. Since they consisted of a hollow bullet envelope filled with phosphorous, they would bore out and follow a normal course until they became unbalanced by their uneven burning and careened all over the sky. Inexperienced aerial gunners often dispensed with their gunsights and "fired on tracer," meaning that they simply aimed so that their tracers seemed to be going into an enemy machine. This was a sad fallacy, as the gun drums were usually loaded with one armor-piercing round, one tracer, and one regular bullet in that order. If one fired on the course being taken by the tracers, it was more than likely that the armor-piercing and regular rounds would be wasted. Tracer bullets were fairly accurate up to short distances, but usually went off on erratic courses.

As Skipper toured about seeking an emergency landing

field, he could identify no known area; there were vague
patterns of open space, but he did not know whether they
were plowed fields, or meadows that had seen heavy ground
action and were pocked with shellholes or patterns of old
barbed wire. He cruised about searching for a friendly sign,
and realized that a murky night was setting in; the hangar at
Cachy was no longer sending out dancing flame, and there
were only trails of smoke and indistinct patterns of ground
areas.

He reset his air valve and manipulated the butterfly carburetor of the rotary until the Le Rhone was just ticking over
and keeping him in the air. In this manner he clung to the
last few feet of altitude until a faint promise of dawn drew a
finger of gold across the eastern sky. Paul held his breath and
waited, the prop still ticking over, and then as some uncertain
detail of the ground came up, his engine conked out for good.

It was neck or nothing, and Paul risked the misty half light
and made a dead-stick landing without bursting a tire or
breaking a wire. He had come down within the British lines at
a village called Martainville nearly forty miles from Cachy.
Ten minutes later a heavy fog closed in, but he was found,
and taken over by the officers of a British regiment who at
the time were billeted at an old château. He had to stay there
four days, but his Lafayette companions were delighted to
know that he was safe and unharmed. Most of them had been
betting that he was down somewhere in the German lines,
possibly killed in a crash, or taken prisoner.

From that time on Paul Pavelka seemed to be fascinated
with the prospects of night flying, and he made more than
twenty flights, sometimes accompanied by Lieutenant de
Laage. These forays did not reward them in any way for no
enemy planes were intercepted or destroyed, but they must
have added some knowledge of the art to the many experiences of the Lafayette. In time night signals were devised. A
set of "lighthouses" that could be turned on to mark certain
areas were used—particularly by the British night-flying

squadrons—and aircraft were better equipped for this kind of work. Certainly Paul Pavelka contributed his share to the new aerial science.

A short time later a call went out for volunteers to serve on the Salonika front in Greece, and being interested in geography and exotic cities of the world, Paul offered to go. It was said, too, that Kiffin Rockwell's death had affected him more than he would admit. Although poles apart in social and intellectual stature, the war had quickly eliminated all barriers, and Paul and Kiffin had become fast friends. Paul had kept a stiff upper lip at the time of Kiffin's death, but those who watched him closely sensed that he was becoming dull and morose, and when a change of scene was made available, Paul responded eagerly.

IIe arrived in Salonika in February of 1917 and soon enjoyed the new life. The picturesque background of the Near Eastern front fascinated him, and he was pleased to learn that the polyglot enemy forces there were easier to attack, and their aerial gunnery practically non-existent. Skipper proved to be a valuable man here, and his work was soon recognized. He was cited in the Allied dispatches and decorated with the Croix de Guerre.

Paul flew a Nieuport single-seater and an Italian A. R. Caudron-like two-seater that was used for observation and artillery spotting. He had an unnamed Greek officer as his observer but this gentleman was not too familiar with machine guns and Paul, then a sergeant pilot, had to show an officer the sequence of firing and the art of using aerial gunnery sights.

On November 12, 1917, Paul met an untimely and quite unnecessary death. That day, while taking a walk in the Salonika area, he met a British cavalry officer whom he had once known in the Foreign Legion. He was invited to visit the British regiment for a drink and meal, and during his stay, Skipper, who was an excellent horseman, asked permission to ride a remount that had just been sent to the regiment.

This beast was a vicious devil and did its best to unseat Paul, and failing in that reared up suddenly and rolled over on its back, crushing the rider beneath it. Paul's neck was broken in the mishap, and he died a few hours later.

Laurence Rumsey was another of the early arrivals. He was born in Buffalo, New York, and soon after the outbreak of war volunteered for the American Field Service. On September 9, 1915, he transferred to the French Aviation and was brevetted on a Caudron in February 1916. He was assigned to the Escadrille on June 4 and was on the roll until November 25, 1916. He was plagued with ill health, however, and took little active part in any of the chief missions; most of the time he was under hospital care, and was released finally by the French as physically unfit for further active service.

Perhaps the most self-effacing member of the Lafayette Escadrille was Dudley Lawrence Hill, a native of Peekskill, New York. Few World War I buffs could identify the name, for he managed to keep out of the war-ace limelight, although he put in nearly twenty-eight months of active-service flying with the French, and later with five different squadrons of the U. S. Air Service.

Hill deserves unusual credit since he was physically unfit for active-service flying. He had defective vision in one eye, but like the famous Mickey Mannock, another one-eyed wonder, Dudley had a dozen tricks to fool the medical examiners.

He joined the American Field Service in 1915 and made the transfer to aviation by August 3 of that year, going through the usual tour of aviation schools from September 25, 1915, until he took his brevet on a Caudron on March 17, 1916, all the while hoodwinking medical experts who were convinced that Dudley was a semi-invalid. Now and then Dr. Gros would examine him and declare him fit for service, but when he got to a training squadron other doctors would discover more alarming defects. He was proposed for a medical

discharge several times, but apparently Dudley's eyesight was
so bad he couldn't read the order. Later on his flight instructors all agreed that this invalid American was totally
unfit to risk acrobatic training, and made out reports to that
end. But French military matters moved as slowly as those of
other belligerents, and Dudley had taken up and passed his
acrobatic course long before the report that stated he couldn't
had reached an important level.

Groggy and perplexed with the varied opinions as to his
physical being and flying ability, Dudley finally arrived at
Luxeuil after N.124 Squadron had returned there for the
Mauser arms factory raid. Over the next nineteen months he
served with modest distinction with the Lafayette, never missing a mission or failing to volunteer for any risky assignment.
Still, nothing spectacular seemed to happen to Hill; he was
just there day after day, wearing his old French uniform with
no gaudy decorations, cords, braid, or particular insignia.
Whenever American correspondents arrived looking for a new
story Dudley usually was curled up in a corner reading a
week-old newspaper, obviously trying to find out how the war
was progressing.

Something in the pattern got out of register, however, when
Adjutant Hill was awarded the Croix de Guerre with Star, but
for the life of him Dudley never could explain it, and there
seems to be no photograph showing him wearing either the
ribbon or the cross.

When the Lafayette was transferred to the U. S. Air Service,
Hill was assigned to the 103rd Pursuit Squadron with which
he served until June 1, 1918. He then went to the 139th and
flew regularly for two months. On August 1, 1918, he became
the commanding officer of the 138th Pursuit Squadron, and
ended his war as CO, 5th Group, a command he held for only
eleven days.

We can find no official or unofficial report stating whether
Hill ever destroyed an enemy aircraft. He would probably
deny any such accomplishment, if we could.

Chapter IX

DOWN ON THE SOMME

Cachy Wood and other fields on the Somme were the scene of much action and considerable discomfort throughout that bleak winter, and those of us who remember that war will docket those heartbreaking months as the worst of all. By then all the regulars on both sides of the line had been wiped out or retired to training schools at home, and the civilian armies were having to take over. The line was established from the Swiss border to the English Channel, and looking down from the air one could see the scars of battle—areas that once had been Ypres, Loos, Poperinge, and other names that have appeared in military history for centuries.

Mass graves and small rectangular cemeteries were everywhere; some bodies had received decent burial, but in many instances shellfire disinterred the dead, for high explosive had no respect for graveyards or hallowed acres. The trenches ran through old churchyards, disturbing those in their long sleep. Ancient monuments no longer marked final resting places since they were more valuable as defense buttresses, and as a result there were a dozen Coffin Corners on every front.

The battles of Loos, Neuve-Chapelle, Festubert, and a dozen other minor but deadly attacks, which gained some ground but more often set up new salients to be straightened out by less experienced men, had broadened the science of ground slaughter. Historians can find little meaning today in these bloody forays; at best they were emotional diversions of impatience, plotted to break up the monotonous routine of stalemated warfare. France, too, endured some of these grievous battles, for all through 1916 she had been hurling her reserve regiments against the enemy around Verdun. In fact, she sustained the greater load of the German offensive along the Western Front during that year until at last, bleeding but defiant, she had to stand by while the British took up the gage and staged the Blood Bath of the Somme.

Six hundred thousand Empire troops were sent into that carnage, the bulk of them from English towns and villages, and back in Britain immense reserves waited to fill the gaps made in the ranks before that summer's foliage had taken on the dull browns of stale ale. They were now strong in the power of artillery, particularly in the heavy category of 9.2s (eight inchers), and the 4.2s which were well-handled howitzers. The long-muzzled sixty-pounders had incredible range and destructive accuracy.

At the same time Allied aircraft had improved greatly, and new squadrons were arriving to back up every sector. General Sir Hugh "Boom" Trenchard was demanding the best to be had in men and machines, and, although few of us realized it, a Great Tradition was being developed. Young men were taught to fly, to scout the enemy, to fight his circuses—and to die like gentlemen. At last, Allied knights-errant of the air were challenging the German aces on equal terms, and whenever the odds were reasonably even, were beating them back. There were times when Allied airmen gained absolute supremacy by greater daring combined with equal skill. As a rule, and perhaps by order, the German pilots flew with more caution, not wasting their lives and equipment in unequal contests. This proved to be a sound policy for often it enabled them to come back again in force and hold the air for a time with powerful concentrations. But in the ensuing battles of the Somme, Allied airmen, at tremendous sacrifice, kept the enemy's pilots pinned down, and "blinded his eyes."

After the Blood Bath only the airmen seemed to retain some spirit of flight, and whenever the weather permitted they were in the sky fighting to retain some vague standard of control. Gunnery was improving, and fighting tactics, so long talked about but strangely lacking, were being worked out. Fixed weapons no longer shot away the propellers, and Britain's Scarff mounting enabled observer-gunners to give as good as they received from enemy single-seaters. As a matter of

record, the aerial gunners were racking up rewarding figures,
and many a young air knight who was well on his way to
being an ace was cut down by some unnamed gunner before
he had served out his apprenticeship. The famed Max Immelmann was downed by Corporal J. H. Waller, a volunteer
machine gunner who had come out of the trenches a few
days before. Before being counted out, the great Baron von
Richthofen was shot down three times—twice by NCO gunners. The two-seater fighter was slowly but surely coming into
its own.

Although the winter was dreary, the Somme provided a
new scene and rewarded the men of the Lafayette squadron
with a warm feeling of satisfaction since they were at last
accepted, and were members of the first team. No longer were
they the pampered volunteers from a neutral country, who, in
appreciation of their proffered help, had been brought along
tenderly on quiet fronts. All that froth had been blown from
their war tankard. Experienced airmen from other front-line
squadrons who accepted their mess hospitality were sincere
in their praise and generous in their appreciation.

By now "the few" had developed what was known as air
sense, the unconscious art of knowing what was going on in
their particular area. This sense, the antithesis of their early
air-blindness, was a facility that evolved in small subliminal
streams. Its chief components included the immediate identification of enemy aircraft, the quick decision of whether it
was a single- or two-seater, and the automatic reaction of first
moving for the shield of the sun, calculating the wind, fuel,
and distance from a friendly area. In other terms it might be
called the strategy of salvation.

Those who were articled in the air conflict knew when to
wait, when to move in, or better still when to turn for home.
Only if they were hallowed with unjustified luck, did the
impetuous ones live through the working-in period, scoring
victories or escaping the penalty of brash behavior. The art of
waiting was a tedious skill, but one that usually was rewarded
with another meal with comrades, another evening of pleasant

reflections, one more night wrapped in one's own blankets beneath a hospitable roof. "If you get through the first six weeks," the veterans assured us, "you will one day go home. You won't be the same, but you'll go home—and wonder how you lived through it all."

During their first few weeks war airmen were charged with one or two resolves; to live long enough to justify their ideals and to put up a respectable strip of ribbon (civilians cannot know the inspiration of a military decoration), to live, and once again know the peace of sleep untortured by soul-searing nightmares. By the time they had survived the various levels of training, all the romance, the spirit of adventure, the glossy novelty of being a fighting pilot, had long dissipated. The man with any degree of intelligence knew that his chances of seeing the end of the war were hellishly slim.

As an aside, few of us had any idea at the time how the war would end. The word "Armistice" was not mentioned until a few hours before that morning, November 11, 1918. We had often wondered how the hostilities would be concluded. We tried to remember how the Boer War was closed out, what means were contrived to end the Spanish-American War, or how the Civil War was stopped. At best, we could remember the testimony of old dusty engravings that showed someone handing over a sword, but who fought with swords today? We visualized men signing a large, curling sheet of paper, or the classical figures of defeat standing in an obsequious attitude before a portal of regimental drums while their dejected troops piled their arms in rows of peaceful pyramids.

That was how half-remembered wars were said to have ended, but any such theatrical tableau was out of the question in a carnage of this breadth and magnitude. None of us could know that one day a party of German officers would gather in a railway car outside Paris, that was assigned to General Foch, and gratefully sign to halt the invasion of *their* homeland. Had anyone told us that less than a quarter of a century later another German, Adolf Hitler, would play the opposite role in the same historic piece of rolling stock on the exact spot

in Compiègne Forest, our half-formed dread that our war
would not be finished properly, would have had shattering
conviction. But it was years later before we realized that
politicians, masquerading as diplomats, and quaking sentimen-
talists had wickedly betrayed us.

There were other experiences and customs to be learned
and absorbed, and once the Lafayette had been accepted by
members of the first-line squadrons, it was soon apparent that
patriotism and service loyalty did not of necessity come pack-
aged in heroic proclamations or emotional displays. Their
French compatriots were unlike the Alphonse and Gaston
caricatures in the comic sheets back home; they were less
explosive and volatile, and their love for France was as sincere
as that of any other soldier, their determination to win and
drive back the Hun as fierce as that of any British lad. These
French airmen did not consider it necessary to mouth plati-
tudes, declaiming they were willing to fight and die for their
country. They knew they were engaged in a cruel business
that had to be faced in a calculating manner, and once the
Americans learned that actions spoke louder than words, they
soon slipped into important slots of the military jigsaw.

About this time, too, they were embarrassed or enraged
by the few American journalists who, wearied with penning
the continued heroics of the French and British, made the
most of the modest contribution by the Lafayette Escadrille.
From their reports one gained the impression that each one
of this handful of volunteers was bringing down a Hun a day,
or dying gloriously while fighting against tremendous odds.
Some of the articles implied that whenever the Lafayette
Escadrille moved into a new sector, the French and British
packed up, went off on leave, and left the war to the gallant
Americans. This image possibly did more harm than good, for
it took considerable "living down."

Their acceptance also carried the burden of having to fly
all kinds of missions. All assignments that were committed to
the 13th Chasse Group included N.124, along with the Storks

and other top-flight Nieuport squadrons. The Lafayette was expected to fight and act like a first-line organization, to take its turn in the air no matter what the mission.

This particular Somme area, a vital junction of the French and British lines, afforded some hair-raising actions, and this period of the war saw the growing strength of the German flying-circus system, and the enemy's new Albatros and Fokker machines. Bloody April was just around the corner.

New American volunteers, neophytes in experience, arrived charged with enthusiasm. The others, comparative veterans, knew that war in the air was no picnic; the aviation service might furnish more basic comforts, cleaner uniforms, drier beds, and meals served in a civilized manner, but it was far more deadly than the trenches. The enemy still fought his war according to his schedule, and selected the aerial battlefields well inside his own lines.

Early in 1917 three new candidates, who were to contribute much to the history of the Lafayette, turned up soon after the billets at Cachy were ready for occupancy. The first was Edwin Charles Parsons, a gay cavalier type who was born at Holyoke, Massachusetts, September 24, 1892. It was Parsons who set such a high standard as a fighting airman. He was a striking figure, a fashion-plate on leave, a veritable Scarlet Pimpernel, who ended his war with eight confirmed victories. In addition, Ted, as he is still known, proved to be a valuable, reliable, and lively historian of the Lafayette. His book, *The Great Adventure*, published in 1937, is a colorful account that misses no tricks, rollicks with gay, good humor and should be read by anyone at all interested in the Escadrille. It may be out of print, but deserves to be reissued and take its rightful place on everyone's World War I bookshelf.

Ted Parsons is still a delightful companion and he does not disguise the fact that he was an unreserved adventurer, a happy-go-lucky knight-errant. He has never displayed any Gallic sentimentality, nor has he written paeans to his own gallantry. If there are men who seem to glory in war, Parsons is one of them.

He received his early schooling in Springfield, Massachusetts, and at Phillips Exeter Academy, after which he attended the University of Pennsylvania for about two years. What particular impression he left there has not been recorded, but the betting stands that his classmates still remember him. In his youth he was not an outstanding physical specimen, being continually tormented by enlarged tonsils, and at times one eyelid would droop producing a piratical sneer even when he was in a most benevolent mood. He had lost most of one little finger as the result of an infection from a signet ring of questionable alloy, and he had early consorted with My Lady Nicotine, so that medicos inspecting his respiratory system were often bewildered. To top all this Ted also had a touch of color blindness.

"If I had ever tried to get into the U. S. Aviation Service in those days," Parsons explains, "I would have been booted out on my ear. I mean to say, how could I expect to fly a Wright biplane with a couple of joints missing from one pinky, two eyes that could never seem to make up their mind, and a respiratory complication that would have been diagnosed as the heaves by any second-year veterinarian?"

It should be noted here that during World War II, Ted contributed his trembling frame to the U. S. Navy—and wound up a rear admiral!

The wanderlust virus bit Ted in 1912 and he left home, his undergraduate days of ease, and the puritan policy of his relatives. He took Horace Greeley's advice and went to California where he encountered a fascinating complex known as a flying school at Dominguez Field just outside of Los Angeles. From this point on history becomes misty. We can only presume that Ted took some tuition if he had the money. He may have turned out to be a first-class aviator of that day, but he himself makes no such claim. Whatever he picked up, it enabled him to take a captain's commission in the Mexican Aviation Corps and from various sources we learn that he may have led the aerial might against General Obregón's legions, for Didier Masson refers to Parsons as one of his aerial opponents during this comic-opera uprising.

Once his first campaign had closed down, Ted returned to Massachusetts, and learned that a much better war was being staged in Europe. This was in 1915 and the belligerents were flying real airplanes and shooting real machine guns at one another. It occurred to Ted that although he was supposed to be a physical wreck he might be accepted as an ambulance driver, and he put the proposition to his father hoping that he would shell out for a first-class ticket to Paris, but Dad Parsons remembered the Boer War and couldn't see his semi-invalid offspring mixed up in anything that was going on along the Marne or in Flanders. He flatly refused.

Drifting about, Ted learned of the cattle-boat routine, and signed on as a veterinary surgeon—one sure way of being accepted. Fortunately, his equine charges were fairly healthy and there was no need for his skilled services. On arrival in France, Ted was so entranced with his ability to endure the cattle-boat regimen, he threw all caution to the winds and offered his services to the French Aviation. He was told that he would have to serve at first with the Foreign Legion, a stipulation that shook him back to his original infirmity. He tottered away to join the American Field Service and there so built up his drooping strength he was able to take charge of a complete ambulance section at Mrs. Whitney Warren's hospital near Juilly behind the Soissons front.

By April 1916 Ted had wangled his way into aviation, but only after faking through an almost unbelievable medical examination. To appreciate the details, I will present them just as Ted relates in his book, *The Great Adventure:*

I walked into a room partially filled with a number of tough-looking specimens of every race under the sun, including a couple of blacks and one or two whose real color I was unable to distinguish because of a most effective disguise of plain ordinary dirt.

My name was called and I popped into a small office, occupied largely by various charts and a much-harassed, black-beavered, beetle-browned individual with a booming voice and the caduceus of the Medical Corps on the deep-red tabs of his uniform collar. I blushingly complied with his order to strip. As impersonally as if I were just another horse, he gave me a short once-over and saw that I was equipped with the regulation torso, head, arms and legs. Satisfactory grunt. The first hurdle had been surmounted.

Then he laid a large dirty, grease-spotted towel on my lily-white chest, and I shuddered with the thought of how many chests like those in the ante-room that same towel had already covered. It didn't take me long in the French Army to get over my squeamish ideas.

He ordered me to breathe deeply. I did, surprising even myself. Although my heart was beating like a triphammer, a long-drawn sigh had no trace of the heaves. With his ear to my chest, protected by the towel from contamination, he listened for waterfalls and volcanic upheavals, none of which, fortunately, were forthcoming at the moment. Briskly he nodded approval, and I drew another sigh of relief, to which, as luck would have it, he wasn't listening. A slight grating, as of steel rails dragged across a graveled yard, was produced by that exhalation.

But the most difficult portions of my test were yet to come. Standing me off at ten feet in front of a chart whose letters looked as large as the Corticelli (a popular silk product) sign in Times Square, he commanded me to read.

"The second line," he'd say, "the third letter. I see there a B. What do you see?"

Sure enough, it was a B, and I'd say so.

"*Bon,*" he'd explode enthusiastically.

Then we'd do some more of these silly exercises, he calling the letters as I checked on him. He was right every time. He never tried to cross me by calling the wrong letter. He wasn't taking any chances I'd be wrong, and his "*Bons*" grew bigger and better with every answer.

Then we passed to the color charts where we repeated the same delightful process.

"I see red. What do you see?"

"Red, Major."

"*Bon.* I see green. What . . . ?"

But why go on? In two shakes of a lamb's tail it was all over.

He gave me a friendly pat on the bare back that sent me staggering across the room, and, signing his name to my papers with an official flourish, he congratulated me on being a perfect physical specimen and said that as far as he was concerned I could go out and get myself killed at any time "*pour la France.*"

I fooled him, though, and didn't get killed. Despite my tremendous handicaps, including the fact that my college education was of very brief duration, I served three years with the French pursuit and got more than my fair share of victories. The physical examination was a farce, and no mention was made of mental requirements. I couldn't even speak the language well at the time.

How right Parsons was. To the French it was a self-evident fact that a candidate did not have to be a genius or a physical marvel to fly a war plane. Good health was an asset, but it was by no means an absolute requisite. Courage and marksmanship were more important qualities.

Georges Guynemer, who scored fifty-four official victories, was frail, consumptive, and weighed less than one hundred pounds. Nungesser was so battered he literally was wired together with silver, but he lived to down forty-five enemy planes. After months of cruel incarceration in an enemy prison camp, Georges Madon crawled back, and went on to score forty-one victories. Mickey Mannock had but one eye and a limited education, but he downed seventy-three Boche. Jimmy McCudden, who was born of poor parents in a military barracks, had little formal schooling, but he too more than earned his keep with fifty-eight downed planes. René Fonck, France's greatest ace, started out as a young peasant boy with a sketchy education, but he led his country's ace pack with seventy-five confirmed victories. To close this reflection it is interesting to note that more than 70 per cent of all flying men in the French Aviation were noncommissioned officers, many of them with only primary school educations, and the majority from good peasant stock. Their magnificent records speak for themselves.

Ted Parsons eventually wound up in aviation, was brevetted on a Caudron on August 23, 1916, but did not get an assignment to a front-line squadron until January 24, 1917, when he was sent to the Lafayette Escadrille at Cachy.

Another young American who arrived with Parsons was Ronald Wood Hoskier, the son of a New York financier who lived in South Orange, New Jersey. At the outbreak of war the Hoskier family was in France, and the father, Herman C. Hoskier, served with the Norton-Harjes Ambulance Corps, a Franco-American group. Mrs. Hoskier acted as an auxiliary nurse in a Paris hospital. Fired by the example of his parents, Ronald, who was a gentlemanly young student, drove an ambulance for a time before responding to the appeal of military aviation. He was accepted on April 5, 1916, and brevetted on a Blériot by August 13 that same year. He was a skilled and daring pilot, and was assigned to the Lafayette Escadrille on December 11, and served with some distinction until his death on April 23, 1917. This young man lived less than four months amid the hellish action on the Somme. Paul A. Rockwell, official historian of the Lafayette, told the author recently that "Hoskier was an outstanding pilot, a gallant young man, and equally important, a gentleman in the true sense of the word."

Young Hoskier was unlike any of the other members of the Lafayette; in the first place he seemed to be too youthful to be included in such a hazardous mission. He was refined, cultured, with an above-the-average intelligence, and seldom raised his voice. Like Dudley Hill he was modest and self-effacing. Apparently he had access to private funds, for his uniforms were neatly tailored and outstanding. That winter he arrived wearing a sky-blue greatcoat of excellent material, topped off with a warm fur collar. He was one of the few Americans to adopt the French beret, and it must be admitted that he looked very smart in his equipment.

The varied types, styles, and combinations of uniforms worn by the French, American, and other airmen in the aviation service require some explanation. Actually, the service did not have a uniform of its own until after World War I, and since the pilots and observers were drawn from various arms of the service—infantry, artillery, cavalry, engineers, Zouaves, colonial troops, and the Foreign Legion—the trainees usually wore the uniform of the branch in which they had served previously.

In fact, pilots, gunners, bombardiers, and aerial observers could wear any French military uniform that appealed to them. They would simply order one and have the insignia to which they were entitled stitched or pinned to the accepted portion of the jacket. For instance, Kiffin Rockwell liked the French artillery uniform and had one made for him when he obtained his pilot's brevet. Later, he adopted the khaki of the Foreign Legion officer, and when he was killed he was wearing the new horizon blue of the French infantry, a uniform that he had just had made by a Paris tailor.

The third newcomer at Cachy was a very small, pink-cheeked lad named Edmond Charles Clinton Genet from Ossining, New York, a direct descendant of Citizen Genet, the ambassador of the French Government to the United States in 1792. The Genets were descended from Edmé Jacques Genet, secretary and interpreter to the Count of Provence, later Louis XVIII. Having lived a long while in England, Edmé Jacques became an authority on English affairs and a publicist of some renown when he returned to France. Two of his children also distinguished themselves, the first Edmond C. became the famous Citizen Genet who was sent to America, and who, according to John Jay Chapman, was recalled later, owing to his diplomatic indiscretions. He did not return to France, however, since his political party was out of favor, but remained in America, bought a small farm on Long Island and in 1794 married Cornelia Tappen Clinton, the daughter of Governor George Clinton of New York. Later he became an American citizen.

Citizen Genet's sister Henriette, who became Madame Campan, began life as an infant prodigy, and received her early schooling under distinguished instructors, poets, and musicians at the French court. At fourteen years of age she was governess to the children of Marie Antoinette with whom she was a friend and lady in waiting for more than twenty years. When the king and queen were imprisoned, Henriette asked to be allowed to accompany them, but her offer was denied. The King, Louis XVI, entrusted his most secret documents, family valuables, and other heirlooms to Henriette before he entered prison at Feuillants in 1792. Among these mementos was a brooch, Marie Antoinette had ordered sent to Citizen Genet, which Edmond's mother wore during World War I. After the fall of the French monarchy, Madame Campan founded a school for young girls, which was turned later into a national academy by Napoleon. On the fall of the First Empire, the Bourbons, with harsh ingratitude, persecuted Madame Campan for having accepted the protection of Napoleon. She died in disgrace and poverty in 1822 at the age of seventy, leaving personal memoirs of the old court, considered to be among the most valuable extant.

Young Edmond was a great-great-grandson of Citizen Genet, and despite the treatment his forebears had suffered at the hands of the French Government, there lay beneath his quiet demeanor a burning ambition and a love of France that few people divined. He was born in November 1896, the traditional youngest son, predestined to achievement. He grew up independently of his three older brothers, finding his pleasures and interests for himself, ever free in thought and action.

He was educated in several private and public schools, and at Mount Pleasant Academy. He had an unending love of the sea and was often photographed playing with ships on nearby ponds in the current junior seaman's outfit. He was musical, could paint well in oils, and from his earliest days wrote down everything that happened to him. His letters from the Foreign Legion trenches and later from the hangars and cubicles of the Lafayette Escadrille furnished valuable and well-written material for historians. A kindly boy, thoughtful of everyone and imbued with good manners, he was soon known as "Smiler" to the other American pilots who took him to their hearts with rare warmth and sincerity.

Smiler Genet once made an application for entrance to Annapolis, but failed the entrance exams, since he was sadly lacking in mathematics. The rejection made a deep impression on him, and in desolation he enlisted as a seaman in the U. S. Navy, but when he was denied a role in the Mexican affair, any role in which he would become a fighter, he lost interest and made plans to desert. He had made routine applications for a formal release, but none of these was granted, so he jumped his ship January 8, 1915, and took passage aboard the S.S. *Rochambeau* for France. By a strange coincidence Norman Prince was aboard the same steamer, and it was from him that young Genet first learned of the proposed squadron of American volunteers. (It should be noted here that in November 1919 Josephus Daniels, Secretary of the Navy, formally absolved Edmond Genet of all charges of desertion, chiefly through a generous interpretation of the facts, and in consideration of his service and sacrifice.)

Edmond enlisted in the Foreign Legion on February 3, 1915, and after two months of training was sent immediately to the front. Young Genet, who seemed hardly big enough to wear a greatcoat and carry a rifle, won the praise of his officers and companions in this rugged infantry organization, mainly for his boyish enthusiasm and willingness to undertake all kinds of tasks, disregarding his own safety. In the deadly Champagne offensive through September and October of 1915 Edmond's battalion attacked the enemy in the Bois Sabot, and during one charge he was stunned and hurled into a hole by the explosion of a large-caliber shell. When he regained consciousness he saw a regiment of Zouaves continuing on in support of the Legion, and asking no questions he joined them and fought manfully. Three days later he rejoined his comrades who had mourned him for dead.

On another occasion Genet was in a bayonet charge with his company that bored into a storm of machine-gun fire until he was the only man left in the advance, the others being killed, wounded, or taking shelter in nearby holes or trenches. Genet found another member of his regiment and together they decided to work their way back. Edmond made it simply because he kept cool; his companion lost his head in the furor and was cut down and killed.

He served fifteen long months in this kind of activity, but he still remembered Norman Prince and his talk of a possible American air squadron, and eventually one of his applications for a transfer was acted on and he turned up at aviation head-quarters on May 24, 1916. He was as happy as a lark, although he realized that war flying was more dangerous than general infantry activity—or so it seemed to him. "Still," he pointed out in one letter home, "if I am killed while flying you will know all about it almost immediately. If one is killed in the trenches there are a dozen chances no one will ever know anything about what actually happened."

With Genet went Herman Lincoln Chatkoff, another American in the Legion who had been in the thick of the ground fighting since late August 1914, but who, on transferring to French Aviation, did not manage an assignment with the Lafayette before it was turned over to the American forces. This was because, after gaining his brevet, he requested permission to go back to the trenches and spend two more months with his old comrades where he fought the Germans and vermin until an opening was found for him with the French C.11 Squadron, flying Caudrons.

Edmond also made the acquaintance of Dennis Dowd, the New York lawyer who had served in the trenches for about eighteen months, and was killed in a training-flight accident at Buc.

Throughout his flying training Genet was beset with the full realization of his obligations to the United States Navy, and as letter after letter from home contained some dreary or disturbing reference to his desertion, the young man was at times on the verge of hysteria. Then he had a crash aboard a training Blériot, an accident that put him in the hospital for several days where he fumed and fretted, certain that he would be dismissed and sent back to the Foreign Legion. While he lay there he heard that Dennis Dowd had been killed on the same field, a shock that made him positive that any American who so much as broke a guy wire would be eliminated quickly from the training course. Around this time he grew a full-sized mustache to give him a more mature appearance.

But good fortune now awaited the young American as his training proceeded along a smooth course. Boylike, he was fascinated by the various aircraft he encountered and marveled at their speed, mechanism, and delicacy of handling. He passed through the Buc, Pau, Cazaux, and G.D.E. schools with flying colors and gained his brevet on a Caudron on September 3, 1916. He made one of the best training records of any of the American volunteers. At one time, after graduating, he volunteered to serve in Rumania with a French air service operating there, but his offer was not considered seriously, and while waiting he put in two or three weeks at the Cazaux *chasse* school where he was eventually passed out on Nieuports. He was transferred to the Lafayette Escadrille on January 19, 1917.

Once the Escadrille was settled at Cachy the work was intensified and patrols were carried out whenever a gleam of decent weather permitted. These included routine offensive patrols well inside the enemy lines. They flew escort for two-seaters assigned to photography or visual reconnaissance tasks, and in regular order they sat over the artillery-spotting planes that were flying their tiresome figure eights between their gun emplacements and the enemy targets. There was little glamour or glory, and successful fights were few and far between.

Lufbery downed a German somewhere south of Chaulnes on December 27, and an hour or so later Georges Guynemer, flying from the same field, sent down another startlingly close to the spot on which Lufbery's victim had fallen.

Although a severe frost chilled the hands and feet, it at least hardened the mud around the hangars and made the surface of the field more adaptable for landings and take-offs. Some of the French squadrons at Cachy were being equipped with the new Spad fighter, but the cold weather considerably cut down their vaunted efficiency. The Hispano-Suiza engine, a water-cooled power plant, was not as yet fitted with radiator shutters, and it was almost impossible to get it running without some makeshift panels that were ripped away when the engine finally warmed up. The rotary engines of the Nieuports had none of this trouble, and the Lafayette pilots were often called on to fly missions originally assigned to the Spad squadrons.

Around this time Bill Thaw returned from a short trip to the United States and turned up just in time to oversee still another move when the squadron was ordered to take over a new airfield located at Ravenel near St. Just-en-Chaussée. Everyone was expecting an Allied push the following spring, and the British and French were realigning their air squadrons and preparing for this all-out campaign. Much of this activity took place in February 1917, at which time Frederick Prince, Norman's brother, was returned to Pau as an instructor, and his place was taken by Harold B. Willis, a native of Boston, Massachusetts. Another Bostonian, Stephen Bigelow, and Walter Lovell of Concord, Massachusetts, were added to the New England contingent. Before the month was ended Edward F. Hinkle of Cincinnati, Ohio, was signed on. He was well over forty years of age, far beyond the limit for front-line fliers, but he had entreated, pulled wires, and called on friends until he was able to take and complete the training course, and put up a creditable record. After about ten weeks at the front, however, where he had carried out three or four patrols, he suffered a physical collapse and was eventually released from duty.

Raoul Lufbery, who was now a lieutenant with the Legion of Honor added to his list of decorations, was downed by weather, which aggravated an old rheumatic condition so that he could scarcely climb into his aircraft. He was advised to take a long furlough and go to the South of France to bask in

the Mediterranean sun and sea, but he did not stay long for
he was back at the squadron as soon as his knees had limbered
up.

During the ground activity that was necessary to get the
organization settled once more, three of the newcomers—
Parsons, Hoskier, and Genet—anxious to get some action, obtained permission to go off on what they termed a general
look around.

Once they were aloft, however, they soon forgot their good
intentions since they were anxious to run up a score. There
were no Boche over the French balloon-line and they decided
—or perhaps Ted Parsons decided—that they might as well
go over and have a look at Hunland. Their renowned an-
cestors, the American pioneers, had courageously investigated
the great unknown Indian country, so why shouldn't three
American volunteers venture a little farther?

All went well for about ten minutes. The enemy spanked
the sky with a few antiaircraft splotches just to let them know
they were "offside" so to speak, but that only added to the
general interest. A few minutes later they ran smack dab
into a couple of fast two-seaters, and the courageous ancestry
had a quick revision. All three suddenly realized that they
were cold, but Parsons at least kept his head, and, flying as
leader, remembered enough of his training to move up into
the sun. Once he took Hoskier and Genet down on the enemy,
however, he swears he forgot all he had learned.

"In the first place we must have started firing at them from
about fifteen hundred feet, a ridiculous distance that blanked
out all the getting-into-the-sun strategy. They saw us in plenty
of time and the gunner sprayed us beautifully. I felt colder
than ever. Bullets were splashing all around and some were
pecking through the fabric of my wings. My engine roared
as I continued my dive, but like a fool I kept on firing my
gun—at empty space! I guess I was paralyzed with fright,
and then went past the tail of one of these enemy planes
and soon found myself well below them both.

"I tried to remember what they had taught me at Cazaux.

What was I supposed to do in a case like this? For the life of me I couldn't recall one word of that instruction. I should have pulled up in a steep climb to get under one of them, a position in which at least one gunner could not fire at me. Instead, I floundered around down there, a sitting duck for both. Bullets were zinging all around me, and there like a fool I sat until at last I found myself in front of one of the pilot's guns. Boy, was I proving to be a bright boy! This jerry had a wonderful time with me. He could take his ease and decide which control cable to shoot away next. I just sat there and let him.

"Later, I learned that young Hoskier, that perfect little gentleman, had taken pity on me and had tried to rescue me from these two Germans, but they chased me well into our lines before giving up the game."

As usual, there are several versions to this story. In a more recent report there were five enemy two-seaters, and Parsons seems to have forgotten that it was Hoskier and Genet who went out with him. He was cut off well inside the enemy lines and had about given up hope when, to his amazement, he spotted a gleaming Nieuport, sporting a brand-new Indian-head insignia, taking on all and sundry. Flying like a dervish of the wind, this unknown airman soon scattered the enemy machines and led Ted home, and tenderly helped him up to the bar. It was then that Parsons realized that he had been saved by Raoul Lufbery, the invalid who was supposed to be convalescing at Nice.

Two days before Christmas of 1916, Jim McConnell, still far from a whole man, arrived at Cachy and demanded to be returned to active service. His back still bothered him, but Jim was convinced that the best embrocation would be for him to get back into harness. Since there was a jovial air of good fellowship everywhere—except over the lines—Bill Thaw and Captain Thénault agreed that Jim might pick up where he had left off and get his hand back in.

Once the squadron had settled down at Ravenel it was told

to play it safe and not appear too often on the front. A new ground offensive was in the making, and HQ decided that through the month of February the Lafayette Escadrille should simply maintain a program of practice flying, and get in some ground courses on engines and machine guns. As a result, the month provided more recreation than usual. Bill Thaw went to Paris to pick up a Spad, one on which the squadron pilots might get in some time and learn the peculiarities of this new biplane and its Hispano-Suizo engine. Bill took Whiskey with him, hoping to get some medical attention for the young lion's injured eye, but no veterinarian in Paris would go near the animal, and as a form of surcease Bill managed to pick up a female cub as a companion, the one known as Soda.

With the German retreat and the "planned withdrawal" to the new Hindenburg line, French aviation returned to increased activity. The enemy movement over this wide front required considerable aerial observation, photography, and emergency spotting for the field artillery, which in turn demanded *chasse* escort, resulting in numerous air battles.

On St. Patrick's Day, a dull gray day with a threatening storm moving in, a 10 A.M. patrol was ordered, and Jim McConnell, Ted Parsons, and Edmond Genet were selected to carry it out. Their engines were started after heated oil was poured into the lubricating systems, but even with this assistance Ted Parsons' Le Rhone became obstinate. He was hardly in the air when his oil line clogged, and before he could get back to the field the engine seized and was almost useless. Genet and McConnell went on alone.

They crossed the line at a point northeast of Ham and then flew on toward Saint-Quentin. Over Douchy they were intercepted by two German Albatros two-seaters, and, although short on experience, the two Americans each took on an Albatros. A wild melee followed and once more there were reports of "explosive" bullets, but they obviously were light-cased tracers that broke up on impact with anything. At any rate one of these bounced off Genet's main spar and splinters of it spattered his face and cut a gouge in his cheek. The shock put Edmond out of the play for a few seconds, and he started to head for his own line not certain how badly he was hurt. During this time he lost track of McConnell, and although he circled about over Ham for more than a quarter of an hour, Jim never turned up.

Some time later Genet told what he could remember of the incident. Apparently their patrol was assigned an escort mission and they had spent some time circling over some friendly two-seaters that were carrying out a reconnaissance task. In this version Jim McConnell suddenly hared off and flew toward Saint-Quentin, and as Genet followed he soon noticed that they were well north of Ham and fairly deep inside the enemy lines. Genet saw the two enemy machines first; they were not flying together but were some distance apart. One seemed to be maneuvering to get into a position for a dive on Mac, so Genet, after making sure that Jim was aware of the situation, started to climb to engage the second. It was during this activity that he lost sight of his partner, since he was fully occupied in working out a position for an attack. It was cloudy and misty over Ham, and Genet had to keep his attention on the enemy two-seater. Once, the Albatros cut across on a diagonal course, and Genet could see the dark green outline of the gunner who opened fire.

The first enemy burst spattered through Genet's wings, and one tracer bullet bounced off an aileron bracket and a portion of it clipped the young American in the cheek. Almost at the same time Genet opened fire as he raced at the Albatros. He was certain that he had the enemy two-seater on fire for a few seconds, but evidently one of the crew extinguished it.

The circling fight continued for some minutes with no particular effect, until at last they passed within seventy-five feet of each other, at which point the German turned away for his own back area, and Genet, finding himself alone, decided to return to the line and see if McConnell would rejoin him. He was given a warm reception by the enemy antiaircraft guns, and knowing that his main spar had been pierced, he was not too certain of his chance of getting back. But he put in fifteen minutes of search, and then, wishing to have his wing structure checked, returned to his field.

McConnell had not come back, but some days later a French cavalryman out on patrol at Petit-Detroit, recently abandoned by the retreating Germans, came upon a crashed Nieuport. Jim McConnell's completely stripped body was beside it. A farm woman came out of a nearby cottage and explained that she had seen the air fight and that the French machine had been engaging a German airplane when a second enemy plane dived down on him from behind. Whether this was the one that had previously engaged Genet could not be confirmed, but it was discovered that Jim had received several bullets in his body, any one of which could have killed him.

Once his companions knew his loss was certain, they opened a letter Jim had left in case he was killed. It read as follows:

My burial is of no import. Make it as easy as possible for yourselves. I have no religion and do not care for any service. If the omission would embarrass you, I presume I could stand the performance. Good luck to the rest of you. God damn Germany and *vive la France!*

J. R. McCONNELL

Edmond Genet was awarded the Croix de Guerre and cited in the Order of the Army.

⌐ James McConnell was the last American wearing a French uniform who was killed fighting the enemy before the United States entered World War I. Edmond Genet was to be the first American to fall after the United States declared war on Germany.

The international situation in which the United States was still attempting to remain neutral with President Wilson walking a precarious political tightrope, made many of the volunteers bitter and discouraged. It is understandable that they would be influenced by French and British opinion, and as the war progressed their explanations, arguments, and excuses carried less and less conviction. From their point of view it was apparent that the behavior of German diplomats in Washington, the continued arrogance of U-boat captains, and the repeated evidence that Germany was fomenting trouble in Mexico to keep American forces occupied along the border, left no doubt that the United States could with honor join the Allies.

On November 9, 1916, Edmond Genet, along with dozens of Americans then on leave in Paris, received the news that Charles Evans Hughes, the Republican candidate, had been elected President, defeating President Wilson who had run for a second term on the platform that he had kept America out of war. The news was premature, but the same report had been received throughout most of the United States, and it stood until the last California vote was tabulated, and the decision reversed in Wilson's favor—by the electoral votes of one state.

For a few hours, however, the American volunteers were in a seventh heaven. Edmond Genet wrote to his mother, giving three rousing cheers for a new administration in Washington when March 1917 came along. "I'd like to know whether Teddy Roosevelt will be on Hughes' cabinet as Secretary of War. If he is, then there will be lots of hope. Also, there's going to be a big boom in aeronautics in the U.S. now," he added hopefully.

All these warm reflections were dashed the next day when the revised figures were published, and the Americans in France were again downcast and disconsolate. Hughes had lost, and the United States was in for another four years of the wishy-washy behavior of Woodrow Wilson. "Peace at any price," was the attitude at home, or so these young men believed. It was difficult for them to understand the actions of the American voter in the face of Germany's invasion of Belgium and France, the dread threat of U-boat warfare, and German outrages against all neutral countries. But they realized gradually that it was difficult for Americans across the

Atlantic to visualize the full impact of the war, as did the Americans in France.

It was a bitter pill, that re-election of Wilson, but they swallowed it, went on fighting, and hoped that their own actions on the Western Front would one day put the whole picture in a new focus.

On March 27 Edmond Genet received a number of letters from the United States, one of them from his mother in which she explained as tenderly as she could that the young lady he had hoped to marry when he returned from the war had become engaged to someone else. The pink-cheeked young man was desolate for some time as he had known the girl for about five years and had written loyally to her whenever he had a few minutes from his duty.

Although Edmond had set his heart on marrying this young lady, once the world returned to its normal course, she had given him few cheerful thoughts and very little encouragement, seldom answering his correspondence since he had been fighting in France. When he knew that she had deserted him completely he reacted like a lover who has been wounded grievously. He fell into deep moods and periods of depression, and seemed to have lost much of his original bounce. He expressed the view that there was little chance of any of them surviving the war. McConnell's death, in particular, affected him, and at times he berated himself for not having acted more decisively in the patrol that had seen Jim's finish.

Then he became unduly wild and reckless over the line, and on several occasions had to be warned that his impetuosity would be his undoing, and that he had better revise his tactics and act more conservatively. There was also a period when Edmond was obviously homesick, but he knew that in his case leave to the United States was out of the question, but he became petulant and complained that certain members of the American Field Service who had had only a few months in France were being sent home to be "petted and idolized," whereas others who had put in many months with the Foreign

Legion were being ignored. Everyone knew that even if he were selected, Edmond could not accept such a *permission*, for once he was back in the United States he would have to face the penalty for his desertion from the U. S. Navy.

We know now that young Genet was in poor health, but he refused to go into a hospital for a check-up, nor would he take time for a short rest in Paris. One wonders what sort of discipline prevailed in the squadron when junior members could decide whether they would undergo a physical examination, or accept the medical officer's recommendation for furlough or rest.

Genet did attend a memorial service in Paris for McConnell, and later on when the news came through that President Wilson had reversed his field and asked Congress for a declaration of war, Edmond displayed no particular enthusiasm. So many disappointments and frustrations were certain to have some effect on his moods and manners.

He was killed on April 16, 1917—not by an enemy airman, but by a direct hit of an antiaircraft shell, the million-to-one chance everyone took almost daily. It had to be young Edmond Genet who had made so many sacrifices already, and who was obviously at the end of his physical tether.

On this doleful day Genet and Lufbery were sent out on a patrol between Saint-Quentin and La Fère. By this time the Lafayette Escadrille had been moved up to Ham to keep pace with the German retreat. Luf led the patrol, of course, and he reported later that once they were in the vicinity of Mouy, German antiaircraft batteries began to shell them. They had been in the air for about thirty minutes when Lufbery noted three shells that burst uncomfortably close to Genet's airplane, and although it was accurate shooting, Luf, who had been through this a hundred times, took little notice of the bracket. However, when he looked at his companion again he saw that Edmond had turned and apparently was heading for the French lines. He followed to make sure the youngster was flying in the right direction for Ham, and once convinced that he was safe, although his Nieuport may have suffered some damage from the ground gunfire, he turned back to their original patrol area.

By this time Lufbery remembered that Genet had not been feeling well, but that when Edmond had seen his name up for the patrol, he had refused to be excused. He had been out earlier in the morning, but on his return had gone to bed. Concerned, Lufbery decided to go back to make certain that Genet had returned home safely, but owing to a sudden over-cast of low cloud he could not find him.

Later Lufbery learned that Edmond might have fainted in the air, or died from some wound from a shell while trying to get back to Ham. A group of soldiers explained that they had seen this particular Nieuport go into a corkscrew spin at about five thousand feet, and as it continued on down a wing ripped away and the aircraft crashed just a few hundred yards from where Jim McConnell had piled up. The Nieuport was a complete write-off, for it had gone in with the engine full on, indicating that Genet either had fainted or died some time before the crash.

He was buried at Ham during a sudden, blinding snow-storm, and at the funeral service it was announced that he had been awarded the Croix de Guerre, and it was explained, furthermore, that the plane Edmond had attacked on the day McConnell was killed, had been so badly shot up it had had to land in French territory. The captured crew had made statements that indicated that Genet had done well, and that McConnell's death in no way reflected on him. It was un-fortunate that the troubled young man could not have known of this before.

When Edmond's loss was announced officially, many trib-utes came to the Genet home in Ossining, and one—some-what belatedly—from the White House, signed by Woodrow Wilson, expressed the President's sympathy, and admiration for the fact that Mrs. Genet had contributed two other sons to the Great Cause. The French ambassador in Washington offered the condolences of his country, and stated that the memory of Edmond Genet would long be cherished by all in France and America. Other tributes came from many important sources, all speaking glowingly of the young man not yet twenty-one who had looked like a schoolboy.

Matters continued apace at Ham while the international situation recoiled to another upheaval. America declared war on Germany on April 6, 1917, the Germans continued their headlong retreat across the British front, Cuba and Panama joined the United States in her pact with the Allies, and Austria-Hungary declared war on America.

By now someone decided that the original Indian head insignia of the Lafayette was not distinct enough, so Harold B. Willis and Edward F. Hinkle collaborated to brighten it; in a few days the old Seminole was banished and a Sioux head, made suitably ferocious with streaks of red, white, and blue, was substituted. This official design was taken over when the Escadrille became the U.S. 103rd Pursuit Squadron.

Lieutenant de Laage de Meux downed two enemy planes on April 8 just north of Saint-Quentin and was awarded the Legion of Honor. Lufbery continued to peck away until by now he had seven or eight to his credit, but his rheumatic condition still troubled him. William Dugan, Kenneth Marr, and Thomas Hewitt joined the Escadrille at Ham.

Dugan, a Rochester, New York, boy was working as the assistant manager of a banana plantation in Central America when the news of the war came through. He gave up this United Fruit Company sinecure, made his way to France and enlisted in the Foreign Legion early in 1915 where he served long and well, and lived through the German offensive at Verdun in 1916. Like Victor Chapman, Dugan loved action, was always loud in his praise of the exploits of others, but rarely mentioned his own. Later on he transferred to the French 107th Infantry Regiment, an outfit that was especially active and tough. Around this time Bill was advised of the Escadrille Américaine, and decided that a change was in order, but his French commanding officer declared that he had never heard of such an organization, and in that way hung on to Bill.

When a light wound put him in the hospital at Saint-Etienne for a time, Bill made contact with Dr. Gros who worked in his behalf and soon had him transferred to the French Aviation. His training began on June 9, 1916, and he was brevetted by late September and assigned to the Lafayette Escadrille on March 30, 1917. He served with them until February 18, 1918, although his papers indicate that he was commissioned in the U. S. Air Service on January 11, 1918. He was assigned to the 103rd Pursuit Squadron from February 18 until June 1, after which he was appointed officer in charge of repair and testing at the American Acceptance Park, Orly, until the Armistice brought an end to hostilities. His brother Charles joined the First Canadian Contingent and served in France as an infantry sergeant.

In June 1918 while he was on a short leave in America, Bill introduced an innovation in the service. He married his sweetheart, brought her back with him, and had her living nearby the field while he went on with his test flying. American overseas services have never been quite the same since.

Kenneth Marr, affectionately known as Si or Siwash, hailed from San Francisco but had spent considerable time in Alaska where he had picked up his nickname. He worked for some time in a lumber camp and eventually specialized in the training of Eskimo dogs. At the outbreak of the war he went to France, herding a shipment of these tough animals that were to be trained for use in the Vosges by the Alpine Chasseurs. Si soon picked up a weird patois of French that would fascinate or astonish the natives, and became a famous character in that area of the war front.

Once the dog deal was over, Ken decided to stay on and capitalize on his linguistic ability. He joined the American Field Service and bewildered all and sundry with his Gallic double-talk. After a long enlistment with the ambulance service he made his way into the French Aviation by July 20, 1916, and was brevetted on January 7, 1917. Discounting his freakish vocabulary, the Lafayette Escadrille took him in on March 29, 1917, where he remained until February 18, 1918, creating something of a record in establishing Franco-American cordiality, based chiefly on his ability to cause linguistic confusion and/or amusement.

In March 1918, Marr, along with Captains Peterson and James Norman Hall, was transferred to the U.S. 94th Aero Squadron, the first American unit to be placed on combat status after the Lafayette. A few weeks later Ken was promoted to major and commanded such stars as Eddie Rickenbacker, Douglas Campbell, Jimmy Meissner, Reid Chambers, Alan Winslow, and others. Late that summer Marr was posted to the United States to hold down an executive position. After the war he returned to the lumbering business, and at this writing is retired and living in Phoenix, Arizona.

Early in September of 1917 Ken suffered one of the most hair-raising experiences on any front. He was on a routine patrol with Douglas MacMonagle and Harry S. Jones when the squadron was covering the Verdun-Argonne sector. These three were attacked by four Albatros scouts, two of which selected Marr as their particular target, but Ken gave one a bad time and drove him out of the skirmish. The other, however, got on his tail and shot all elevator controls away. This is a situation no airman cares to contemplate. With no elevator control you have nothing to prevent you from nosing straight into the ground. Today, an airman would ask no questions, but would immediately step out and take to the silk. Unhappily, there were no such life preservers for Allied airmen in those days, so Marr had to figure out matters for himself, hoping to come up with a solution before Gabriel blew the horn on him.

Through the process of experimentation and a gambler's choice, he used his ailerons to get the plane into a steep bank. In this position, considering the force of gravity, this reversed what controls he had and his rudder became his elevator. This was satisfactory up to a point, but it was, to say the least, an unorthodox manner of flying. However, making the most of what he had, Ken stayed in this position until he was in a friendly area, by which time he discovered that by jazzing his throttle he could fan the dangling elevators up to a neutral position. With that temporary arrangement he worked his way well into his own lines, maintaining level flight, and when he decided it was safe to lose altitude, performed tricks with his propeller stream, or tilted over on one side to employ the rudder routine until he lost more height. This went on in gentle stages with Ken sweating it out all the way down. He managed to get somewhere near his field, but decided not to risk this unorthodox manner of flying any farther, and pancaked into some small trees in the area known as the Forest de Hesse. He was unhurt, but admitted he had learned a lot about the principles of flying in those few minutes.

About this time Raoul Lufbery had an extraordinary experience, one which compelled him to pen another of his almost-classic reports for *Guerre Aerienne,* the original copy of which has been made available to me by Paul Rockwell. It will be interesting to note Lufbery's continued love for the countryside, his use of the word "motor" for engine and "accelerator" for throttle. This was probably one of his last flights aboard a Nieuport, for the Escadrille was soon to be equipped with the Spad.

My altimeter marked 2000. Beneath me was a marvelous panorama, the Vosges! For a moment the beauty of the landscape caused me to forget the object of my journey, the pursuit of the Boche. In order better to enjoy the view I decided to make a slight detour to the left and to fly again over the Ballon d'Alsace. To the north of the mountain, down in a narrow valley, lay a tiny silver mirror, the Lake of X. . . . I could not resist the temptation to remain there for a few minutes to enjoy its beauty. Gently I spiraled down in my Nieuport trying in vain to glimpse its reflection in the tranquil water beneath.

I might have continued thus for several minutes, had not my motor suddenly attracted my attention by throwing out a discordant note. It was sufficient to arouse my fears. I listened attentively. It seemed to grow more and more irregular. Visions of a treacherous breakdown, a precipitate landing on the borders of one of these precipices whose wild aspect I had admired but a minute before, floated before me. Instinctively I bore down on my accelerator. I was in haste to get away from these parts where I could expect no immediate assistance. But as I drew near to the plain my motor appeared to recover; its throbbing was now normal. Probably it had intended to play me a nasty trick. Or was it I, the pilot, who had been the victim of an unpleasant illusion, or of a primitive feeling of fear? Somewhat ashamed, I called myself to order, reminding myself that any moment I might have to fight a Boche.

As a tired horse that hangs its head after a fatiguing course, so my machine, then at a height of 4000 meters, of itself turned horizontal-wise, as if about to take a header. This meant that it had reached its maximum height.

Almost at my feet lay the great city of Mulhouse, while in a glide a few kilometers to the right was the German aviation field of X. . . .

A glance at my map showed that I had crossed the enemy lines without my having noticed it. It did not matter. Often this happens, especially when the network of trenches is as narrow as in these sectors where there is never an important engagement.

The wind was blowing strongly from the west to the east, a disadvantage to the aviator when flying in this region. I considered it prudent not to venture farther into the enemy's lines but to turn my face northward. As I was about to do so, the artillerists of the Vaterland sent me a few bullets just to show me they were not asleep. But their aim was bad and I decided it was not worth while to change either my direction or my altitude, which I do as a rule when I seek to avoid a more-accurate fire.

My attention was drawn to a mountain top that differed from other summits in that it was a brick-red color. It was the Hartmannsweilerkopf, rendered famous by the heroic defense of the Alpine troops of France. Here, as at Verdun, the enemy's way is barred.

A semi-turn to the right, another to the left, and I am able to get a periscopic view of my surroundings. I discovered nothing abnormal, and reassured, I continued on my way. As I approached

the Hartmannsweilerkopf I tried to recall where I had already seen
the picture beneath me. I remembered. It was in the photographs
of the moon. Yes, the moon in its most uneven parts. Burrowed
by shells, the summit of the Hartmannsweilerkopf stands out in a
striking manner from the verdant tops of the surrounding mountains.

Again I glanced in all directions, and this time not in vain.
Above me and somewhat to the rear was a small monoplace
biplane of the Fokker or Halberstadt type. A glance showed me
that it was alone. I was surprised at this, as it was the first time
I had seen a machine of this type place itself at a disadvantage for
a fight. A ruse, perhaps. One never knows. Or maybe my adversary was a novice with more courage than caution, whose ambition
it was to become an "ace" for the Vaterland.

The wind continued to blow westward, carrying me farther and
and farther into the enemy's lines. It would not do to allow the
Boche to take advantage of my position. I decided to start the
attack without further delay.

I faced about and bruskly made a double turn, thus placing
myself behind my foe. Profiting by this position I opened my gun
on him, but with remarkable skill, he succeeded in getting out of
my range. He had forseen my maneuver and parried the blow.
I was now convinced that I was face to face with a virtuoso. His
first move was proof of this.

As I tangoed from left to right, I saw him once more above
me, but about forty meters nearer. Suddenly, he reared his machine
as if to loop-the-loop, and in this perilous position let fly a volley
of bullets at me, which I evaded by a semi-turn to the right. A
second time I attacked, but again without success. The wind had
carried us both north of Mulhouse, and I was beginning to wonder
if I was not playing into my adversary's hands by delaying longer
with him.

By chance I turned my eyes in the direction of Belfort, some
twenty kilometers within our lines. There, in the air, I perceived
some small white flakes, an indication of the presence of the Boche.

Here was my opportunity. I had now an excuse for honorably
abandoning the match, and I admit I was not sorry. Only, before
leaving my adversary I wished to show him that I respected his
valour. I waved him a sign of adieu. He understood, and with
equal courtesy returned my salute.

I then turned my entire attention to that which I considered my new prey. It was a large, white biplace. I drew nearer to it. What luck! For the first time in my flying career I was to have an opportunity of meeting my adversary within our own lines. This increased my confidence to such an extent that I forgot all prudence or even tactical science. I had another motive for being more reckless than usual. I was determined that he would not escape me. I would make it a point of honor to fire at him until a final victory. If only I could lodge a bullet in his motor or gasoline tank and thus force him to land on French territory! Then I would have the satisfaction of talking to my captive, getting his impressions of the aerial duel between us. Then too, there would be the trophies which would be mine by right, viz, my adversary's compass, altimeter, etc.

There is an old proverb which says that one should not count one's chickens before they are hatched. That day, as will be seen, I had occasion to verify the truth of it.

My time for dreams were over. It was now the moment to act. Quickly I placed myself behind my adversary who was some fifty meters distant from me. I then opened fire and continued to fire until my machine, which is superior in speed, came so near to the biplace that I thought it impossible to avoid a collision.

Bruskly I changed my direction, rose in the air and leaped over the foe, gliding down on my right wing to my former height. Increasing my speed I recovered my balance and sought to try my luck a second time. But this was impossible. My motor, the soul of my aeroplane, was mortally wounded and about to breathe its last.

I turned to find the stabilizer also seriously damaged. My enemy appeared not to want to take advantage of the situation. He continued his flight in the direction of the lines. Perhaps he too was in a critical condition. I hoped so. In any case his flight left me master of the field. That was some consolation, but it was of short duration for my machine began rapidly to descend. Finally I reached the aviation field. Pilots, observers and mechanics came up to question me. They had witnessed the combat and were eager for details. I was anxious to examine the wounds of my Baby Nieuport. I found it badly damaged. Three bullets in its motor, its gasoline tank smashed, part of its fuselage out of commission, several holes in its hood, and the left side of the stabilizer cut and torn by bullets.

"Poor Baby! In accord with my mechanics, I decided it was irreparable. It had flown its last flight and its days of combat were over."

This is typical of so many wartime reports written by airmen immediately after any particular combat. Luf gave many interesting details but forgot to explain that the German two-seater pilot, or gunner, had fired at him as he approached, or passed over. Nevertheless, the story gives many other facts and features of interest to non-flying men, who would not notice the omissions, or consider them important.

Chapter X

AMERICA GOES TO WAR

The long-awaited news of America's entry into the war filtered much of the glamour from the activities of the Lafayette Escadrille. French and British heroism no longer was news, but Allied defeats were proclaimed widely for political expediency, since these setbacks furnished an explanation for the necessity of America's participation. This became the practice for the rest of the war, and the pattern was repeated, almost to the letter, in 1941.

For months the American volunteers had been the one bright gleam in their country's lukewarm interest in the European conflict, but from that late afternoon of April 6, 1917, it was evident that the sharply focussed spotlight was to be switched from their activities to those Americans who, for obvious reasons, had decided to wait until Congress voted them into the war.

At first, public interest back home was centered on those who had enlisted willingly, but national policy demanded that the ponderous machinery of conscription, cautiously termed "selective draft," be glamourized for public acceptance. Newspapers and rotogravure sections torrented off the presses plastered with the activities of the new recruits, the standard scenes at the training camps, the tearful farewells at railroad stations, and the ubiquitous tableau of the indignity of KP. The war had finally struck home, and its opening scenes were played to the limit. All the stock shots of 1914 were repeated; the only difference was the geography, the uniforms and the professional clarity of the photographs. The same old jokes, rewritten for American consumption, were greeted with shrill enthusiasm. For instance; "Halt! Who goes there?" "Who the hell wants to know?" "Pass, American!" It was never explained that this chestnut had started out in 1914 with the snapper, "Pass, Fourth Blobshire Rifles!" As soon as the First Canadian Division arrived in Flanders it was revamped to close with, "Pass, Canadian!" After the Australians came out of Gallipoli to fight at Pozières, you know who first said, "Who the hell wants to know?" "Pass Aussie!"

The old war songs of 1914–15 were dusted off and presented as brand-new numbers. *Mad'moiselle from Armentières,* who had been slandered by British Tommies for months after the retreat from Mons, suddenly appeared in American training camps with revamped lyrics that ran into dozens of improbable verses. By that time the British had taken up *Mad'moiselle from Bully-Grenay* . . . the one who was assaulted nightly "in the hay," and thus was the progress of the war marked.

Lieutenant Gitz Rice, who composed the music of the lugubrious *Dear Old Pal of Mine,* probably made a fortune from an old London music hall ditty, the chorus of which ended with, *And you told me that you'd never kissed a girl before. Hold your hand out, you naughty boy!* Gitz Rice revamped that into, *If you want to join your father in the Fatherland, keep your head down, Fritzie-boy!*

And so it went. Friends and relatives in the United States

who had not written to us in what seemed years, patriotically
took up the pen. We were deluged with letters, boxes of
chocolates, newspapers, and enough sweaters, socks, and
knitted scarves to have outfitted a mountain division. From
all accounts, the war enthusiasm back home soon reached an
unprecedented pitch, and the climactic decibel was no doubt
attained when the immortal George M. Cohan proclaimed:
And we won't come back 'till it's over, over there!

On the Lafayette field at Ham, America's entry into the
war triggered several diverse viewpoints. One small group
predicted that it would be only a matter of weeks before the
skies would be filled with American airplanes, and oversized
United States Army divisions would occupy wide sectors of
the Allied front. Unfortunately, it was not until the following
October 23 that a lone American artillery battery moved up
into a quiet sector on the Lorraine front and fired the first
shell from a United States' howitzer—six months after the
declaration of war!

Another group, less optimistic, especially after the defeat
of Charles Evans Hughes, took the attitude that America
might provide more food, ammunition, some primary weapons,
and conceivably take a hand in the antisubmarine campaign,
but it expected no great effort from an active military stand-
point. At least one gathers all this from their letters written at
the time.

A short time previously, a few of the volunteers had been
back home on short leaves and these airmen had encountered
the general attitude of many Americans toward the European
war. They returned to the front with the grim realization that
it would take some great emotional upheaval to sting certain
sections of the country into any patriotic fervor.

There were a small number who decided by now that service with the French, rewarding as it was from their original
idealistic point of view, left something to be desired. In a
few cases it was the tang of disillusion, or the realization that
military flying—after the first heady thrills had simmered

down—could be something of a suicide club. Several pilots considered the possibility of their being transferred immediately to the U. S. Aviation Service. Colonel William Mitchell, who had arrived in France just as America declared war, had assured them that he soon would have half a hundred fighting squadrons at the front. There was the prospect of higher financial reward and perhaps a boost in rank. However, thanks to the continued efforts of the Executive Committee of the Escadrille, the volunteers were receiving a reasonable monthly pay.

Only a few men nurtured the hope that America would immediately produce a glittering aviation service, complete with new and more efficient aircraft—and perhaps a higher standard of living. Those who had served in the trenches with the Foreign Legion could appreciate, of course, how well the Lafayette Escadrille lived, but there were some who believed, or hoped, that they would be called on to help form and build up a United States Air Service—a hope that was quite understandable.

On the other side of the ledger were a number of idealists who could not conceive of deserting the Lafayette Escadrille or any of the French squadrons. They argued that France had listened to their appeals, accepted them, provided their training, and, as far as possible, had turned over their latest flying equipment to them. It was unthinkable to "desert." The same viewpoint was standard with Americans who had volunteered and were serving the Royal Flying Corps. These airmen seemed to know that it would be months before the United States could furnish adequate training, reliable airplanes, or an efficient ground organization. All that their homeland might offer when the time came was possibly a boost in rank and a higher rate of base and flying pay. Whether a man would consider foregoing the satisfaction of flying Spads, Camels, Bristol Fighters, S.E.5s, or Nieuports for some yet-to-be-produced wonder plane became one of the general topics of the day.

There were many predictions and rumors, but, generally

speaking, it was believed that any American with military aviation experience of any kind would be approached and invited to take over important executive jobs until some basic organization could be established. Colonel Billy Mitchell, who became the United States Air Service's stormy petrel, was already on hand hoping to learn how an air war was fought. He, too, had high ideals, but he saw immediately that the service he represented had no idea how far military aviation had advanced. He was amazed at the aircraft the Allied pilots were flying, and astounded by their speed, the progress of aerial gunnery, and the high degree of training afforded by the Allied aviation schools. Before leaving America he had taken a short flying course, but his mount was prehistoric when compared with the fighters and two-seaters flown by the French and British. He had to start all over again in order to handle a school-type single-seater, but, to his credit, he willingly undertook the course, and for months his lone Nieuport was the only aircraft on the roster of the U. S. Aviation Service in France.

Billy Mitchell, the indomitable organizer, soon saw that the Lafayette and several French squadrons could furnish a wealth of American experience and technical ability. He wrote anxious requests for their transfer to his jurisdiction. Up to now he had been an Aviation Service colonel without an aviation service to command. His appeal shocked other executives a grade or two higher, for they saw no reason to entice these men out of their "foreign" uniforms to help build up an American air force. Next thing they knew, Mitchell would be asking them to adopt French and British fighting machines. Now that America was in their war, hers would be an All-American effort. They had plenty of time.

Back in Washington a handful of ex-cavalrymen, engineers, and administrative officials were running an air arm that, at the time, was a minor affliction of the Signal Corps. These men still lived in an era of telegraph wire, semaphore flags, and heliograph instruments. They wanted no part of the Wright brothers' invention, or men who had actually flown.

They did not wish to risk any association with aviators who might have opinions contrary to theirs. There were several among these high-ranking officials who were convinced that powered aircraft were unnecessary to carry out aerial observation. They pointed out that airplanes were too noisy, and argued that kite balloons were to be preferred since they could be flown in almost any weather, day or night. Three years of modern warfare in Europe, a war that had brought the airplane to a peak of high efficiency, had seen the tank developed to break the trench-warfare stalemate, the use of poison gas, and flame throwers, and the most practical use of artillery and machine-gun fire, had not made an impression on this collection of Top brass that was in full command of American military operations.

A few weeks of this, and the members of the Lafayette Escadrille realized that they were destined to fly and fight in the azure blue of France for a long, long time.

Meanwhile, along the Hindenburg line, the ground activity continued with increasing ferocity. The enemy had moved back to well-prepared positions, and both sides settled down to a new slugging match. It was impossible to dislodge them from these new redoubts, pillboxes, dugouts, or trench systems. Campaign after campaign was touched off, and a few paltry yards gained, but these thrusts only created new and dangerous salients. The British tanks were not yet ready for an all-out attack, and the French had devoted their efforts to a smaller whippet-type vehicle that at best was capable of short-range reconnaissance; it was not designed to take and hold important areas. The bayonet and machine gun had been tried on many sectors, but the problem was too great for mere men and rifles. Obviously, the air war had to be stepped up to more deliberate tactical planning, and there were some men, notably General Sir Hugh "Boom" Trenchard among them, who were already advocating strategic warfare. That is, they would as soon as suitable long-range aircraft could be designed. Fortunately, the British had the twin-engined Handley Page that was capable of eight-hour flights, carrying eight 250-pound bombs. In the works, too, was the large four-engined night bomber, the Handley Page V/1500 that had a range of more than one thousand miles, carrying thirty 250-pound bombs.

All this nurtured considerable hope, but in the meantime routine reconnaissance, artillery spotting, and offensive patrols had to be carried out to keep the enemy pinned down. Both sides took to the air in new fury, and for a few weeks the Germans made the most of their new Albatros, and later their Fokker triplane fighter, largely because—at least as far as the British were concerned—first-line aircraft like the Sopwith Camel, the S.E.5, and the famed two-seater Bristol Fighter, had been held back for some mysterious air thrust that was planned for the late summer of 1917. When these new air weapons were released, the infamous Bloody April came to an end. From then on the German Air Service never regained the upper hand, but in maintaining the initiative, Allied flying men had to put on some heartbreaking performances. Small as it was, the Lafayette Escadrille assumed more than its share of this air offensive.

Bill Thaw, in particular, provided an outstanding example, being in the air hour after hour. He never allowed new or inexperienced pilots to take too many chances; he accompanied them, or led them on patrol after patrol. On one occasion while covering a formation that was supposed to be doing a corps observation show, Bill spotted some very interesting and important activity going on just ahead of a French advance. Unable to contact the ground forces by radio or signal flare, he risked an almost impossible landing well forward, hurried across some fields and warned the French commander of the situation. He began to make a habit of this sort of caper until the French troops looked forward to seeing Bill's Nieuport screeching along just over their steel helmets. He provided more than information; his presence brought a new warmth of morale.

At another time Bill landed in the main street of a small

village that had just been evacuated by the enemy, and the villagers, particularly the schoolchildren, were able to give him valuable information as to the strength and equipment of the retreating forces. A short time later the Lafayette adopted this village—especially the youngsters—and saw to it that they seldom went hungry while they were in that area. This benevolence assumed several expressions, depending on the age and sex of the youngsters concerned, but it was no time for hair-splitting or Grundyism.

As the military activity continued and the front rolled back, all Allied airfields had to move up to keep pace and stay within flying distance of the enemy back areas. This meant they landed on fields that only recently had been abandoned by the Germans, and in many cases they took over complete fields that a few hours before had been used by enemy *staffels*. Ham turned out to be such a place, and amid the damage and desolation the best that could be said for that particular field was that it was a bonanza of German souvenirs. I remember flying to Ham with a fellow airman of the R.F.C., simply to obtain some German bombs and potato-masher grenades with which to decorate our officers' mess at Chipilly, a few miles to the north. This was the first time I encountered any of these volunteer airmen, although several members of the Lafayette Escadrille visited us regularly from that time on.

During the various moves from field to field the Lafayette had been saddled with an assortment of aircraft, mostly Nieuport 17s and 27s, castoffs from other *chasse* squadrons that were being equipped with new Spad-7s. It was a period of transition in so many ways. Included in this boneyard collection was a vintage Morane Parasol, still fitted out as a two-seater, and used for area reconnaissance, gunnery training, an aerial taxi, and in times of unrelieved drought, delegated to move in wine, beer, spiritous liquors, and the latest selection of Kirchner pin-up prints from Paris. Everyone liked to fly this old crock, and at times some joker would take it over the lines for general observation, or simply as a gag.

But this bus turned out to be a tragedy tumbril when, on

April 23, 1917, Ronald Hoskier took Jean Dressy, Lieutenant de Laage's orderly, over the line on a general offensive mission. Dressy had long yearned to become a flier, and whenever he could get an hour off he worked in a short course of aerial gunnery. Once he had been checked out, he would volunteer to fly with anyone simply to get in combat time.

Orders had come through to get rid of this heterogeneous collection of aircraft, with a promise that new 140-hp Spads would replace them. Hoskier decided to have one last flight aboard the Parasol before it was banished to a training school, and Dressy asked to go along. All went well for a while but just as they were beginning to turn back, the Morane was attacked by three Albatros fighters. Hoskier and Dressy held their own for more than a quarter of an hour, but the odds were too much. Dressy fired every round in his drums and succeeded in sending one of the enemy airmen down in a tight spin, but the end was inevitable. In all probability Hoskier was so badly wounded he could not remain conscious long enough to get down safely, and Dressy was not capable of taking over the dual control, if the old hulk had any. The Morane was seen to start down in a tight spin from which it never recovered. It crashed in the French communication-trench area and both occupants were killed instantly.

As usual, there are several variations of the Hoskier-Dressy tragedy. In an interview, conducted late in 1960, Harold Buckley Willis stated that Hoskier and Dressy were not alone, being part of a fighter formation. Hoskier had often said that the two-seater could create more damage in a dogfight than a fixed-gun plane, and with this idea he was allowed to take a tail-end-Charlie position in a formation that was led by Willis. They headed for Saint-Quentin and searched through some cloud cover and flushed out several German fighters with the result that every plane in the flight was engaged, darting in and out of the vapor banks with little practical result. When Willis went down to reorganize the formation, Hoskier failed to join them, and it was learned later that the Morane had fallen close to the Allied line in front of Saint-

Quentin from where both bodies were recovered when Ted Parsons, Dudley Hill, and Robert Rockwell went up the line that night in an ambulance to bring them back to Ham.

Ronald Hoskier's parents in Paris were advised and they gained permission to go into the battle zone for the military funeral. Lieutenant de Laage and Ted Parsons went to the nearest railroad station to meet them. It will be recalled that Dressy's family had been in service to Lieutenant de Laage's for generations and the lieutenant was as almost broken up over the deaths as were Ronald Hoskier's parents.

For anyone fascinated by wartime superstitions, it might be added that a short time previous to this tragedy Edmond Genet had adopted a black mongrel pup, one of a litter whelped by a loose-moraled animal owned by de Laage. Since this pup was smoky black and possessed no discernible intelligence, it was named Archie, the contemptuous term for the enemy's antiaircraft barrage. Strange that an Archie shell finished Genet.

After Edmond's funeral no one seemed to want the pup, but Hoskier took him over in compassion. Ronald "went west" soon after, and the poor pup was cold-shouldered and booted out of sight. Eventually Lieutenant de Laage, who said he had no time for war jinxes, gathered up the friendless mongrel and gave him a place under his bed. A few days later de Laage was killed in the accident mentioned previously, and once more Archie wandered about the field. By now he was a complete pariah until Sampson, the squadron cook who wasn't drawing flying pay, took Archie in and fattened him up. Later that week Sampson was caught in an illegal deal, swapping Lafayette food for village *bistro* wine, and he wound up with fourteen days, inside, looking out.

Lieutenant Maison-Rouge was transferred from another squadron to replace de Laage, and since everyone was in a black mood over the losses of that month, no one warned him about Archie. Maison-Rouge was glad to associate with anyone, and Archie seemed the most responsive, with the result that the new addition to the squadron found himself in a series of near accidents that broke his nerve and put him in the hospital. Apparently this was too much for Archie, for after Maison-Rouge left, the mutt considerately developed some unfathomable disease and died. The Lafayette staged the most joyous funeral in dogdom.

The Spad fighter, that bulldog-inspired French biplane, became the standard mount for all air-war romancers, and probably financed the pulp-aviation magazines of the 1920s. The scriveners who wrote these fictional adventures relied on a standard plot, and did all their flying with just two models in the hangar—the Spad and the Fokker. When I broke into print with a yarn that involved something called a Sopwith Camel and an Albatros, and later wrote a series about some hellions aboard a night-flying Handley Page, many pulp writers turned their attention to science-fiction literature. At the time the editor of a thriller called *Flying Aces* called me into his office and asked me if there were such aircraft, or had I made them up. When I assured him that we had flown warplanes other than the Spad and Fokker in the Big War, he hired me as his technical editor. If I never made any other contribution to aviation literature, I at least put the brakes on the hackneyed Spad-versus-Fokker plot.

But the reverence for the Spad lives on, and today World War I buffs are convinced that military aircraft design began and ended with that airplane. But when the first Spad-7 models were delivered to the Lafayette Escadrille pilots, the over-all impression was just the opposite. After zipping about the sky in their precision-controlled Nieuports that they had learned to love and fly with no effort, the heavier, cumbersome Hisso-powered Spad seemed to move like an asthmatic truck. Years later it became the aviation photographer's dreamboat, but to most of us it looked like a boxy crate with wings that had been manufactured by the mile and sawed off by the yard. It had no dihedral and no forward stagger to the wings which resulted in almost negative inherent stability. Its flat wings, intended for speed, demanded a high

landing approach, a quality seldom recommended for wartime airfields. It could not compare with the Nieuport for
maneuverability, but it was rugged, tough, and could take a
beating. Perhaps its name is responsible for its postwar favor,
since Spad has a soft explosive sound and an eye appeal in
print. Its name was compounded of the initials of the manufacturing plant, Société pour Aviation et ses Derives.

In fighting maneuvers the Spad was nowhere near as nimble
as the Nieuport or the Sopwith Camel and it was foolish to
duel for any length of time with Fokker or Albatros single-
seaters. The routine was to attack from advantageous levels
and if the pass did not come off, it was wise to remember the
rugged construction of the Spad and keep on diving. Pilots
who had graduated from the Nieuport also noted the limited
downward visibility, since the lower wing of the Spad proved
to be something of a handicap in contrast to the sesquiplane
feature of the Nieuport. However, the Spad's improved speed,
climb, and ceiling perhaps made up for these other considerations.

The Spad S-7 was the first of the series of Spad single-
seaters to go into service and they were initially employed
in the midsummer of 1916. This model with the 140–150-hp
Hispano-Suiza engine was the first of a long series of experimental designs to fill the war-front requirements. By that
autumn the S-7 was being accepted by the leading French
fighter groups.

Interestingly enough, this new scout-fighter attracted the
attention of the British Royal Naval Air Service and orders
were placed for one hundred or more. Before they were delivered, the R.N.A.S. learned that the Sopwith Triplane, for
some unaccountable reason was proving to be "unsuitable" for
Royal Flying Corps operations and an agreement was reached
whereby the R.F.C. took over the R.N.A.S. order of Spads and
gave the Naval fliers their triplanes. It was this rejected batch
of three-wingers that were to make air-fighting history for
Major Raymond Collishaw and his Black Triplane squadron,
which ran up such an amazing record against Baron von

Richthofen's Flying Circus. The Royal Flying Corps, on the other hand, provided their Nos. 19 and 24 Squadrons with French Spads, but the model never enjoyed great popularity with the British and wherever possible, the Spad was replaced by Sopwith Dolphins. British designers experimented to some extent with the machine and four hundred were actually built in England; some with 175- and 205-hp Hisso engines and eventually the wing area was slightly increased on the 205-hp model which is said to have been flown at 132 mph.

In the late summer of 1917 an improved French model was produced and listed as the Spad C. XIII and commonly known as the Spad-13. This model came into being almost by accident, for it was to be developed from a cannon-armed Spad known as the Spad-12. It will be remembered that a 37-mm. air cannon had been under development for some time and a special Hisso engine with a hollow airscrew hub was produced, which allowed the fitting of this weapon. Georges Guynemer and René Fonck were the first to be provided with these machines and scored a few individual victories with this type of armament. Unfortunately, the mounting required considerable modification of the cockpit, since the weapon had to be placed between the pilot's feet. Reloading was difficult and slow and the recoil of the weapon offset whatever advantage the higher caliber ammunition provided. In addition, fumes from the breech, swirling around in the very compact cockpit proved dangerous and often nauseated the pilot.

This Spad-12 then was abandoned but because of its improved flying characteristics was eventually revised to take twin Vickers guns. The wing area was increased slightly and first a 200-hp Hisso was fitted and later a 235-hp engine. The wings and tail assembly had rounded tips, a great improvement over the angular features of the Spad-7, and as such the new scout became a worthy member of the Allied fighter program. A still-later version, known as the Spad-17 was specially designed for high-speed reconnaissance work and was fitted with a wide-angle aerial camera.

A two-seater version of the Spad, officially known as the Spad XI A2 went through a long course of development, starting late in 1915 and reached production line status by September 1916. M. Becherau, designer of the Spad line, almost ruined his reputation with this monstrosity, for it turned out to be one of the most unpopular aircraft of the war. Like the single-seater versions, the XI A2 was most photogenic and looked particularly racy in the company catalogues, but it was a menace to fly. Basically, the machine was well designed, but French authorities made so many unreasoning demands for extraneous equipment, hoping to use the plane for half-a-dozen different missions, that the 235-hp Hispano-Suiza engine had trouble hauling it off the ground. It was a lumbering hulk in the air and in tight turns showed a distinct tendency to fall off into a spin. Its longitudinal stability was erased by the weight of bomb racks, cameras, guns and other military incidentals. The landing speed was ridiculously high and a very shallow climb was necessary if a stall was to be avoided.

French authorities persisted in equipping their two-seater squadrons with this machine, in spite of continued crashes, losses in action and the complaints of the crews. By June. 1918 a second version appeared that was powered with a 250-hp Lorraine-Dietrich engine and was intended as a two-seater fighter. It was armed with two fixed Vickers guns and a flexible mounting carrying two Lewis guns for the observer. This model attained a top speed of 121 mph and would climb to 21,700 feet but the S-XVI, as it was listed, was as hopeless a performer as its forerunners. It should be added too, that as fast as the earlier Spad two-seaters were discarded they were awarded to some unfortunate American squadrons.

At Ham hardly anyone liked the Spad, and when it was learned that the Nieuport firm was now producing their Nieuport-28, a new biplane that was powered with a Gnome 160-hp rotary engine, there was a wild rush to dump the Spads and take on the "28." This aircraft had several of the design features of the Sopwith Snipe, and had it been constructed more sturdily, it might have become an important factor in the air war. Instead, it soon developed dangerous structural weaknesses, and in addition had a nasty habit of shedding its wing fabric during steep dives.

Delighted to fly anything in preference to the early Spad-7s, the Lafayette pilots had a fine time making the transition and for a while buzzed around, happy as larks. Then one day there came a sharp note of warning from the Issy-le-Molineaux, Nieuport factory; the 28s were suddenly withdrawn, and the pilots had to go back to their Spads.

About a year later, the U. S. Aviation Service, abandoning all hope for a miracle fighter to come off any American production line, bought up every Nieuport-28 available, defective wings, molting fabric and all. With such equipment were many of Billy Mitchell's pursuit squadrons equipped until a few Spads were made available. Over the previous years American know-how had discarded the expediency of borrowing the blueprints of the Nieuport, the Sop Camel, the S.E.5, the Bristol Fighter, or even the early Spad-7, and whipping them out along modern production lines. They selected a British DH-4 instead, a model that had been in the discard for months, burdened it with the new Liberty engine, and created the original Flying Coffin.

During this period of heavy air action, and amid the turmoil of adopting new equipment, an additional furor was dumped on the Lafayette tarmac. The squadron had been under heavy night-bomber attacks, it had recovered from the deadly plague of Archie the mongrel, and by now all hands were immune to the French decorations parades with their mustachioed affection, but just as they were getting their breath following their Spad trial flights, destiny delivered Andrew Courtney Campbell, Jr., of Chicago, Illinois.

This bundle of hilarity and action had been a professional dancer before the war, and from his photographs must have looked like a very mischievous Robert Benchley. He was as much a fashion-plate as Ted Parsons, but although these two

men became bosom playmates, there were times when Campbell drove Ted stark, raving mad. It was that kind of a companionship.

Courtney Campbell had enlisted in the French Aviation on
July 20, 1916, and whatever capers he cut at Buc, Juvisy,
Avord, Cazaux, and Pau where he took his training, were
carefully deleted, probably to maintain the morale of the
service. At any rate he was eventually transferred to the Lafayette, arriving at Ham on April 15, 1917. The squadron had
recently suffered the loss of Hoskier, Genet, and McConnell,
and whatever Courtney may have done to lift the gloom,
must have been welcomed warmly.

No sooner had he arrived, dressed to look like the "intrepid
birdman" of those fabulous times, than Courtney began to
show what could be done with a Nieuport—by intent or total
ignorance. Because of his ability to do the unexpected in any
simple situation, he was given the job of test-hopping a new
engine. Few men still alive care to remember this exhibition,
but Ted Parsons put it all down on paper later, possibly on
the assumption that no one would believe it until it appeared
in print.

Courtney Campbell took the ship off, performed a few
hair-raising banks over the windsock, and then went up for
a little altitude. He nosed her over, gave the new engine all
she could gulp, came down in a terrific power dive and
yanked her back into a loop. At the top of the screaming
figure, guy wires began to twang, struts took on unbelievable
curves, and chunks of wing structure went skimming off in
all directions. Sitting there—upside down, of course—Courtney
studied this interesting phenomenon.

"I wonder what's going on," he pondered.

In her agony, the Nieuport hung there at the top of this
torturous loop and tossed a few more parts away. Several
flying wires gave up with high-pitched pingings and then, to
Courtney's amazement, the lower left wing panel tore itself
from the longeron and folded outward. It flapped its farewell

for some seconds, and then departed, fluttering away toward Chaudun.

"*Very* interesting," Courtney added and decided that measures should be taken to cope.

It must be said to his credit that Campbell behaved with rare coolness and skill. Granting that Providence took a hand until the crippled Nieuport had completed the loop, Courtney kept his head and found some mysterious counterbalance that allowed the plane to glide under reduced power and at such an angle that he was able to slip into a beet field almost ten miles away. Had he attempted any form of a turn, or put any unnecessary stress on the "one-wing" side, it is certain that the remaining panel would have been torn away, resulting in a deadly, tight spin.

In a short time the squadron ambulance arrived to bring back his battered body, but he was found giving a lecture on aerodynamics to a group of bewildered peasants who had gathered to inspect this strange bird. He rode back in triumph, took some restorative and sustenance from the bar, and in thirty minutes was in the air again, still proving that the Nieuport would put up with almost anything.

Kindred spirits in some respects, Campbell and Parsons teamed up for various flights and frivolities. Both men put in ungodly hours of flying time trying to rack up a confirmed victory. At last one fell before Parsons' guns, although most of the afternoon had been consumed in trying to avoid Campbell who delighted in tucking his wing tip between his leader's trailing edge and tailplane. He had Parsons completely bewildered with this form of wingman association; Ted was never certain whether he was listening to enemy bullets whistling past his head, or the hissing whirl of Campbell's propeller. It was impossible to plead with him. At times when Parsons threatened to punch his brains out, Campbell would respond with a delicate soft-shoe routine or a cakewalk, and the next time they went on patrol Courtney would discover a new way to inch in on his companion. It was all in good fun—but at times hair-raising.

Around this time the very sensitive Lieutenant Maison-Rouge who had taken over the late Lieutenant de Laage's post, began to assume some of the patrol-leader work. The young Frenchman had been mildly astonished by the capers and gaiety of some of the Americans he was supposed to command, but Courtney Campbell practically finished him.

During one of these "precision formations," conceived by the Chicago dancer, Campbell's wheels somehow touched down on Maison-Rouge's top wing and his tires actually sank through the fabric of the upper surface. They flew along in this manner for a few seconds with the French lieutenant almost passing out with fright, and as they came to their own field Campbell maintained this liaison. Locked together like aerial Siamese twins, the two machines made one complete circuit of the field. Klaxons screamed, bells rang everywhere, and an ambulance raced out to pick up the remains.

Finally, when Maison-Rouge looked as though he was ready to leap overboard, Campbell took a wild chance, rammed the throttle well up the quadrant, worked his elevators to hoik his nose up, and finally got his wheels clear, and pulled away. Why he did not take his leader's top wing with him is a mystery.

Deathly white and understandably frightened, Maison-Rouge gingerly landed while Campbell, apparently delighted to be free, put on another acrobatic exhibition that almost lifted the canvas from the hangars. When he landed, he ignored the general admonishment and could not understand what all the excitement was about. Shortly after, Lieutenant Maison-Rouge had a nervous breakdown and was replaced by Lieutenant Verdier-Fauvety.

Verdier-Fauvety contributed considerably to the enthusiasm and excitement of the squadron. He was a skilled and daring pilot and could tell a good story. Shortly before joining the Lafayette, he had had an amazing escape from death when during an air combat near the front line he had a mid-air collision with a Lieutenant Ciecomski, his squadron armament officer. This took place at an altitude of about eleven thousand feet, and the two planes remained locked together during the time it took to fall about six thousand feet. Then they broke apart. Verdier-Fauvety's had lost half of its elevator surface and most of its fin. For a time he had no control of his aircraft, but it somehow fluttered into a series of flat spins and sideslips until at last it piled into some heavy treetops in a large wood. The plane broke up in small segments, but the pilot had only a split lip and a bruised forehead.

Lieutenant Ciecomski, whose airplane had lost both blades of its prop and had a damaged wing, was not too difficult to handle. He held her in a powerless glide and made for home, but he unfortunately tripped over some high-tension wires and suffered a roll-over landing from which he crawled with a fractured collarbone.

Ignoring America's entry into the war, the Lafayette Committee in Paris, through its agents and representatives in Washington, continued to lure young Americans into this branch of the French Air Service. There were several now inducements, besides the offer of free transportation across the Atlantic Ocean on first-class liners. Finances had been improved, and more money had been added to the original $20,000 donated by the Vanderbilts. Also a new scale of prize money was announced. These funds were offered for military decorations, awarded by the Allied nations. In general the plan was set up as follows:

1500 francs ($300) for Legion of Honor
1000 francs ($200) for British Military Medal
 500 francs ($100) for Croix de Guerre
 200 francs ($ 50) for each additional palm, bar,
                        or citation.

Considering the earlier financial arrangements of base pay, allowances for mess bills, gratuities for leaves and furloughs, few men would have much to complain about. True, many were still serving as corporals and sergeants, but since the Lafayette had maintained a very democratic attitude toward rank, commissions simply meant more responsibilities and few material advantages.

New candidates appeared regularly in Paris and were soon shunted along to the flying schools. Most of them, because of their ingrained spirit, and willingness to serve, combined with some appreciation for even being considered, ran through the training schedules with little trouble. Very few failed to make the grade, and many who were to come after the Lafayette Escadrille had been absorbed into American aviation, willingly served with French Air Service squadrons until the end of the war.

Early in May of 1917 three more candidates, John Armstrong Drexel of Philadelphia, Ray Claflin Bridgman of Lake Forest, Illinois, and Henry Sweet Jones of Harford, Pennsylvania, arrived at the Lafayette field. Drexel was one of the aristocratic family of the City of Brotherly Love, and had been a sportsman aviator in the early days. He took part in the British air race of 1910 between Bournemouth and the Isle of Wight, a distance of twenty-one miles, mostly over water. This race was won by Leon Morane of France with a time of twenty-five minutes, twelve and two-fifths seconds. Drexel was second and Claude Grahame-White of England third. Later that year Drexel was again among the topliners who flew in the Belmont meet that featured a flight from Long Island around the Statue of Liberty. A prize of $10,000 was put up for this race which was won by Count Jacques de Lesseps who flew a Blériot. Some of the most famous names in aviation were on the entry list, including Roland Garros, Glenn Curtiss, Frank Coffyn, Arch Hoxsey, Claude Grahame-White, Ralph Johnstone, John B. Moisant, and Hubert Latham. Drexel usually was an important figure at any international meet held anywhere in the world.

He joined the French Aviation in October 1916, willingly took the full course although he had had years of exhibition flying, and naturally became a very skilled airman. He was brevetted on a Blériot on March 6, 1917. He joined the Lafayette at about the time the United States Air Service sent a small staff to Paris and opened offices on the boulevard Haussmann, and Drexel therefore spent only a month with the Lafayette, being assigned to the American headquarters as a liaison officer since he spoke French fluently. He later transferred to his own country's service, was made a major, and served in executive capacities in France, England, and the United States until the Armistice. For a number of years he lived at Baten Farm, Kent, England. He died on March 4, 1958.

Ray Bridgman proved to be a skilled, courageous, conscientious pilot who hated war wholeheartedly, but nevertheless willingly volunteered and enlisted in the French Aviation on July 24, 1916. He made excellent progress at all the training schools and arrived at Ham on May 1, 1917, after serving a few weeks with N.49, a French Nieuport squadron. Bridgman was on active duty at the front from the early part of April 1917 until the close of the war. He did not run up a lengthy victory list, but he was always available, and his companions could rely on him. When he became a patrol leader, every man in his formation enjoyed an unusual sense of confidence. He was particularly adept at breaking up enemy observation patrols, and many a jerry photographer went back without an exposed negative, due to Bridgman's harrying tactics. Bridgman's problem was to live up to the loftiness of his ideals, but he was a keen pilot, a courageous fighter, and fiercely loyal.

He was always in the heat of action and his aircraft could be picked out of the line on any day by its general appearance. The most battered, bullet-slashed, fabric-torn heap on the rank would be Ray's. He might take over a brand-new one for a dawn patrol, but by nightfall it would always be the most battered and torn. He had combats by the dozens, but seldom a real confirmation. Perhaps he never tried too hard.

On February 4, 1918, Ray Bridgman was commissioned

a captain in the U. S. Air Service and assigned as a flight commander with the 103rd Pursuit Squadron. He flew with this group until August 15 when he was made commanding officer of the 22nd Pursuit Squadron, which post he held until the Armistice.

Henry S. Jones was a graduate of Lehigh University, and had served with the American Field Service throughout most of 1916. He was accepted for aviation training on October 27, 1916, and became famous almost overnight for his wild antics aboard early Blériot trainers. While he was at Buc, Henry could do the most amazing things—in the air—with these pre-historic birds, but once it came time to put them back on the ground, Henry was even more miraculous. There are some who swear that Jones could outfly the great Pergoud, the gentleman who first looped-the-loop. Henry is said to have done an outside loop and repaired a recalcitrant engine at the same time. It is still admitted in hushed tones that Henry Sweet Jones was the greatest acrobatic pilot World War I had known . . . that is, until he had to land. At that point it was simply a matter of how many parts the Blériot could be broken into. According to legend, Henry's Blériot, after one such display, was picked up and taken away in three old horse nosebags.

Once he was allowed to glance at a Nieuport, however, Henry reformed and became one of the finest *chasse* pilots on the front. After his arrival at the Lafayette on May 12, 1917, he put in more than seventy hours of combat time during his first two months on the front. This was the period when some of the fiercest air fighting of the war was taking place. His name has never appeared on any list of American aces, but like Bridgman, he more than justified his place and rank.

More important to his comrades, Henry was a gay soul who brightened any mess or cubicle. He never bowed to homesickness, and during bad weather could content himself with an ancient magazine, a couple of wornout phonograph records, or the pleasure of just sitting about without fretting. He admitted that he liked rainy weather and enjoyed the respite it brought, but when the weather cleared he usually was one of the first out on the line—ready to go.

After nine solid months with the Lafayette, Henry was transferred to the U. S. Air Service, commissioned a lieutenant and assigned to the 103rd Pursuit Squadron. He served in that capacity for four months and was returned to America where he became an instructor and test pilot until the Armistice ended hostilities. After the war he managed a chain of Woolworth stores throughout New York State. He is now retired and living in Florida.

Another New Englander had moved in most unobtrusively, settled down, and taken over several important ground chores, as well as his regular flying assignments. This was Walter Lovell of Concord, Massachusetts. This candidate was somewhat mature for the work, having been born on September 9, 1884, at Newton, Massachusetts, and after an early education at public and private schools, entered Harvard where he graduated in 1907. A natural leader, on enlisting with the American Field Service early in 1915, he was soon made second-in-command of Section 3, but like so many others he also yearned for more active service. He was accepted for the French Aviation in May 1916, but owing to slack programs and many delays, Walter did not gain his brevet until October 1, 1916. He proved to be such a reliable and skilled airman, he was posted to the Lafayette by February 26, and served with them until October 24, 1917. After more delays and frustrations, he was finally commissioned a captain in the new U. S. Air Service, was later promoted to major and attached to American GHQ at Chaumont where he served until the following July. He then was returned to the United States where he held several executive positions until the end of the war.

During his time with the Lafayette, Walter Lovell was credited with two enemy airplanes, and awarded the Croix de Guerre. He put in ten heavy months with them, and took over as a patrol leader after McConnell, Hoskier, and Genet were killed.

Chapter XI

CASUALTIES AND COMEDIES

The war produced all forms of savage conflict through the late spring and early summer of 1917. General Henri Philippe Pétain replaced General Robert Georges Nivelle as commander-in-chief of the French Armies after a series of defeats and military blunders had ruined Nivelle's career. The British were still hammering away along the Arras front and managed to take Bullecourt. Following the greatest mining operation in military history, the Messines-Wytschaete ridge fell into the hands of the war-weary Tommies on June 6. General John J. Pershing, Commander-in-Chief of the promised American Expeditionary Forces, arrived in England to show the flag.

Four days before the Lafayette Escadrille had been moved from Ham and relocated at Chaudun, a field nestling halfway between Villers-Cotterets and Soissons. It was a brand-new establishment with space and hangars for at least six other squadrons.

As usual, the aircraft were flown in and Thomas Hewitt had the misfortune to wreck his new Spad in an encounter with a drainage ditch. Captain Thénault was provoked with Tommy's carelessness and, as a penalty, ordered him to motor all the way back to Ham and pick up Bob Soubiran's airplane. Bob was on leave at the time. Tommy had no trouble taking off, and made the flight back to Chaudun with ease, but then, with rare skill and precision, put Soubiran's ship smack-dab into the same ditch, completely wiping out another plane.

Tommy couldn't seem to do anything right, and the French decided eventually that he was not emotionally equipped to become a fighter pilot, although he was given every opportunity to settle down and learn the tricks. He was released from the service by October 1917, and he returned to the United

States and enlisted as a private in the U. S. Army. From that point on Tommy maintained little touch with his friends and relatives, and after the war wandered about the country, completely at loose ends. He died some years ago, and is buried at Arlington National Cemetery.

The war continued its monotonous course and those men who had been out there since the early months of the conflict and were still alive, had lost their original interest. No matter what rank one gained, or what honors and awards were meted out, the glamour had worn off, and one simply carried on, hopeful of nothing, believing nothing, except the possibility of a leave. The short-term spirit of a newcomer was but slightly amusing, and only those who were doubly inspired with the ideals of young knighthood, or alive with the drive of intense patriotism could continue on day after day with determination and resolution.

It may be difficult for the present-day military aviation enthusiast to accept, but in France the flying services were no longer considered the elite corps. There were hundreds of squadrons and thousands of airmen on the front, and the flying man with his silken or silver wings was no longer the glamorous figure he had once been. There were too many of him in circulation, and the other services had long resented the high regard in which he was held by the civilian population. In referring back to histories *written at the time*, it is interesting to note how little space was given to the flying services. In Sir Philip Gibbs' well-known *Now It Can Be Told* volume, which was based on his wartime dispatches, he devoted only a few brief paragraphs to the activities of the flying men during the fateful battles of 1916–17. The plethora of aviation histories, the gaudy biographies of the various aces, and the chauvinistic books hastily written *well after* the war, give the impression that the aviator was accepted as the savior of our civilization.

But on the contrary, many of us were beginning to realize that we were not fulfilling our mission. As a matter of fact, few of us had any idea what our mission was. We had not

been enlightened by postwar experts. Giulio Douhet had not
lectured us on the tactics and strategy of air power. Only a
few men in Europe had any concept of true strategic aviation.
Command of the air was a condition that was widely discussed *after* the war, but in 1917–18 few squadron commanders had ever uttered the phrase.

A handful of people insisted that the two-seater fighter was
not fully appreciated, and what few were available were not
being employed in an efficient manner.¹ We were shooting
down other airplanes, but in no way were forwarding the
advance of the all-important ground troops. It was the Germans who first produced a true ground-attack aircraft, one
that could co-operate with tanks, but, unfortunately, they
had failed to realize the full value of the armored vehicle,
and did not have such weapons to use with their Halber-
stadts and Junkers all-metal aircraft.

We sensed that despite the publicity being given to the
top-scoring airmen there was something lacking in the military
air arm. We felt that we were doing little to help the poilu or
Tommy, but we did our best with what was available. Hind-
sight tells us that the military airplane was hardly out of its
cocoon, and what we were doing amounted to little more
than the first fumbling efforts to build up the science of
military aviation. If the truth be known, or admitted, many
of us were now casting invidious eyes on the men who drove
tanks, or fought from their armored sponsons, since these
heroes rapidly were becoming the new glamour boys of the
war. I, for one, remember having a twinge of envy the first
time I saw a Tank Corps man sporting his silk-embroidered
lozenge insignia on his sleeve. I would have traded cockpits
then and there. I may have had a revision of viewpoint after
the Battle of Cambrai, but in the early summer of 1917 the
flying men were in a partial eclipse. This overshadowing of
effort was not fully dispelled until well into 1918 when American airmen and American publicity methods put the "ace"
back in the spotlight. However, the heroes of the two-seater
squadrons were seldom mentioned.

Once the dust of take-over activity had subsided at Chaudun, the routine work was continued. Three new recruits arrived to fill out the required roster; James Norman Hall, Douglas MacMonagle, and David M. Peterson. The Lafayette Escadrille in France had attracted such wide attention in America and the Franco-American Volunteer Committee representatives had made such a persuasive appeal that large numbers of candidates were swarming into the French flying schools, and the Lafayette soon discovered that the squadron could not absorb them all. Many of them had to be assigned to other French squadrons.

Officially, the Lafayette Escadrille was known as Spa.124, since the pilots in most cases were flying Spads. The term "Lafayette" was retained and this created concern with other Americans who could not be accommodated in Spa.124, but had to be posted to French squadrons. They wished to have some special designation, one that would indicate clearly that they were Americans and that they had volunteered. (It will be remembered that during World War II Americans who volunteered to serve with the Royal Air Force or the Royal Canadian Air Force were permitted to wear an identifying strip, "U.S.A.," stitched to the upper curve of their sleeves.) This yearning for national identification was fulfilled by the establishment of the Lafayette Flying Corps. In other words, whether an American volunteer served with Spa.124 or with any other French squadron, he could consider himself a member of this offshoot organization.

Over the ensuing years, this dual organization created considerable confusion. Proud parents or relatives of men who had flown as volunteers with the French usually proclaimed that So-and-So had served with the Lafayette Escadrille. Later on these people were puzzled or chagrined when no trace of their hero's name could be found on the forty-two-member roster of the squadron. The hero in question may have joined up, taken the training and actually flown on the Western Front, and could have run up an impressive score. For instance, David Putnam and Frank Baylies, both ranking

high in the ace list, were never members of the Lafayette
Escadrille, but both are still presented proudly on the roll of
the Lafayette Flying Corps.

Nevertheless, there always has been some disappointment
when it was pointed out that Such-and-Such an airman had
never been a member of the Lafayette. By the same token,
there were a number of men who signed up, started the
training course, and failed to make the grade, but when they
returned home several of them brazenly declared they had
been members of the Lafayette Escadrille. Others who had
served with the Lafayette Flying Corps became careless in
their explanations and often allowed their listeners to assume
that they had been bona-fide members of the original organization.

Both services gave much and displayed the finest spirit in
maintaining the great tradition, and for this reason a short
history of the Lafayette Flying Corps will be presented later
on in this book. However, it is well for the reader to be
clear on this point, for while the Lafayette Flying Corps
pilots contributed as much to the cause over the months in
which they served, it was the Lafayette Escadrille that conceived and first carried out the idea of volunteering and
serving with the French Aviation squadrons.

As will have been noted, the Lafayette seemed to attract
the most unusual personalities. Consider James Norman Hall.
Few people today realize that Hall was an outstanding member of the Escadrille, being best remembered for his telling
the story of the ship Bounty—Mutiny on the Bounty, Men
Against the Sea, and Pitcairn's Island—written in collabora-
tion with Charles B. Nordhoff, a member of the Lafayette
Flying Corps.

James Norman Hall was born in Colfax, Iowa, April 22,
1887, and graduated from Grinnell College in 1908. He later
did some post-graduate work at the University of Chicago,
took a vacation trip to Scotland, and returned from the High-
lands to take up social service work in Massachusetts. He

stayed with this absorbing employment for about five years, but returned to Great Britain in 1914 to have a year of travel and research. Shortly after his arrival in Britain the war broke out, and promised a more interesting experience. Hall joined the 9th Battalion of the Royal Fusiliers on August 18, 1914, and after a stretch of infantry training in England, was sent out to the front on May 30, 1915. Jimmy served well through those early days of trench warfare, and was relieved and discharged in December of that year.

This release apparently came about when Hall requested an emergency leave to visit his father who was seriously ill in Iowa. This was a military consideration totally unknown in the British Army of those days, particularly in respect to private soldiers. But influential friends in the United States added their intercession and influence and Hall was given a definite discharge—some said because he was an American citizen. However, there were hundreds of other American citizens in the various British services, and it is hard to accept this explanation. The essence of opinion might be found in the attitude of anti-war groups in America that frowned on any United States citizen who volunteered for service with any of the Allies, usually harping on the fact that these men were jeopardizing their national status. It is interesting to note that this American citizenship objection did not come up later on when Hall volunteered for and was accepted for the French Aviation.

After making his visit to Iowa, Hall returned to Boston where he spent the early part of 1916 lecturing on the war and writing a book detailing his experiences with the Royal Fusiliers. It was titled *Kitchener's Mob,* and enjoyed some success. Following this, the editors of the *Atlantic Monthly* suggested that he return to Britian and do a series of articles on the war. This appealed to Hall who made plans to return to England and rejoin his old regiment, but before he left the same editors brought up the subject of the Lafayette Escadrille, and added that it might be a good idea if he wrote

two articles on the American fliers before he again tied himself up with the British regiment.

Hall returned to Europe with this general plan in mind
and first made a contact with Paul Ayres Rockwell who was
working in Paris. Paul was the accepted Boswell of the Lafayette and he introduced Jim to his brother Kiffin, Bill Thaw,
Raoul Lufbery, and Jim McConnell. This association in turn
brought in Dr. Gros who was fascinated with the publicity
idea and offered to provide every assistance possible.

A few days later it occurred to Dr. Gros that Hall might do
better by actually joining the Escadrille and thereby see the
whole story first hand. This turned out to be a fortunate
inspiration, for a few years later James Norman Hall completed the famous two-volume history of the Lafayette Flying
Corps. Although he was intrigued with the idea, at first Jimmy
felt that he was perhaps a little too old to learn to fly; he was
pushing twenty-nine, and wartime fliers were supposed to be
harum-scarum schoolboys, at least those he had encountered
in the British service appeared to be scarcely out of their
teens.

Dr. Gros brushed aside all of Jimmy's protests, gave him a
quick medical examination and assured him that he would
have no trouble at all. With the ways greased in this manner,
Hall, the correspondent, soon found himself a student pilot,
starting at Buc by October 11, 1916. He had progressed
through Avord, and the G.D.E. routine by the following April
when he took his brevet on a Caudron. He was posted to the
Lafayette, arriving at Ham on June 16, 1917, but after serving
with his countrymen for a few weeks, was for some reason
transferred to the French Spa.112 squadron with which he
served until October 3 of the same year.

By this time it occurred to Jimmy that he was supposed to
write a couple of articles about the Lafayette Escadrille, but
while he was with Spa.112 he had little or no contact with
the Americans. Dr. Gros was consulted, a few wires were
pulled, and by the end of October 1917 he was transferred
back to Spa.124, and everyone was glad to have him.

Jimmy Hall had a most exciting career and his articles that were written for the *Atlantic Monthly* portrayed clearly his adventures. These features were incorporated later on in a book titled, *High Adventure,* and published by Houghton Mifflin Company. His combat record has been difficult to put in chronological order; so many historians of varying abilities have tried to write Hall's story, and he himself set it down in short installments for magazine publication, most of which were tempered by Jimmy's uncommon modesty. Also various writers and editors apparently rearranged some incidents to build up an accepted form of suspense, so that few of these historios or records coincide. However, no matter how it is presented James Norman Hall's war-flying career requires no padding or editorial build-up.

Paul Rockwell wrote in a recent letter: "Jim Hall was one of the finest all-around persons I have ever known, a great and honorable man in every way. He had just about everything, intelligence, courage, looks, talents of many sorts, and was most modest and withdrawing. Everyone liked him, but he did not give his friendship and consideration to everyone. He actually was shy, and one had to learn to know him.

"Another feature of Jim Hall was that he whistled beautifully. He told me that he was walking back to his hotel alone during one of his first nights in Paris through the darkened and virtually deserted streets, whistling for all he was worth. An *agent de ville* stopped him and asked what he meant by his exhibition, and almost took him to the police station. In France it was not against the law to whistle in the streets, but it was considered undignified and almost a breach of the peace."

When Hall first arrived at Spa.124 he was given a war-weary, beat-up Spad that was about ready for the training-school roster. This was regulation procedure. The veterans took over the new aircraft as fast as they arrived, and the newcomers had to wait their turn. Jimmy made no comment, but accepted the hulk and actually flew a couple of defensive patrols in this hand-me-down.

A few days later his name went up for a late afternoon show that was to be led by Bill Thaw. Lufbery, Parsons, Dugan, and Bridgman were also assigned. Thaw ordered everyone to take off and get to about twelve thousand feet over a nearby reservoir. Jimmy was cautioned to stick close once they went over the line since this was only his third time over.

Thaw and the rest of the pilots got off on time, but Hall's crock would not start, so they left without him. They knew that if he could get away within a few minutes, he would try to meet them at the rendezvous.

Ten minutes later the old coffee-grinder decided to perk, and Hall clambered in and started out for glory. The engine was running but the ancient Spad took its own time getting any altitude and by the time Jimmy reached the reservoir rendezvous Thaw and his group had gone on. He tooled about for a few minutes, then realized what had happened and rather than waste fuel in this manner, he nosed around and crossed the line, knowing that he had only to find a five-Spad formation and all would be well.

For another five minutes or so he watched the general activity; there were some two-seaters carrying out an artillery shoot, someone was having a whack at a kite balloon, there was much two-seater reconnaissance but no other Spads anywhere. There did not appear to be any enemy ships either. Then suddenly he spotted a number of black specks in a neat formation about six miles inside the German lines, and as he studied them for a few seconds, he was positive that this was Bill Thaw and his group. Fine! He nosed around and gave the old crate a few more notches and headed for them. Then he saw that there were six—not five—planes! But on some reflection he presumed that some lone-eagle type had joined up, and the more the merrier.

Jim timed his turn-in beautifully and came around to nose in for a space to operate. It was then that he realized these "Spads" had very narrow lower wings, and also sported vee-type interplane struts. Strange. On a closer look, after edging one of the pilots over, he saw that none of them carried the Indian-head insignia, nor were there any red-white-and-blue cocardes; instead, these "Spads" were daubed with black-barred crosses.

Spads? . . . Holy smoke! These were Albatros ships, and there were six of them. Men in black helmets and massive goggles glared at him, some in amazement, others in grim anticipation. Hall knew immediately that he had joined the wrong mob, and wondered how one eased out of such a situation. For an instant he felt an urge to salute, bow, and withdraw as a gentleman should, but these black-helmeted clods had other ideas and he had to duck out unceremoniously.

He went down like a dart, followed by streams of Spandau fire. Pulling out to reorganize, he went into a number of acrobatics, but somehow every turn or twist took him into a new cone of enemy flame. Torrents of lead slapped through the wings and fuselage of his ship, one creased his forehead, another cut a gash across his groin, and a third pierced his shoulder and paralyzed his left side. These three blows knocked Jimmy unconscious and he toppled over against his belt and rammed the stick well forward. Before he passed out the last thing he remembered was flying at fourteen thousand feet still heading in the general direction of the French trenches. His speed was so great that none of the Albatros fliers dared to follow him. They were probably satisfied that he would never pull out.

With his engine screaming, and all flying wires taut as violin strings, Jimmy's Spad continued down. Anyone watching this wild corkscrew dive would have bet it would end with a terrible smash, but for a few seconds Hall came out of his stupor, and more by instinct than intent shut off his engine and hauled back on the stick. With that accomplished, he passed out again. By some freak of luck, the wings stayed on, the plane wabbled into a sloppy glide, swung into a series of flat turns, one minute heading for the German lines, the next turning to head for home. It wavered from one side to the other, and then decided on the trickiest set-down of all. Before Hall regained consciousness again, the Spad fluttered along the top of the French front line, its wheels fitting neatly between the wall and parapet. Gradually it eased down, and its wings slithered along the sandbags until they folded up and dropped the fuselage gently into the trench.

When Hall came to he was on a stretcher and being taken away from the trench area. He squinted, and tried to figure who had him and where he was going. The bearer in front was wearing a bluish-gray uniform, but it was so muddy, Jimmy found it difficult to decide whether the man was French or German. When he could squint again he was relieved to notice that the stretcher-bearer was wearing a French steel helmet, not a German coal scuttle.

At the dressing station it was learned that the crash hadn't even scratched Jimmy; his only damage was from the three Spandau bullets that proved to be not too serious, and he was soon back and available for patrols again.

Hall soon provided another adventure for the boys of Spa.-124. It was not such a thriller, but is interesting since it concerned an assignment to destroy a kite balloon, and involved the use of Prieur rockets, rather than incendiary ammunition that was fired from rifle-caliber machine guns.

New and intense ground activity was introduced on all fronts in the latter part of 1917, and the observation balloon came in for more critical attention since up to a point and over an important trench-operations area, it could furnish reasonably accurate information. Whether the destruction of these gas bags was as dangerous or as important as some writers have led one to believe, has long been a matter of argument.

As I recall, balloon-busting was not especially dangerous, but it certainly was frustrating at times. It was part of the general routine of my squadron to have a special Sunday afternoon game in which all aircraft took part. We would take off, our guns loaded with special Buckingham ammunition, and start down the enemy-balloon line where it began near the Belgian coast. We played follow-the-leader, diving on the gas bags, firing into the observers' baskets, and when fortune favored, shooting them down. This was kept up as long as there were balloons up, or until we ran out of ammunition or fuel.

But balloons were not easy to shoot down, no matter how large they were, or the fact that they were inflated with hydrogen. It was our experience that it usually took one telling burst, and if some metal fitting or grommet were hit, that sort of spark would more likely ignite the gas than a whole drum of incendiary ammunition. I have flown directly over a balloon, watched my twin streams of sparkling ammunition bore into the upper part of the envelope leaving a perforated impression as though some giant sewing machine were stitching the bag—and nothing would happen. On other occasions, I would scarcely press my trigger than the whole thing would go up, seemingly before any of my bullets had reached the bag. As I said, it was most frustrating, and few of us enjoyed it.

In the early years of the war the British did not take balloon-busting seriously and few of their aces appear to have had outstanding success in this particular field. Captain Andrew Beauchamp-Proctor, the South African who was awarded the V.C. for downing thirty-eight enemy aircraft, was also credited with destroying sixteen kite balloons, but it should be noted that in their official records the British did not consider the gas bags to be in the same category as powered aircraft.

It was not until late in the war when Lieutenant Michael Coiffard and Major Willy Coppens ran up impressive balloon scores that their importance became newsworthy. The exploits of Lieutenant Frank Luke, the Arizona Balloon-Buster, enlivened aviation activities somewhat, and later built the feature into an exaggerated adventure.

From my point of view, gained while flying on the British front for many months, attacking balloons was not very hazardous. I knew that some of them were sent aloft with dummy observers aboard, dummies that carried a lethal ballast of explosive that could be detonated whenever an enemy plane approached, but I never saw one of these traps touched off, nor heard of anyone being brought down in that manner. The real danger, as I saw it, was in becoming entangled with the looping steel cable that tethered the balloon to the ground winch. In attacking a balloon, one had to make certain which way the wind was blowing, and in which direction the cable was looping up toward the balloon harness, for, if after making the attack, one continued on down below the level of the bag, it was easy to tangle with the cable.

I saw an S.E.5 encounter this hazard, and a frightening affair it was. The pilot had made a beautiful attack and actually torched the bag, but he continued down, apparently forgetting the cable. In the next few seconds, everything possible happened. First, the scout's wing seemed to be undergoing a hacksaw treatment, a large section was sliced through for some distance, and in a second or so the jagged portion fluttered away. Next, the balloon cable somehow slid along the leading edge, scraped up to the engine cowling and became entangled between the propeller and the radiator shutters; the poor devil was completely trapped. The S.E.5 began to fight this steel leash and flailed itself into a dreadful twirling movement as it slid down the cable. By now the burning balloon had been snubbed into a position dead over the trapped airplane, and the end was inevitable. The doomed plane went down in this horrifying twirl until at last it piled up in a crazy flat spin on top of the cable winch. The crash in itself was bad enough, but then what was left of the burning balloon, its basket, and the two dead observers fell on the wreckage. Hours later it must have been difficult to sort out anything recognizable from that charnel heap.

Jimmy Hall's introduction to balloon-busting came about when Spa.124 was included in a special all-out program that was planned to eliminate four enemy kites that had been noted in a very important sector. The French were planning a new attack and wished to make sure that the gas-bag snoopers would not notice any unusual back-area operations. This is an interesting incident since it introduced the famous Prieur rockets that were now being brought into general use. They had been designed originally to stop German Zeppelin attacks, but when the big dirigibles were gradually withdrawn from the raids on Paris and London, someone conceived the idea of using these early missiles against observation balloons.

The patrol orders indicated that there were to be two protection formations composed of five planes, and there were to be four four-plane flights of attack. Two of these attack ships were to carry the rockets and attempt the kill while the remaining two were to follow them down and keep defensive aircraft off their tails. All in all, the attack was to involve a force of twenty six airplanes. The whole formation was to rendezvous over a nearby town around 10:45 A.M. at an altitude of about ten thousand feet. Each force had its own set of orders and duties, but as will be seen, there were only two rocket-carrying Spads assigned to each target. If the number 1 pilot failed to get his bag, the number 2 man took over to finish the task.

Hall and another man, whose name was not given out at the time but who was identified as "J.B.," were selected to fly the rocket-carrying planes. Their Spads were prepared for this task by lashing three heavy cardboard tubes to the outer-bay wing struts, and a sheet of tin was tacked down over the fabric of the lower wing to eliminate any danger from sparks. The rockets, which were about two inches in diameter, and about eighteen inches in length, were tipped with steel points, and to the rocket casing was added a regular stick-tail that was inserted in the rocket tube. A firing system, composed of a set of batteries and some primary form of ignition was carried in the pilot's cockpit.

Before they took off Hall and his companion were given an opportunity to try out this device against a marked-out ground target. A suitable ring sight was also provided, with graduated circles that would indicate how far away the enemy bag was while the Spad was being flown at it. On the ground everything seemed simple, but in training practice, Hall found that it was difficult to dive at the required speed, keep a true course, get the target within the rings of the sight, and then ignite the rockets at the correct instant. However, they kept at it, and finally were able to satisfy their instructor, Lieutenant Verdier-Fauvety, that they might possibly do some damage to something.

When the time came for the attack, Bill Thaw, accompanied by Whiskey and Soda, sauntered up and in his casual style repeated the orders and instructions to send them off.

"Get going, you sausage-spearers." Bill grinned. "We're having lunch at twelve. That will give you time to wash up after you get back."

Then the squadron joker came up, waving Jimmy's toilet case to remind him of the possibility of landing in Germany with a damaged plane. It takes all kinds to send off a combat formation.

Once in the enemy-balloon area, it was seen that French artillery was giving its all to the cause; the enemy ground sector was taking a wicked strafing, most of which was intended for the German antiaircraft batteries that might harass the Spads. As a result antiaircraft defense was fairly light and none too accurate.

The plan was good so far. The railroad line that was to be their chief guide, was easy to find as it led into a small town, gleaming with red-tiled roofs. Above an open area nearby Hall spotted their gas bag, and as he and his rocket partner moved to get into position for their attack, they saw two large oily blobs of smoke curl up. Great spear-tips of flame snapped through the black design, and they realized that two balloons already had gone up. Their turn was next.

As the two Spa.124 men moved in the enemy sent up a number of flaming onions, deadly missiles that emitted a greenish glare, and balls of fire that seemed to be chained together to entangle if the main charge missed. But there were other things to catch the eye. Jimmy saw two dirty-white blossoms flash out below their balloon, and knew that the observers had been ordered to jump. "J.B." went down, hoping to get it before it had been drawn all the way to the ground. Hall followed, his throttle wide open. For a second or two his partner's plane blotted out all view of the gas bag, and Jimmy had to ease to one side to find out what was happening. By then the balloon was oscillating against the winch tug and the speed with which it was being withdrawn. Hall had to work his Spad back into position, and in the meantime "J.B." had fired his rockets. There were several wavering lines of smoke, but the balloon was still intact. It was very close to the ground now, and to Hall it looked as big as an ocean liner. It would be impossible to miss, so he thought. He let the big gray-black mass pass from his sight and slide somewhere beneath him. Then he nosed down to the vertical and brought the bag well into his sight. Standing on his rudder bar he finally ignited the rockets, and the whole battery screamed out.

He missed!

The rockets had ignited properly, Hall was certain he was dead on with his sight; the missiles had screeched away with a glorious roar, but when he had pulled out and was curling away, the old gas bag still shuddered over her winch. A beautiful attempt, but an artistic fizzle.

But there was no time for regrets. Both "J.B." and Jimmy were down to about seven hundred feet, after they had zoomed away from the attack. They were some miles behind the German lines, and a faulty engine could put them in the stockade for the rest of the war, so they concentrated on racing home. When they landed and told their doleful tale, Bill Thaw said, "Don't let it worry you. Better luck next time. We bagged two out of four, and someone shot down a jerry plane. Not too bad for about thirty-minutes' work."

"I don't think we're worth much to the Allied cause," Jimmy said, and wandered off to wash away the "sweat of fear."

Late in October, just after Jim had returned from his short assignment with Spa.112, he put on a combat display that had the veterans of the squadron goggle-eyed. Along with Walter Lovell and Bill Dugan, and with Ted Parsons leading, Hall was sent on a high-altitude patrol over the Chemin-des-Dames highway. They got away neatly and were soon in a classic formation, heading across the enemy lines. It was a beautiful day, there was no real enemy opposition over the trenches, so Parsons took them on well beyond the Boche-balloon line. The antiaircraft assault was hot, but there were no enemy aircraft to be seen anywhere as the foursome droned on and on. Then suddenly Ted spotted three enemy two-seaters that were churning up toward the French lines, apparently taking no notice of the Lafayette formation.

"Here we go!" Ted said, and waggled his wings to alert his brood. He knew that although he had four Spads against three enemy airplanes, the Albatros machines had flexible guns that could give them trouble if they were properly employed. Parsons, Lovell, and Dugan each selected a target while Hall was given the task of covering and watching out for attacks from above—he was something of a roving sentinel.

But things did not work out according to pattern; none of the three two-seaters was bothered in any way. Although they tried every method of attack, they always came under the whiplash of the rear gunners. Then Parsons decided to go down and come up under and in that way block off the flexible weapons. They made several futile stabs, but again the gunners kept them dodging about so that no true bead could be drawn. Parsons was hot with fury, but the best they could do was to harry the enemy and hope to keep the observers from carrying out any special plans.

In the middle of all this action Ted suddenly saw that a fourth Spad, with a gaudy Indian head insignia, was coming down like a lightning bolt. To Ted it looked like a real professional job with the Spad zinging down at the trailing Albatros. If the gunner was still intent on the three Spads below he might miss this streaking fury completely. As he watched, Parsons realized that this pilot, whoever he was, had no intention of missing. He was now within a few dozen feet of the two-seater and had not fired a round as yet. In the next split second a collision would be unavoidable. Either that, or the crazy Lafayette pilot was staging a suicide crash in his attempt to down one of the enemy planes. Parsons was stiff with awe.

The enemy gunner, too, saw that the Spad was getting too close for comfort, and he was seen to duck down and huddle below his gun mounting just in time as the wild Spad was yanked out with only inches to spare. Ted could see its wheels almost ride over the enemy's center section, and then the Spad climbed steeply, fell off in a pathetic stall and started to spin. By this time Parsons and his wing men realized that this wild pilot must be Jimmy Hall, and presumed that during his attack he had received a bullet or a burst from one of the defensive gunners. As they watched, it was obvious to them that Jimmy was completely out of control, and finally the spinning single-seater disappeared into the low haze below. They naturally thought that Hall had crashed.

But we are getting ahead of the story. When Hall saw that Parsons and his wing men were getting nowhere, he took matters into his own hands. Knowing that the three two-seater crews would be well-occupied by their tormentors below them, Jimmy went down in an almost perpendicular dive, but was so intent on getting one of the Albatros ships full in his sight, forgot to fire his guns. When it was almost too late, it took all he had to yank the speeding Spad out and avoid a headlong collision. Air-blind, and under the stress of the pull-out, Jim lost complete control and found himself in a tight corkscrew spin. He knew what should be done in that situation, but he was so shackled with anxiety and fright, he allowed the ship to fall for another thousand feet, until he realized that he was heading straight for enemy territory. By this time some latent resolve bubbled to the top, and he managed to level off and start contour-chasing until he came upon some real estate that he recognized. The pull-out was terrific and should have yanked off the Spad's wings, but the old hulk held together somehow, and Jimmy was able to keep her intact until he picked out his field.

When Parsons and the other two pilots landed they were astonished to find Hall hale and hearty, but were more perplexed when they took a good look at his plane. Despite all he had been through, there was but one buckled wing tip, one wing rib was broken, and there were two bullet holes, yards from any critical section. The greatest damage suffered was Parsons' outraged emotions, but Hall soon lived down this misadventure and in a short time was one of the Lafayette's leading scorers. On one occasion he found and picked on four enemy planes, roaring in and out for more than twenty minutes as he matched wits, guns, and attacks with them all. He flew like a veteran and never let up his offensive; one of the Germans was driven down in flames, two more were so badly damaged they had to withdraw from the fray, and the fourth lost interest when his pals decided they had had enough.

With the coming of the U. S. Aviation Service, and the transfer of the Lafayette men to their own colors, Sergeant Hall was taken over by the 94th (Hat-in-the-Ring) Pursuit Squadron. His further adventures will be related in subsequent chapters.

Douglas MacMonagle was the son of Scottish parents who lived in San Francisco. Doug was another of the classic type who made up the bulk of the Lafayette roster. He was handsome, had an aristocratic bearing, and spoke softly with cultured diction, a true gentleman of the period. He had a quick tongue, a caustic wit, and the ability to detect a phony at twenty paces. He had no use for the ones who "talked" their flying skill or combat courage, and was the first to put a stop to any boastful statements some men made, particularly when they were on leave in Paris. A valued and respected man, Doug had the most tragic death of all.

He did the accepted stint with the American Field Service during the summer of 1916, but by October 3 of that year was accepted by the French Aviation. He went through Buc, Avord, and the G.D.E., and was brevetted on a Caudron by April 10, 1917, and joined the Lafayette Escadrille on June 16, 1917.

On September 24 when autumn was painting her first harvest tints of brown and gold over the war area, Mac was selected to fly in a formation that was led by Raoul Lufbery. It so happened on this same day that his mother had traveled all the way from California to the war area to see him. How this was arranged has never been made clear, but at any rate Mrs. MacMonagle arrived in Paris where she gained permission to visit her son's squadron at the front. Doug had planned to motor over to Ravenel, the nearest railroad station, to meet her, but when he saw his name on the duty list, he induced someone else to meet his mother while he went on patrol.

According to Lufbery's report, they went up to the line, and shortly after spotted a flight of enemy single-seaters about fifteen hundred feet above them. Since they had the advantage of the sun, Luf took his pilots back inside the French line with the idea of first gaining some altitude and then reversing the up-sun position. When he turned away to carry out this plan, MacMonagle did not stay in the formation but instead seemed to be making directly for the enemy grouping. By the time Mac's intent was realized, he was too far away for them to give him aid or to head him off. Lufbery came to the conclusion later that Doug hadn't seen the main enemy force, having missed it in the sun, but why he left the formation was hard to explain. He may have spotted a bait "sitter" that no one else had seen, and being impetuous and determined had gone in to take it on. Who knows? He may have decided that this was the day to score his first victory and had seized what appeared to be a heavenly chance.

Before Luf and the others could interfere, two German single-seaters were on Doug's tail and one of them got him cold with its first burst. They saw his plane spin down until it fell just inside the French lines. When the body was recovered Mac had two bullets in his head, but the Spad, as if in reverent compassion, had pulled out of the spin, and leveled out to make as gentle a landing as it could. The body was not mangled or burned. Other members of the Escadrille brought Doug's remains in and laid them out in a spare shed only minutes before Mrs. MacMonagle arrived at the field.

After her long trip across U-boat-infested waters and up the torturous wartime railroad to the battle zone, she missed seeing her son by only a few hours. Her courage and demeanor in the face of that tragic blow, however, were magnificent, and set a brave example for every airman present.

A small group of American Engineers, one of the first U. S. Army organizations to appear at the front, provided a firing squad, and a bugler to blow Taps. Douglas MacMonagle was the first American to be buried at the front with military honors by his own uniformed countrymen.

David McKelvey Peterson came from a fine family living in Honesdale, Pennsylvania. An uncle was a general in the United States Army, but Dave showed none of the accepted dash and thunder of the professional soldier. From all accounts, he was another Dudley Hill, for he found no thrill in any of his many adventures, and no event of the Great War aroused his tranquil nature. It simply was not in Dave Peterson to be elated, depressed, overjoyed, or frightened, and perhaps because of this immunity to shock or excitement, he lived to see the end of the war. He was killed in a postwar flying accident at Daytona Beach, Florida.

Dave made his way across the Atlantic in the late summer of 1916 and enlisted in the French Aviation early in October, started his flying course at Buc on October 16, went through Avord, Pau, and the G.D.E. schools, and took his brevet on a Blériot on April 16, 1917. The Lafayette Escadrille received him, along with Jimmy Hall and Douglas MacMonagle, on June 16, and he flew with the American squadron until February 18, 1918. He was commissioned a captain in the U. S. Air Service, and served at various times with the 103rd, 94th

Ronald W. Hoskier of South Orange, New Jer-
was living in Paris with his parents at the out-
: of the war. For some months he drove an
rican ambulance and then volunteered for fly-
He was killed while flying a Morane Parasol,
ing a French officer's servant as his gunner.
A. Rockwell)

dmond Charles Genet, who deserted from
. S. Navy to fight in the Foreign Legion.
ent more than a year in the trenches before
ng for French Aviation. He was killed
16, 1917, the first American to be killed
America declared war on Germany. A short
ter the Secretary of the Navy cleared his
of the formal charge of desertion.
Air Force)

19. Playing with the lion cubs, Whiskey and Soda. The day America entered th
the men of the Lafayette Escadrille put on a celebration. Here are seen Will
Dugan, Captain Thènault, Thomas M. Hewitt, Bill Thaw, Raoul Lufbery, Lieu
deLaage (with shoulder turned), Kenneth Marr, Ted Parsons and Edward F. I
Whiskey is the larger lion on the right. *(U. S. Air Force)*

20. Down on the Somme. Raoul Lufbery gets a send-off in his Nieuport scout
lion cub Whiskey being held by Didier Masson. Bob Soubiran stands by. Th
Indian head insignia is interesting since it shows the original primitive design.
(U. S. Air Force)

The famous Courtney Campbell, the best
remembered playboy of the Lafayette Escadrille
his renowned three-winged Nieuport. Court-
out on a stunting trick one day, came out of
ht loop and found one of his lower wings
ring away. With rare skill and cool-headed-
he brought the machine back to the ground,
rles H. Dolan II)

d Parsons who destroyed eight enemy air-
levised his own flying gear. A crash helmet
d by a British airman, suitably decorated,
topped off his college campus mackinaw
Thus arrayed he went off to meet the foe.
C. Parsons)

23. In a more military outfit, Parsons
here wearing the *Medaille Militaire, C*
Guerre, Cross de Leopold and the *I*
Croix de Guerre. He did not transfer
U.S. Air Service but stayed on wi
French and flew with the famous
squadron. In World War II Parsons se
the U. S. Navy and became a Rear A
(*Edwin C. Parsons*)

24. Douglas MacMonagle of San Francisco
was killed under most tragic circumstances.
His mother had gained permission to visit him
at the front. About two hours before she arrived, Doug was shot down only a short distance from his own field. She stayed on to
attend the funeral. (*Paul A. Rockwell*)

...rance's early 1915 Voisin bomber which was flown by several members of the
...ette group before they became single-seater pilots. Raoul Lufbery, Norman Prince,
...Balsley, Chouteau Johnson and Elliott Cowdin all began their careers aboard this
...ner. Victor Chapman started out as an aerial gunner on a Voisin.
...*nal Archives)*

...here Raoul Lufbery fell after jumping from his burning plane. His body struck
...p of the picket fence running through a cottage garden. The peasant woman ran
...d tried to pull the airman off and then found a piece of picket had pierced Luf-
...throat. She pulled it out hoping to save his life. She is seen here with the piece
...et wrapped in a piece of paper. *(LeRoy Prinz)*

27. James Norman Hall, who was to bec[ome] a renowned author, served a year with British infantry. He joined the French A[via]tion in October 1916. After a spell with [the] Lafayette Escadrille, Jim transferred t[o the] U.S. Air Service and was shot down [and] taken prisoner May 7, 1918. He was cre[dited] with destroying three enemy aircraft. (*National Archives*)

28. Robert Soubiran, a New Yorker, [went] into action with the Foreign Legi[on] August 28, 1914. He fought for mor[e than] a year as an infantryman. After [being] wounded he transferred to the F[rench] Aviation, served with the Lafayette [Esca]drille for sixteen months and at the A[rmis]tice was still flying, and wound up a s[quad]ron commander with the U.S. Air S[ervice] (*U. S. Air Force*)

29. David Putnam, New England's most popular airman who destroyed twelve enemy planes while flying with the Lafayette Flying Corps. A direct descendant of Israel Putnam of Revolutionary War fame, David logged one of the most dramatic of war careers. Impetuous and fearless, he attacked no matter what the odds. He was killed during a fight with five enemy aircraft. *(National Archives)*

30. Another New Englander who scored an even dozen victories was Frank L. Baylies of New Bedford, Mass. Here was a keen cool-headed fighter who had every skill that would make him a great ace, but like David Putnam, there were times when he took on more than he could handle and he died while fighting a large formation of Fokkers single-handed. *(National Archives)*

31. The early Spad-7, a model flown by Georges Guynemer of Spa. 3, the famous S
squadron. Here is shown the famed classic insignia typical of the designs preferre
French aviators. *(U. S. Air Force* [Soubiran])

32. The ultimate in the wartime Spad line. This is the famed Spad-17 which
equipped with a fixed wide-angle lens aerial camera and used for quick intr
observation missions. It was powered with the 235-hp Hispano Suiza engine and
attain top speeds of 135-138 mph. (U. S. Air Force)

and 95th Pursuit Squadrons. He was promoted to major on August 29, 1918, and by October 8, 1918, was sent back to the United States to assume an executive position. He remained with the U. S. Air Service until his death the following year.

Nothing seemed to impress Dave. He signed on for the conflict, whistling a popular war ditty. His first solo flight brought no expression of any kind. Passing through the school of acrobatics with rare skill caused not a smile, and his first patrol over the line, and his first confirmed victory were just events in a normal man's day.

He was soon selected as a patrol leader, and it is on record that Dave led more patrols over the line than any other member of the Lafayette. He had a blue pennant painted on his Spad, and was ever in the thick of battle. He had unbelievable eyesight and usually spotted enemy aircraft long before his men had any idea there was danger nearby. He was so nonchalant, he would simply waggle his wings to draw his pilots in closer, and then roar in for the attack. Most of the time the others just wondered what Dave was up to now. He was skilled in flight and fighting maneuvers and never put the men he was responsible for in any unnecessary danger.

If the war was quiet and there was no opposition over the enemy back areas, Dave would cruise up and down, gradually inching in deeper and deeper until at last he would taunt some jerry formation to come up and take him on. Under such circumstances, the invaders, with the advantage of height and time to pick the up-sun spot, usually sent the defenders down again, sometimes in flames, sometimes completely out of control. On his way back Dave would delight in chasing enemy trains and shooting up road transport, but usually he went back to about six thousand feet to annoy the German balloon observers. Sometimes he shot one down, but more often he just had the satisfaction of watching the frantic activity around the ground winch.

When Peterson's flight came in the other fliers would often swarm up to learn what tricks he had been up to this time, but his pilots would have to tell and illustrate the story, for Dave usually sauntered off to make a very routine combat report that generally read *"Rien á Signaler"* ("Nothing to Report").

In contrast to his disinterest in the combat, Dave believed in making himself comfortable. He was clever with tools and had dozens of ideas. His cubicle was one of the most comfortable, and certainly the best equipped on the field. He put in bookshelves, made a table, and contrived a washstand. Although the Lafayette seemed to be continually on the move, his quarters were always smart and cheerful. While others moped about seeking some warmth and welcome, Dave's room was snug, cozy, and the woodbox filled.

But with all his nonchalance and bent for personal comfort, Dave more than paid for his training. At the close of hostilities he was credited officially with five victories, and was honored with America's Distinguished Service Cross with a Bronze Oak Leaf, and the Croix de Guerre with Palms. In one citation, signed by General Pershing, he was credited with extraordinary heroism in action near Lunéville on May 3, 1918, when leading a patrol of three planes he encountered five enemy aircraft at an altitude of ten thousand feet and immediately gave battle. Notwithstanding the fact that he was attacked from all sides, he succeeded, by skillful maneuvering, in shooting down one of the enemy and dispersing the remaining four.

The Bronze Oak Leaf was awarded to Peterson for extraordinary heroism in action near Thiaucourt on May 15, 1918. On this occasion, while flying alone, he met two enemy aircraft at an altitude of fifteen thousand feet, and promptly attacked and shot down one of the enemy planes in flames. While thus engaged he was attacked from above by a second enemy aircraft, but by skillful maneuvering he succeeded in shooting down that one too.

The last two Americans received into the ranks of the Lafayette Escadrille were James Ralph Doolittle and Christopher Ford. This Jimmy Doolittle must not be confused with the

Colonel—later General—Jimmy Doolittle who commanded the famous U. S. Army Air Force raid on Tokyo in World War II. This Doolittle was a native New Yorker who volunteered to serve with the Norton-Harjes Ambulance Service in 1916. He transferred to the French Aviation in October 1916 and joined the Lafayette on July 2, 1917.

Ralph Doolittle was the hard-luck character of the squadron. He had a painful accident at G.D.E. after he had completed his training, and was confined to a hospital for treatment of severe facial wounds, which deprived him of about eight weeks of front-line action. Shortly after his arrival on the Somme, the squadron was sent up to Dunkirk to join in a British air offensive. During this general shift, Doolittle was selected to fly one of the aircraft up to the new field, and on his way bad weather set in, he became lost and prepared to land on a German aerodrome. But luckily, they started firing at him which warned him of his mistake and he zoomed and escaped. While searching for a more friendly reception, Doolittle came upon a British airman who was guarding an Allied balloon and having a rough time with a couple of German Fokkers that were bent on torching the bag. In this scuffle, Ralph was shot in the calf, and on landing at a nearby field, he lost control and his machine turned over and the crash reopened the old face wounds.

Back he went to the hospital for several more weeks, and in time was relieved by the French to permit him to go home and become a civilian instructor at the Gerstner Field aviation school located at Lake Charles, Louisiana. Again, his luck ran out; he was killed in an accident there.

Christopher Ford, another New Yorker, was more fortunate, although he ended his war in a German prison camp after a very extensive period of air action. Actually, Chris was the thirty-eighth and last American to join the Lafayette Escadrille, but he began with plenty in his favor. In the first place he had learned to fly early in 1916 when he took some lessons on an old Wright Model-B pusher at the Stinson Flying School at San Antonio, Texas, for which he received an American aero certificate Number 462. Thus armed, Chris went to France to chase the von Richthofens out of the sky. However, this civilian brevet scarcely covered the requirements, so Chris had to go through the routine Penguin and Caudron instruction, taking in a little Sopwith two-seater, Spad, Nieuport, and other training whenever there was a mount available.

Amusingly, Ford's student course, one devised specially to rid him of his Wright-pusher technique, went awry. By some strange twist he missed the important acrobatics school, and was switched direct from Avord to G.D.E. without having attempted a spin of any kind. Somehow no one noticed this discrepancy until he arrived at Chaudun, presumably ready for active-service flying.

He could not have picked a worse time, for his arrival coincided with the period when the enemy, suspicious of French intentions in that area, moved in a number of first-class fighter squadrons to keep Allied airmen on the defensive. As a result, Chris learned all the acrobatics in the book, with enraged German airmen on his tail, to make sure he completed every one. Those who remember his first few patrols, still speak in awe of the amazing things he did with a Spad so as to get home for lunch or dinner. And to add to these freakish maneuvers, Chris had a fistful of lightning bolts, glaring with France's tricolors, painted on his fuselage and wings. When he started "stunting," these flaming decorations added some noteworthy effects to his hair-raising performances.

Ford's career was most colorful from start to finish. He served with the Lafayette from November 8, 1917, and stayed with the organization after it was absorbed into the American Air Service. He flew all through the Aisne, Champagne, Saint-Mihiel, and Argonne Forest engagements, and then on October 15, 1918, while leading an offensive patrol his engine was damaged by enemy machine-gun fire from the ground, and he had to make a dead-stick landing behind the German lines just south of Buzancy. He was taken prisoner but with the signing of the Armistice, he couldn't wait for a routine transfer and, with a number of other prisoners-of-war, started to walk a distance of one hundred kilometers to the frontier. Chris Ford reached Colmar just as the French were entering the town from the other side.

Chapter XII

IN FLANDERS FIELDS

In the middle of July 1917 the Lafayette Escadrille had to pull up stakes once more and move to Saint-Pol-sur-Mer, a narrow, bomb-battered field that was lapped on one side by the North Sea. Here they were to co-operate with British and Belgian squadrons during the proposed Flanders offensive.

This heroic folly, sometimes known as the Battle of Flanders, opened with a big-gun barrage around Ypres about July 31, that resulted in the greatest artillery battle ever recorded up to that time, for by now both sides were very strong in this department. The Germans concentrated on enfilade fire, while the British had no choice but to center their efforts on the hundreds of concrete pillboxes that the enemy had spotted all over the area. These clever redoubts were staffed by skilled machine gunners who were trained to ignore artillery fire, and to play alert roles from their shelters by halting any ground advances by British infantry.

The Allied tanks that had been moved up into this area were left immobile, since artillery shelling had destroyed the drainage ditches, and when water had spilled out to flood the low plains, the continued shelling churned up the ground until the whole area was a morass of impassable slop. Trenches were thigh-deep in water, dugouts were uninhabit-

able, the dead that had been tenderly interred after battles
fought months before, were washed out and sent wallowing
along these yellow-clay sluiceways.

Both sides fought with heroic frenzy and each assault and
defense offered a thousand incidents of unbelievable courage.
What the British had suffered in earlier battles was completely eclipsed by what they were called on to endure in
the Battle of Flanders. Every agony, every terror, every sacrifice met at Ypres, Arras, Hill 60, Messines, Loos, and
Poperinge was doubled and trebled; not one of war's abomina-
tions was missing.

In spite of careful checking of the weather in order to set
off the attack in good order, one that would allow the tanks
to perform their chief duty in overrunning the enemy's first
two lines, rain started almost as soon as the whistle was
blown. It scarcely ever stopped for more than four months,
and only for a few hours each day were the Flanders skies fit
to fly through. Night after night it torrented down and turned
the Belgian lowlands into one massive bog, little streams became raging torrents, brooks overflowed and ran wild over
large sections. Shellfire added to the quagmire by churning up
the ground and joining up old shellholes, creating a maze of
deep or shallow channels that trapped everything that tried to
negotiate the area. One division took eleven hours to move
three miles. Nevertheless, the Tommies stumbled on, fighting
exhaustion, and continued the attack. Men who were only
slightly wounded could not get to a medical station. Usually
they fell in some ditch or shellhole and were unable to save
themselves. Week after week, month after weary month, the
hapless British Army slogged through this Slough of Despond,
and captured ridge after ridge until at last the heights of
Passchendaele were stormed and taken. The Germans clung
to Staden and Westroosbeke, but the "victory" at least assured that the planned attack for the Channel ports was
never started.

All this reads like ancient history, but we who were in any
way associated with this dreadful campaign, cannot ever for-

get it. Those of us who had transferred from the ground forces and were now flying over these sodden battlefields, could appreciate fully what was taking place below, for we had seen and experienced ground action, had been through many bayonet charges, trench raids, and had huddled deep against the cruel thud of heavy artillery. But none of us had seen semi-amphibious warfare of this kind. None of us wanted to see the like again. We were glad to fly and fight in the clean, cool air, rather than wallow in the muck, blood, and torrent of Flanders fields.

Thrown into this wild cocking main, the Lafayette Escadrille encountered a new type of warfare. Now that they were a part of the forces responsible for northern Flanders, they were engaged with new types of enemy aircraft, and for the first time saw examples of naval aviation—flying boats and floatplanes used by both sides in antisubmarine work, or naval reconnaissance. They saw and had to be able to identify new British equipment, and learn to recognize the red, yellow, and black cocardes carried by Belgian squadrons. For the first time they encountered the famed Hanriot fighter that was flown by many of King Albert's gallant airmen. But more important than these surface changes, was the fact that they might have to stack up against the greatly augmented flying circus packs, headed by Baron Manfred von Richthofen. These *staffels*, manned by hand-picked airmen, roved up and down the British-Belgian front three times a day, and because of their numbers, their first-class equipment, and ability to maintain tight formations, could play havoc with any Allied flights that dared to intrude into their back areas.

It should be pointed out that this is about all the Flying Circus did. These gaudy aircraft had no other mission but to beat down enemy opposition and run up impressive scores. They took no part in artillery co-operation, tactical bombing, reconnaissance, or photography. They did no trench-strafing, nor protected their own attack planes. They stayed well inside their own lines, roved up and down in great packs and picked off smaller formations or stragglers from previous combats. They had their place in the scheme of things, but, as we know now, the German Flying Circus provided more scarehead publicity, than efficient or valuable air power.

For reasons that have not been fully explained, the Lafayette spent only a month on this Flanders front, but they did suffer some damage from night bombers. In all probability they were soon required back on the Verdun front when Pétain decided to make a countermove at his end of the line to increase the pressure against the Boche, while the British Fifth Army continued to slog through the mud of Flanders.

During their short stay up north the pilots of the Lafayette had an enjoyable time—on the ground. They flew three stiff patrols a day, but during their off periods they could bathe at the famed Belgian beaches, mingle with the airmen of British squadrons, and have a pleasant interchange of entertainment and dinners.

While they were in the Dunkirk area, the Escadrille was honored with its first citation, which read:

The General Commandant-in-Chief, cited to the Order of the Army, the Escadrille N. 124 [Escadrille Lafayette]:
An escadrille composed of volunteer Americans who have come to fight for France in the spirit of purest sacrifice. Under the command of Captain Thénault, who formed it [?], it has maintained without ceasing an ardent struggle against our enemies. In exceedingly difficult combats and at the price of severe losses, which far from discouraging it, have exalted its morale, has brought down twenty-eight officially confirmed planes of the enemy. It has excited the profound admiration of the officers who have it under their command, and of the French escadrilles who, fighting by its side, have striven to vie with it in valorous deeds.

PÉTAIN

On their way up for the short stay at Saint-Pol-sur-Mer, Harold Willis and Ted Parsons managed to frighten each other stiff as they searched for their new airdrome. Willis had drawn a map of the proposed route, but Parsons evaded the chore and decided to follow Harold. All would have gone well except that, as we explained in the James Doolittle episode, the weather turned foul and crossed up Ted. As long as the skies were clear, they stayed together, picking out Péronne, Arras, Bethune, and Albert, the last town being easy since it could be recognized by the famous statue of the Virgin Mary that had had its structural support damaged by German shellfire in the Battle of the Somme the summer before, and now hung precariously out over the street.

While shocked at this desecration, the townspeople found some faith in building up a legend. They said, "One day the Virgin Mary and her babe will fall. You'll see, on that day the war will end." Strangely enough, a few hours before noon of November 11, 1918, a wayward shell from a German gun smashed what was left of the statue's precarious support, and the religious figure crashed into the street.

Parsons and Willis were churning along, probably taking in the details of the historic town hall below when they suddenly bored into a light cloud bank. Willis swung over hard and snapped away in a tight turn. Not knowing what had caused this, Parsons instinctively followed, and as his Spad went up on one wing tip, he caught the picture of two ashen-gray faces peering at him over the edge of a wicker basket. Then the mist thickened and swallowed all further details.

What had happened, of course, was that Harold had spotted a British kite balloon and had banked away well in time, but Ted, who was having to figure things out from Harold's behavior, almost flew into the balloon cable. When they came out into the clear once more, both men were fingering great beads of sweat from their foreheads. "But I was three times greener than Willis," Parsons argued when they landed.

The Saint-Pol field, which should not be confused with the town of Saint-Pol west of Arras, was laid out on the coarse grass and sand dunes that ran down to the sea, thus being long, smooth, but very narrow. A high sea wall was in the process of erection to protect a landlocked harbor. Since the prevailing winds came in from the sea, they had to take off and land into them, using the narrow confines of the strip. On take-off they had to have enough climb to clear the sea wall. What bathing area was available was, of course, laced with barbed-wire entanglements to prevent enemy raiders from sneaking ashore to sack the all-important airfield.

Since there were many enemy airfields, Zeppelin bases, and naval establishments just across the line, it was deemed smart to turn the flat-winged Spads into low-level attack planes, by bolting on some bomb racks wherever possible and placing a release gear in the cockpit. Obviously, someone had heard that the British were putting 25-pound Cooper bombs on their Camels and Bristol Fighters, and came up with the query, "Why not on our Spads?"

It was a splendid idea, except that the Spad wasn't designed for any such tricks. It was supposed to be a low-lift, high-speed type, and had the glide-angle of a blacksmith's anvil. Trying to load down a Spad-7 with a tankful of fuel, and a few bombs designed to blow up enemy airdromes—and have it hop over that sea wall—was hardly in the Spad's Maintenance and Operations book.

Ted Parsons and Robert Rockwell were given the honor of flying the first such patrol. Rockwell's engine had a cracked cylinder, but no one considered that to be sufficient excuse to bow out, and by the time it was settled that this fighter-bomber show was to be carried out, both Ted and Doc felt that they'd seen the last of their war, and they mooned about the hangars and billets offering their personal goods and chattels to the highest bidder.

After this pointed display, Captain Thénault took another look at the general situation and agreed that it might be a good idea if they made a trial flight with full tanks and bombs to make certain they could clear the sea wall. If they could scramble over, Thénault suggested that they might try out the armament officer's rule-of-thumb calculations for hitting a target by aiming their bombs against a barrel floating out in the North Sea. The armament officer was the aforementioned Pole, Lieutenant Ciecomski, who had some difficulty in transferring his trajectory ideas to Ted and Doc, and by the time he was through both Americans felt they had been instructed with a foreign cookbook and an old-fashioned steelyard.

On the trial flight both Rockwell and Parsons just scraped over the sea wall and then flew around trying to recall what Ciecomski had told them about the laws of gravity, the trajectory of a Cooper bomb, and the effect of wind and wave. They had a certain amount of success in that their bombs did drop in the North Sea, but the barrel continued to float on undisturbed.

Eventually, the day came for them to hop off and deliver the goods, but fortunately the rains came, and they sat in the shelter of their hangar day after day, unable to see the sea wall. By that time the infantry had gone over the top, and all required objectives were taken without benefit of air power. Parsons and Rockwell spent the next few days buying back their personal knickknacks, and giving thanks for their reprieve.

Because of the dreadful weather, their loggy Spads, and the damned sea wall, the Lafayette did not get in too much front-line flying, although the ground forces were still banging away at the enemy and swelling the casualty lists. When the pilots did get into the air, the jerries apparently had decided it was too damp, so there was little to worry about except to find that ridiculous airfield when the show was over.

Although still uncomfortable with his rheumatism, Lufbery flushed out the Boche now and then and added two more enemy planes to his bag during his stay in Flanders. Lufbery had a special formation that he enjoyed leading, made up of Walter Lovell, Harold Willis, and Ted Parsons, and this foursome would take off whenever a rift appeared in the sky and work its way over the line, touring the enemy fields, daring anyone to come up and engage. When this treatment failed, they'd move in deeper and deeper nosing about simply to entice the Germans to waste antiaircraft ammunition on them. On several occasions Lufbery put on a "straggler" act that brought some reward, and at times started an action that usually gave one of the Lafayette boys a kill.

On these forays, when deep in enemy territory, and after some enemy shelling, Lufbery would stagger out of the formation indicating that he had been hit. He would waddle and flounder until he was some distance from his threesome. They, of course, knew of the deception and would stooge about until some brave jerry decided he had a nice slice of cold meat. Once he moved anywhere near the bait, all hell would break loose, and if Lufbery did not shoot the attacker to pieces, Parsons, Willis, or Lovell would make life unbearable for him.

On one such occasion Parsons had been assigned as top, or sky man, riding high over the threesome while Luf toured about the enemy back areas. This day their leader was particularly nettled by the lack of activity, and he appeared to be heading for Berlin to flush out some business. Finally, they came to a German airdrome, and after studying the situation for some time from a high level, it became evident that six or seven planes were being put through a tight-formation drill. Lufbery flew around looking for a splash of sunshine to use as cover and then took Willis and Lovell down into the party. The Germans were taken by surprise, being intent on their practice patterns, and, having the advantage of altitude and what little sun there was, the Americans scored heavily. Two enemy aircraft went down to crash, another stalled in with a dead prop, and still another checked out with a dangerous spin.

During this wild melee, Parsons maintained his security post above, at times watching the furor and anxious to get into the scrap. He became so interested in the aerial jousting below, he forgot what he was up there for until a swarm of buzzing machine-gun tracers zipped past his head. Apparently others could play the aerial "bait" game. While Lufbery's team had moved in on the formation-flying drill, another patrol had been sent off to move around wide, cut in and try to trap this impudent lot. When everything had been put together, the Lafayette boys found themselves trapped between two layers of jerry fighters.

Parsons was in trouble, but he also knew that he had to warn his comrades who were intent on mopping up the lower echelon. Ramming his throttle all the way up the gate, he went down like a rocket—with a Hun on his tail—and swept past Harold Willis, which was sufficient evidence that the first part of the game was over. Lufbery saw the warning too and reformed his men and started to move for home. Parsons continued on for a couple of thousand feet, hoping his Spad was tougher than the Albatros that was chasing him down.

"When I felt I had outrun him," Ted said on his return, "I muttered a prayer, yanked back on the stick, and . . . hoped. That poor old Spad groaned, the wires shrieked and every spar bent like an archer's bow. The agony nearly finished me, for a few seconds, but everything hung together somehow. I leveled off and looked back. That damned Hun was still after me but he didn't dare yank out as I had done. He had to ease out gradually and was several hundred meters below me before he could consider taking me on again. By that time I had all my courage back, and boldly turned to fire a few bursts in his general direction.

"Now that I was closer to friendly territory, I decided that I might really take him on, and we circled about cautiously for several minutes, and then both concluded we'd had enough, and on that note called it a day. I gave him a derisive farewell, and thank heavens I was belted in, for I nearly fell out of my cockpit when he returned my gesture with interest."

Some years later when penning his autobiography, Ted reflected, "I had read of aerial contestants exchanging personal courtesies in the air, but this was the first and only time I had ever encountered such goings-on. The fiction writers had us practically knowing each others' names and addresses, but how can you recognize anyone muffled in a great leather helmet, chin-piece, goggles, and a wad of winding scarf? You couldn't even see his nose."

The fictioneers also liked to work up a feud with Baron So-and-So who *always* flew the same airplane, the bright red, yellow, or green one with a Death's Head Hussar insignia daubed on the nose, ignoring the fact that it was virtually impossible to fly the same plane patrol after patrol, day after day. The Jolly Baron might use his favorite for an early morning show, but if he got a few slugs in a wing spar, he would scarcely be flying the same plane later in the afternoon, or even the next morning. Of course, to keep the plot together, it is quite possible that the Baron, Germany's leading killer, had half a dozen such red, yellow, or green triplanes at his disposal.

There are times when one wonders why Ted Parsons was ever allowed to return home, for he was always shattering the revered and hallowed clichés of wartime aviation. He was to destroy eight enemy planes, and probably a dozen more unconfirmed, since most of his fights took place deep in enemy territory, but he never acted the hero. He was more likely to wail that he was scared to death, and was the first to admit that he had made a mistake.

One of his best stories concerns his desire to visit England while the Lafayette was flying out of Saint-Pol-sur-Mer. It seemed a reasonable enough desire, but he decided not to mention it for fear the whole squadron would tag along. The fact that strict orders had been posted to the effect that no unauthorized flights were to be made across the Channel, meant nothing, of course. Those orders were for the French members of Spa.124, not for the Americans—after all, was not Britain a sister country to the United States? Hands-across-the-sea and blood ties, and all that?

What was not clearly explained in these orders was that it was a strict military rule that every aircraft crossing the Channel had to check in on the French or Belgian side before flying over. In that manner, the machine was registered and the British authorities would be advised of its departure and estimated time of arrival. This was a precaution against the enemy flying a captured Allied plane into a critical area and bombing the target, completely unmolested.

This ruling had escaped Ted; his idea was to change into a clean uniform, pull on a lightweight coverall, and nonchalantly take off for a routine engine or gunnery test. He felt that if he confided in anyone, he either would be persuaded to give up the idea as highly irregular, or his confidant would want to join the party. Too many pilots can spoil an AWOL foray.

So he took off with a full tank and started down the coast to gain a little elbow room. Once he was clear of his field, Ted turned and began to fly over the beautiful waters of the Channel. That must be Dover, just over there, and those were the famed white cliffs, beyond which ranged green fields and picture-book farms. He could almost smell the foam on the Kentish ale, picture the pubs, tea shops and quaint old English villages—and girls who spoke and understood English. No more of this "Mad'moiselle, Voolay . . . voo?" Ahead was a friendly shore, light laughter, and a language everyone understood.

Right in the middle of this pleasant reverie something hellish went *bang* alongside his wing tip. Then another just below, and one dead ahead. Ted knew all about bracketing fire and figured that the next would go *bang* right in his lap. The reception was very warm—and most accurate. He knew when he wasn't wanted, and he turned fast and beat it back to Dunkirk. The British didn't mind your coming to visit, but protocol had to be maintained. You checked in and advised, so to speak.

Ted's attempt to invade Britain raised quite a hurrah, and several inquiries were started. He had not been low enough or close enough to have his airplane identified, but it was pointed out that only a certain number of planes were aloft at the time, and Ted was really given a grilling until he almost admitted that it was he who had decided to improve British-American relations. He dug up his blandest expression, however, and denied that he had been anywhere near the British coastline. He had no reason to go over there, he had no relatives or even close friends in England. No, he hadn't even thought of crossing the English Channel.

The interviewing commandant did not believe a word of the explanation, but he couldn't break Ted down, and the matter was finally dropped after loud and long protestations of innocence. Ted got even with the British later that day when he sauntered into an R.N.A.S. squadron and suggested a game of poker, a pastime few Englishmen have ever mastered.

But the pleasures and military activities at Saint-Pol-sur-Mer were soon brought to a close. The weather in that section was the worst of the war, and it was decided that the men of the Lafayette were being wasted, sitting around hour after hour with nothing to do but bathe amid the barbed-wire entanglements, or play poker with their British pals. This latter sport had become a trifle one-sided, for after nearly four weeks in this waterlogged sector the American boys had most of the money available, and since there was little to spend it on, a deal was made with a British quartermaster whereby they were given the opportunity of buying fifty cases of British Army Scotch whiskey at some bargain figure.

Fifty cases of Scotch whiskey seemed like an unprecedented bonanza, and it would have been, had not some clod in Paris decided that this was the moment the Lafayette should be transferred back to the Verdun sector, to the flying field at Senard, to be exact. Now they faced the problem of transportation. Fifty cases of bottled liquor could not be stuffed in the cockpits of wartime Spads; at best each pilot might carry two bottles—but they had fifty cases to haul across Belgium and France!

Military regulations did not allow for the motor transport of Scotch whiskey; a small wine caisson perhaps, but not fifty cases of hard liquor. Anxiety, and in some cases mild terror, suggested some extreme arrangements, such as disposing of all spare parts, tools, and even squadron records. One distressed volunteer thought they might borrow a twin-engined Handley-Page bomber from the British and fly the load down, but no one could think of a reasonable address of approach— you know how bomber commanders are when they are busy cooking up a raid on some unimportant Zeppelin base.

Finally, someone had an inspiration. Whiskey was usually served with soda in the best service messes. Whiskey and soda had a familiar ring. Where did whiskey and soda fit in? With the two pet lions, of course, Whiskey and Soda. Those two spoiled brutes had been hauled all over the Western Front in their own special padded trailer. Who did they think they were? Those lion cubs were big enough to walk all the way to Senard, if necessary.

The cases of Scotch were loaded into the lion cubs' trailer, which was well padded and ran on pneumatic tires, and under the guidance of the most skilled driver in the squadron, with two heavily armed mechanics riding shotgun guard, the liquid sustenance eventually arrived on the Verdun front gurgling merrily. Poor Whiskey and Soda, perplexed by the switch in accommodations, made the trip on the front seats of two trucks, sitting between the drivers and helpers. The sight must have startled hundreds of troops as they passed. However, the docile pets soon learned to enjoy this new outlook on life, and, like their bottled namesake, arrived safely, marked RICHT SIDE UP—WITH CARE!

Shortly after arriving at Senard, Raoul Lufbery wrote to Paul Rockwell. The following is one of several such letters, all written in a neat precise hand on small pale blue cards that fitted into thin envelopes. It is interesting to note Luf's style when writing in English, as compared to his almost poetic touch when he wrote in French. His letter reads:

Sector 62

[not dated]

Dear Paul:

Day before yesterday I brought down my eleventh German machine which fell in fire right by the trenches nord est of Vanquois. Parsons got one the same day and nearly the same place. Lovell is also doing fine, and scored his second Boche official. As you see, we have much better luck here than we had at Dunkerque.

Now if you wish you might let Jacques Mortane publish my stories in the *Guerre Aerianne.*

I am afraid that another American has been brought down. Little Barclay [Leif Norman Barclay] of the Escadrille 65 failed to come back from patrol this morning and a machine has been seen falling in flames at the time he was on the lines.

All the boys here send you their best wishes. Give my best regards to Mrs. Rockwell.

I remain your old friend,

R. LUFBERY

It was from the Senard field that Douglas MacMonagle flew off on his tragic patrol, and where Courtney Campbell had his astounding mid-air contact with Lieutenant Maison-Rouge. There was a wealth of work at Senard, and at times the program was exhausting, for no sooner had they arrived and settled down than the weather changed. There were twenty-four successive days of golden sunshine, and the airmen piled up an unprecedented total of flying hours. Three patrols a day were regulation, and within a month the personnel was exhausted. Despite the Scotch medication, they had little sleep, for the enemy was aware of their return, and almost nightly sent over skulking bombers to keep matters lively. Two hangars were totally wrecked, and several Spads completely destroyed.

A new lilt had been added to their lives, however, when they discovered on their return to this Verdun front that American service troops, a couple of regiments of Engineers had been moved into the sector. The Lafayette finally had evidence that America was really in the war, and that her troops were to take an active part. What few Americans they had encountered prior to this were those who had apparently been shipped over to take part in the hilarious Battle of Paris.

During this tour of duty at Senard the Escadrille was called on to fly a fighter-escort patrol, covering a mass raid on Dun-sur-Meuse, a base some forty miles inside enemy territory. The bombers, Sopwith two-seaters that were modified for the mission, were old, slow, and not particularly adapted for the task, but the Spa.124 crew had to accept this duty. Harold Willis and Ted Parsons were assigned a top position on the left flank of the fighter formation, a spot that was to bring some action and grief.

Willis took off wearing a pair of green-striped pajamas, the ones he had on when he was aroused from his bunk for the escort flight. He had just pulled on some shoes, added an ancient pullover sweater and helmet, and had thus gone over lightly dressed, carrying no identification of any kind.

The raid bombers took off, and shortly after their escorting Spads followed and set out the attack formation. Despite every effort to keep this raid on the secret list, the Germans had a strong force of defensive Fokkers in the air to greet them. As the outer defense team, Willis and Parsons took the first sting of venom. Willis, who was flying a hundred feet higher than Parsons, soon flushed a couple off Ted's tail, but then came under attack himself with no one above to give him any relief. Two heavy bursts knocked out his engine and holed his fuel tank, another nipped off his goggles just as he started to spin down with a dead prop. Amid the gunfire going on all around, it was impossible to follow him down to find out what his fate was to be. All they knew was that Harold Willis had gone down in Germany, wearing only his pajamas and a woolen sweater. He didn't have his wallet, money, or a pack of cigarettes; whereas there were many airmen who never crossed the line without carrying a small toilet case. Willis had made his long flight into enemy terri-

tory sartorially correct for a pajama party, but hardly outfitted for an informal call on the Germans.

Ted Parsons was desolate when he realized what had
happened, but he used his head and, in the best way available, made immediate plans for discovering how Harold had
fared. He wrote a message of inquiry, stuffed it into a cardboard container, and dropped it into the German lines with a
small silken parachute. Two days later an artillery outfit
closer to the line picked up an answer. Harold was alive, a
prisoner, and in good health.

Much relieved, Ted made up a bundle of Harold's uniform, boots, a few decks of cigarettes, and what money he
could scrounge, and went over the line again with a neat
package addressed to Lieutenant Harold Willis, POW. Actually, Harold was only a sergeant, but everyone knew the
routine of a prison camp. Commissioned officers did not have
to do manual labor, but noncommissioned men usually
wound up slaving in the salt mines, or working on the German railroads, hauling ties or lengths of track.

Parsons knew that Harold would be wise enough to state
that he was an officer, and who could argue with him, since
he landed without any identification. When Parsons' package
turned up, bearing the all-important rank of lieutenant, Willis was in. His experiences as a prisoner of war, and his several
attempts to escape will be related later.

Courtney Campbell broke into the limelight once more or
the same day that Harold Willis was taken prisoner. This was
his third narrow squeak, and turned out to be his last, for he
was killed in action a short time later.

With some sixty planes in the air to be accommodated or
the landing space in the Senard area, a rule had to be se
up, since the field was long and very narrow, that all aircraf
on landing were to taxi to the very end of the strip befor
turning off toward the hangars. All pilots were told of thi
rule before they took off, and all who returned, obeyed th
edict—except Courtney Campbell. Campbell belted throug

the full pack of fighters and bombers, and made one of his precision landings and wound up exactly opposite his own hangar. Without bothering to continue on, and then turn to run up the aprons of the hangars, he thoughtlessly turned for his shelter. As was to be expected, a Sopwith that had been maneuvering for a spot to land, was just touching down when Campbell cut across the bomber. There was no space or speed to take off again, and the Sopwith piled into the Spad, its propeller eating up the top wing until it came to a halt a few inches from Courtney's head. It then plowed on, rolled the Spad over several times, and churned it into rags and matchwood.

The American volunteer should have been hacked to mincemeat, but still bearing a charmed life, Courtney stepped out of the wreckage without a scratch. He viewed the tangle, selected a cigarette, and sauntered calmly toward his hangar trying to think of an excuse. It must have been good, for he quickly talked himself out of the disobedience and went on to other things.

On October 3, 1917, Raoul Lufbery wrote the following letter in English to Paul Rockwell, who was still working in Paris:

Sector 181

Dear Paul:

Many thanks for your letter and post card. I was very pleased to hear from you.

Here we have changed sectors again. If we keep that up much longer we soon will know every corner of this front.

A few days ago I brought another boche down, this brings my score up to twelve official.

Two more of our pilots have been brought down. MacMonagle and Campbell. The first one fell in our lines and was buried at Triancourt, a little village not far from the Lafayette aviation field. As for Campbell, a French pilote saw him fall in the other side but could not tell if there had been a fight.

Sincerely yours,

R. LUFBERY

THE BATTLE OF PARIS

As I sit on my bunk, arranging my junk,
With thoughts of old Paris in mind,
With vivid reflections and fond recollections
Of the milestones that now lie behind;
Still fresh in my ears are the words of those dears
Who openly, mockingly, dared us
To forget home and friends till this awful war ends,
And take part in the Battle of Paris.

They are strikingly neat from their heads to their feet,
And have eyes like the stars in the skies;
And fresh ruby lips like rose petal tips,
That make your battle blood rise.
Now these camouflaged birds sap the strength from the words;
We are told by the Chaplain to scare us,
So with a vigorous hop we go over the top
To that terrible Battle of Paris.

Now up on the line where the big guns whine,
And the seventy-fives are a'smoking,
The hell in the air fills your heart with despair,
And the gas fills your lungs till you're choking.
But say! On the square! I'd rather be there—
On the Marne or the Somme or at Arras,
For a *vin blanc* snoot full, it's hard to be neutral
In that famous Battle of Paris.

by Hugh Gordon "Scotty" Campbell
Lafayette Flying Corps.

Chapter XIII

PILOTS WITHOUT HONOR

Late in September 1917 activity at Senard came to a halt, and new orders sent the Lafayette back to the old stamping ground at Chaudun from where they had flown through June and July that year. They now were getting a few new Spad-13s, an improved model of this French fighter. It was at Chaudun, too, that Christopher Ford, the thirty-eighth and last American to become a member of the Lafayette Escadrille, joined them before the unit was transferred to the United States Aviation Service.

The flying activity went on apace with all kinds of new hazards, and it was well they had an up-to-date fighter to deal with the wild situations that GHQ in Paris thought up.

In the meantime some mild interest was noted concerning an earlier suggestion that the Americans serving in French squadrons be transferred to the American aviation service. Billy Mitchell had made some such move, and Dr. Gros was prodding U. S. Army men in Paris to speed matters. Although the doctor's interest in this proposed transfer had not been wholehearted, he willingly did his best to bring the situation to a head when some of his protégés explained that they might be of value to the newcomers, or that they yearned to serve under their own flag now their country was in the war. He never lost his love for the original American volunteer idea, however, and long after the Lafayette Escadrille had been taken into the American force, he continued to work just as hard for the Lafayette Flying Corps.

The American intent to take a broad and active part in the war ran into several immediate snags, and produced a pathetic picture of official ineptness. Colonel Billy Mitchell, who was in France, sought authority from the War Department to establish an air headquarters for the American military mission, as a base from which to work. Washington ignored all communications for weeks, and, not to be frustrated in that manner, Mitchell dug down into his own pocket and rented a suite of offices where he presumed to handle everything concerning military aviation. Patriotic Americans who were residents of Paris, contributed more funds to this project and Mitchell's "unofficial" office was soon a whirlwind of activity, preparing for America's promised entry into the air war.

In order to expedite matters, Mitchell next conspired with the French Minister of War to have him draw up a formal communication that "suggested" the size of air force the United States should furnish to "obtain and keep control of the air." This historic memorandum called for 5000 airplanes, out of a total of 20,000 machines, to be on the line by May 1, 1918. These aircraft were to be serviced by 38,000 mechanics, and in addition there was to be a heavy monthly output of aviation engines.

When this communication was received in Washington few people had any idea that the scheme had been devised by Billy Mitchell, and it was accepted in good faith; in fact, it became the basic objective of America's aeronautical program. The whole country was caught up in the enthusiasm of the project, and for weeks many believed that this unprecedented plan was actually under way.

Mitchell next tried to induce the War Department to undertake the manufacture of several of the best Allied aircraft engines, but he was rebuffed openly. The wonder-of-wonder power plant, already heralded as the Liberty engine, was to be America's great contribution to the Allied cause. Why build Rolls-Royce, Sunbeam, Hispano-Suiza, Bentley, Salmson, or Le Rhone engines when this miracle motor was already in the blueprint stage?

Ten weeks after America's declaration of war, General John J. Pershing arrived in Paris with a small staff of officers. H was followed some time later by Major T. F. Dodd, an airman of some experience. Mitchell quickly laid his plans and general reports before Dodd who in turn explained them to General Pershing between banquets, wreath-laying, and visits to Napoleon's tomb. As a result, Mitchell was eventually appointed to serve as aviation officer at Pershing's headquarters, and along with several other officers, was ordered to formulate a complete aviation program for the A.E.F.

At least this was Pershing's hope, but while his aviation board toiled unswervingly, their efforts were completely ignored in Washington, and a new air mission was sent to Europe; one that selected training centers in France and launched several important projects without consulting the Commander-in-Chief, who, in many instances, first learned of these War Department activities from French authorities. Nevertheless, high officials and headline writers of the American press were telling the world that America would soon win the war with an air force that would blacken the skies of Germany with thousands of planes.

Amid all this turmoil and confusion, no one seemed particularly interested in taking over the Lafayette Escadrille, and it is interesting to study some of the ramifications concerning the American volunteers at the time. Major William W. Hoffman, an officer who had been assigned to the U. S. Aviation Service Headquarters, then located at Chaumont, was a member of one mission that was directed to look into the possibility of taking over the Lafayette pilots. In a recent letter to the writer, Hoffman explained some of the routine and the eventual outcome.

I was in England in 1917 representing the Rockefeller Foundation, and in April of that year when we entered the war, I was given permission to train with the Royal Field Artillery. When General Pershing and the U. S. 1st Division arrived in France, I went to Paris and was commissioned a captain in the U. S. Field Artillery, and assigned to the Aviation Service. When our headquarters opened at Chaumont I was ordered there and served on the staff of Brigadier General William L. Kenly, Chief of our Air Force, and was directly under Colonel William Mitchell and Colonel Marlborough Churchill.

We were anxious to organize American squadrons as early as possible and this involved equipment and personnel.

As to the equipment, Lieutenant Colonel Raynal C. Bolling at Air Force headquarters in Paris had arranged with the French to supply us with Spads as soon as our squadrons could be organized and trained for the front. As to personnel, a Colonel Armengaud, a French staff officer assigned to us as liaison officer, arranged with the French General Staff to release all Americans who were then in the French Air Force and who desired to transfer to the American Aviation Service. General Pershing issued the necessary orders to accomplish this transfer.

I, together with two Regular Army officers, one from the Medical Corps and one from the Aviation Service, received orders from General Pershing to proceed from Nancy to Dunkirk, and visit all French squadrons where Americans were attached; to interview these men, and if desirous of transfer, to report on their records, their capacity, physical fitness, and recommend appropriate ranks. Our orders were issued in October and we started from Chaumont with Bar le Duc as our first stop.

In the fading day we drove to Bar le Duc and it looked like a deserted city. We drove into the courtyard of the hotel and a person appeared from the cellar and said there was an air raid warning, and added that if we wanted dinner to help ourselves in the kitchen. After a hurried and sketchy meal, we went to the cellar where old and young were gathered. Soon the raid started with Gothas and their bombs concentrating on the post office where all communication was centered. It was destroyed along with other buildings, but the hotel was not hit.

The next day we visited the Lafayette Escadrille. What a thrill it was to meet these early American combat fliers. All wished to transfer to what, at that time, seemed like an American combat air force soon to be in operation.

I remember well Bill Thaw who had, I believe, already brought down officially five Huns.[1] He was a natural for a squadron com

[1] An error. Thaw did not get his last three Huns until between March and May of 1918.

mander. For this he had to have suitable rank, and was recommended accordingly in our report.

In that fine outfit there were many qualified for flight commanders, and we recommended them for such rank. Lufbery was a pilot with the French, but I do not remember him at that time.[2]

We proceeded along the whole front, interviewing all Americans in French squadrons; I would say about one hundred in addition to those in the Lafayette Escadrille. Based on our report and recommendations, these Americans were discharged from the French Army and were commissioned in the American Army, but not with the rank we had recommended.

At exactly this critical time, General Benjamin D. Foulois was ordered to the A.E.F. by General Tasker H. Bliss, the then Chief of Staff in Washington, to become Chief of the Air Force—A.E.F. It was done without consulting General Pershing.

With this new Air Force—A.E.F. commander and his staff of thirty officers, nearly all infantry, who came with him, everything was to be changed. General Kenly had to return to Washington, and with him went other highly qualified officers. Our recommendations on ranks for the Americans to be transferred were automatically reduced one grade by General Benjamin D. Foulois. Colonel Bolling's arrangement for Spads was cancelled.

Colonel Bolling, in complete disgust, asked to be transferred to a French squadron on the front, and while motoring north, made a mistake in the route to be taken, and was killed by a German patrol when he drove into enemy territory.

As to the gallant members of the Lafayette, they had applied for discharge, which was accepted, in full belief that they would be awarded higher rank and better opportunity for service.

There was nothing they could do about it, and morale was badly hurt. This, of course, also applied to Americans in other French squadrons.

Up to this time all was running smoothly with the prospect of getting American squadrons on the front at an early date. As a result of the changes, we were set back six months.

In May 1918 I was ordered to report to General Kenly in Wash-

Raoul Lufbery, of course, was a naturalized American with the Lafayette Escadrille.

ington and was a passenger aboard the U.S.S. *Lincoln* which was torpedoed, and I lost all my papers. General Pershing's orders and Colonel Bolling's contracts are all of record.

This is obviously a sincere report on the activity of one mission that tried to smooth the path of the American volunteers, and fit them into the planning for a United States Aviation Service. At least Major Hoffman has provided us with the viewpoint of the visiting mission.

It should be added here that the recommendations of this General Kenly board were downgraded when, by mistake, one man was listed for a United States commission, although he had not as yet flown on active-service operations. He had completed his training and had compiled an excellent record. A short time later his French commander sent to the U. S. Aviation Service an unfavorable report of this man's conduct in the face of the enemy, suggesting that if he had already been commissioned, his commission be revoked. On this unfortunate incident, the whole report of the board was questioned, and the French commanders of squadrons at the front were asked to send in new reports. This created a serious and unnecessary delay, but in all cases, except the one mentioned above, the new reports were found to correspond with the original board's recommendations.

On December 14, 1917, Dr. Gros wrote to all members of the Corps as follows:

Knowing how impatiently you must be awaiting the time of your release, I want to tell you that everything is being done to shorten the delay, which is entirely due to the slowness in the ministerial *bureaux*. Your papers are now going through the *Bureau* of the Minister of War, and we expect that in a few days your official release will be granted. At that time you will be notified and asked to come to take the oath as an officer of the American Expeditionary Forces. I want you to know that the delay in your transfer is entirely beyond my control, and that I am doing everything in the world to hasten these steps.

The reports of the volunteers themselves also make interesting reading. For instance, Ted Parsons, who never did get into the new American service, provides us with a hilarious version of the situation as viewed from the other end of the telescope:

Just when we were on the point of despairing of ever hearing from the American brass hats, the American Army finally sent out another delegation of top-rankers in October to make an examination of the Lafayette Escadrille pilots.

After comprehensive physical examinations, which, much to the dismay of some of the boys, included urinalysis and blood tests, we were put through a long series of rather ridiculous physical demonstrations which weren't helped by frequent visits to the bar to bolster up our courage.

Then the awful truth came out!

In solemn, owlish conclave the board decided that not one of us, despite hundreds of hours in the air, most of us aces, all thoroughly trained war pilots with many victories to our credit, could ever be an aviator. Their tests showed definitely that physically, mentally, and morally we were unfit to be pilots. It was truly pathetic.

Dud Hill had one blind eye. Bill Thaw's vision was hopeless, and he had a crippled arm. Raoul Lufbery couldn't walk a crack backwards. Dolan's tonsils were past all redemption. Hank Jones had flat feet! All this was revealed in the light of pitiless publicity. We were simply a broken-down crew of crippled misfits. There was hardly a man on whom they didn't have to ask waivers.

However, while we were waiting to hear the outcome of these tragic results, and while Paris was filled with American aviators and Y.M.C.A. men—with the bars, theaters, and night spots doing a capacity business—the Escadrille continued to carry on with the war.

It was still the only American outfit on active service at the front, but of course not allowed to wear the uniform of its own country. At the same time the Lafayette was again cited by the appreciative French, which allowed us, as members of a twice-cited organization, to wear the *fourragère* in the colors of the Croix de Querre. It was the second escadrille in the French Army to be so honored, the only one preceding being Escadrille Spa. 3, the Storks, commanded by the famous and beloved ace, Captain Georges Guynemer.

A more formal confirmation of this will be found in a telegram sent by General Pershing on November 5, 1917, recommending for commissions the first men to be transferred from the Lafayette Flying Corps. It read as follows:

No. 272. S.
Agwar - Washington

Par. 14. Recommend following American citizens with Lafayette Flying Corps of French Army be commissioned in Aviation Reserve as follows: As Majors, John F. Huffer and Gervais Raoul Lufbery, 32 years of age, recommend waiver. As Captains, Charles J. Biddle, Phelps Collins, Kenneth P. Littauer, David McK. Peterson, Robert Soubiran whose age is 31, recommend waiver. Robert L. Rockwell and Kenneth Marr whose age is 32, recommend waiver. As First Lieutenants, Paul F. Baer, Willis B. Haviland, Charles M. Jones, Granville A. Pollock, Leland L. Rounds, Joseph C. Stehlin, George E. Turnure, Jr., Frank W. Wells, Charles H. Wilcox and Charles C. Johnson. Also recommend William Thaw as Major, waiving defective vision left eye, 20/80 opthalmoscopic left shows atrophy plus pigmentation in focal area, hearing defective 15/20 and recurrent knee injury with limitation of motion, 3 years experience at the Front with French Army: Walter Lovell, age 33, as Captain, very slight defect in hearing, definitely color blind, got his brevet one year ago and has been flying seven months at the Front after completion of course at Pau. In view of his experience waiver is recommended so that his services may be utilized in instruction. Dudley L. Hill as Captain, vision right eye limited to finger perception on account of three years flying with French Army it is thought he would make a useful officer in spite of marked vision defect. Charles H. Dolan, Jr., as First Lieutenant, vision both eyes corrected to 20-30 myopia, on account of experience of 1. months flying in French Army waiver of defect is recommended
—Pershing

This unpleasant situation has been glossed over in several books about the Lafayette Flying Corps. It is also difficult to judge whether most of the American volunteers actually wished to transfer to their own colors. As the war groaned on it was obvious that much of the boasting back home, was just that, and many Americans with Allied squadrons came to the conclusion that as long as they had to fight in the war, they were better off with an organization that was armed, geared, and fitted for fighting in the sky. While a few men may have realized that such a transfer might bring a respite from the daily grind, they also knew that once the American squadrons were properly organized, they probably would go all-out to prove themselves. This was quite understandable from novices and newcomers full of beef and beans, but with a certain number of inexperienced airmen in every flight or squadron—no matter how experienced the ex-volunteers—the prospects were not too rosy.

Once the Americans had been finally—and grudgingly—accepted for service in U.S. aero squadrons, another situation arose. They had applied for and received French Army discharges, documents that were signed about December 1, 1917, but since no American commissions or official acceptances had been received in turn, the volunteers continued to fly as civilians attached to the French Army. This ridiculous position continued until February 18, 1918. At the same time five more American volunteers, who had flown with French squadrons, arrived at the Lafayette field for transfer to American squadrons. They were Phelps Collins, Paul Baer, Charles Biddle, George Turnure, and Charles Wilcox. The point arises; were they to be considered members of the Lafayette Escadrille, or had the Escadrille been written out of existence? Who knows, since it was asserted later that the Lafayette Escadrille ceased to be a French unit on February 18, 1918, and became the 103rd Pursuit Squadron of the American Air Service, the first American pursuit squadron on the front in World War I. They were allowed to keep their battle-scarred Spads and the Indian-head insignia, but unsentimental brass hats refused to have Whiskey and Soda on the squadron roster. The lion cubs were hauled off to a Paris zoo, while the men of the Lafayette unashamedly flicked the corners of their eyes.

Ted Parsons, who had been granted a short leave to the United States, missed all this, but when he returned and learned what had happened, he decided to stay with the French and was assigned to Spa.3, the Storks squadron.

When the commissions did arrive only Lufbery and Thaw were given the rank of major. A few were made captains, but most of them wound up as first or second lieutenants. There was dissatisfaction, argument, and heated debate in both the Lafayette Escadrille and the Lafayette Flying Corps, for these experienced airmen with splendid records were all shunted about and had little or nothing to fly. While they were thus inactive they came under the temporary command discipline of the ninety-day wonders of that day who treated them as the rawest recruits. This was their reward for experience and heroism.

When all papers had been signed, and the transfer made, the pilots of the Lafayette Escadrille found themselves disposed in the following manner:

Name	French Rank	Assigned	U. S. Rank
William Thaw	Lieutenant	103rd Aero Sqdn.	Major
Raoul Lufbery	Sous-Lieut.	94th Aero Sqdn.	Major
Clyde Balsley	Sergeant	U. S. Pursuit Div.	Captain
Charles C. Johnson	Adjutant	Instructor	Captain
Dudley L. Hill	Adjutant	103rd Aero Sqdn.	Captain
Robert L. Rockwell	Adjutant	103rd Aero Sqdn.	Captain
Robert Soubiran	Adjutant	103rd Aero Sqdn.	Captain
Willis B. Haviland	Adjutant	U. S. Naval Aviation	Lieutenant
Walter Lovell	Adjutant	U. S. Air Hdqtrs.	Captain
Kenneth Marr	Sergeant	103rd Aero Sqdn.	Captain
William E. Dugan	Sergeant	103rd Aero Sqdn.	Lieutenant
Ray C. Bridgman	Sergeant	103rd Aero Sqdn.	Captain
Charles H. Dolan	Sergeant	103rd Aero Sqdn.	Lieutenant
Henry S. Jones	Sergeant	103rd Aero Sqdn.	Lieutenant
David M. Peterson	Sergeant	103rd Aero Sqdn.	Captain
James N. Hall	Sergeant	103rd Aero Sqdn.	Captain
Christopher W. Ford	Sergeant	103rd Aero Sqdn.	Lieutenant

Didier Masson remained with the French Army, retaining his rank of adjutant, and served out his time as an instructor at Issoudun.

Elliott Cowdin was released from French military service in January 1917, but later joined the U. S. Air Service and was commissioned a major and attached to the Board of Aircraft Production.

Frederick C. Prince, Jr., ended his tour of flying duty as a ferry pilot, after which he transferred to the U. S. Army and served out the war in the Quartermaster Corps.

Edwin C. Parsons, a sous-lieutenant, was on leave in American when the Lafayette Escadrille was finally taken over by the U. S. Aviation Service, and on his return he elected to stay with the French and served out the war with Spa.3.

When the time came for the actual change-over, there probably were many pangs and periods of uncertainty. To most men it was quite a wrench, for the transfer meant a new mode of life, new standards to comply with, and a code of discipline that was alien to them. With the French they had been treated as highly respected volunteers and, regardless of noncommissioned ranks, had been welcomed in all military centers as trusted companions. Their rank had nothing to do with their social status. In the new American Army they soon discovered that class consciousness was rampant, and that there were distinct levels for all ranks—a military climate they had not known before.

They also discovered that there was one—and only one—uniform. "If it ain't GI, it'll never get by!" As explained before, they previously had been permitted to express themselves, or pay homage to their previous regiments, by having their equipment and outfits based on French infantry, cavalry, or artillery uniforms, and as a result had some personal pride in their appearance and retained their individuality.

Once they were taken over by the U. S. Army, they soon realized that the accepted uniform was totally unsuited for front-line operations. The tunic, called a blouse, came with a high stiff collar, under which was worn a white starched linen lining. This fancy dress indignity was reminiscent of the braid piping worn by austere bankers and businessmen back home. The hat was stiff, heavy, and fitted with a brown leather visor that had to be polished to match the parade-ground boots. Smart breeches were unknown, and the lower legs were encased in shapeless leather leggings, or field boots of questionable design and leathers. There were no short field jackets, such as the famed British warm, or the French service cape, and the Army overcoat was so long and bulky it was more suitable as a blanket for a horse than an active-service soldier. But more unbelievable, many of the American new-comers actually wore what campaign ribbons had been issued, on these greatcoats, and later on decorated the sleeves with gold chevrons that indicated each six months' service overseas.

The Lafayette men soon discovered that the high collar blouse caused painful abrasions and rubbed their necks raw after one short patrol over the lines, since it afforded no free-dom to swivel the head in order to watch for enemy aircraft. When they attempted to discard these "strait-jackets" for clothing more suitable for war flying, the non-flying disci-plinarians read out the Articles of War, and often imposed stiff penalties.

The airmen revolted eventually, and selected more suitable clothing, despite military restrictions. Many of them resur-rected their old college jerseys and football turtle-neck sweat-ers, and the more daring who had served or trained with the British squadrons evolved an open-type blouse or tunic, while those who had flown with the French dug out their poilu jackets, and by stitching on U.S.A. insignia and U. S. Army wings contrived to evade the uniform restrictions of non-flying brass hats. The flamboyant Billy Mitchell, who had adopted British breeches and open-necked tunics, did much to relieve the American "tight-collar" situation.

But there was more to the transfer than the matter of clothing. Their former liberties were shackled in so many ways. In the Lafayette Escadrille they had lived fairly well on the funds provided by the American Volunteers Committee, and over the months had learned how to live, play, and purchase simple recreations at cost levels enjoyed by the French and British. Americans with their high standards of living, even on active service, and their more generous pay soon undermined the military-social economy. Although their new commissioned ranks resulted in higher pay, as is usually the case, the extra money seemed to go nowhere when they mixed with the big spenders of the new A.E.F. As French soldiers they had been able to buy good wine, champagne, and cognac at reasonable prices. Food in restaurants was cheap, and when they went on leave in Paris they paid the same prices as did the men of the French forces. But once the Americans arrived with their fat wallets and brash behavior, the prices shot sky-high, and French and British troops were soon relegated to the third-class hotels, restaurants, and theaters.

The men of the Lafayette Flying Corps resented all this, but they were so few and had little influence. When they complained, or pointed out the ridiculous, or unfair situation, they usually got such answers as, "Aw forget your frog ways. You're an American again!" Or they might be reminded, "We didn't wanner come over here and fight their gardam war, but we got sucked into it. So, now we're here, why don't we enjoy it?"

The change-over also brought a loss in personal prestige. As volunteer Americans wearing the uniform of the French Aviation, they were a group of men apart. In all modesty, they had enjoyed the adulation they had received from both the French and British. Lafayette volunteers were standouts wherever they went, first because of their colorful uniforms, and because they spoke English among themselves. A few of them had picked up enough French to mingle freely with their Gallic compatriots, but when they spoke English in hotels, theaters, restaurants, or on their airfields, they were spotted immediately as fighters of a different breed. They were heroes to everyone simply because of their status as foreign volunteers.

By the time they had signed in with their own compatriots, much of the early bloom had been brushed off the Americans in Paris, and the ex-Lafayette men soon discovered that they were just additional members of a force that so far had done very little fighting, but already a lot of talking. Although they still wore their French aviation insignia and the Lafayette Escadrille crest, they were now in American khaki, and their previous service was quickly forgotten, and in many instances their foreign insignia and ribbons were looked upon as the marks of the "sucker," men who had willingly gone to fight someone else's war months before they needed to.

"You mean to say you came over here in 1915 . . . and you fought with the frogs with a rifle and bayonet for French Army pay? You sure lost most of your marbles, pal. I got my bellyful of war already. I can't wait to get home and get a real home-cooked meal again."

The Lafayette men were weeks breaking in to the new rules, regulations, standards, and viewpoints. They felt like aliens amid this new high-pitched social order. They had no idea what their companions were talking about. They hadn't been home in months, and on reading the newspapers from America, publications that flowed in like a torrent of printed pulp, were amazed at the war news as it was being presented to the American public. Upon some reflection, however, they conceded that it was natural that the news should be slanted to the American effort, since the American public was paying the bill. It was understandable, but somewhat strange to the newcomers.

The frenzy and high-speed impact of everything left them bewildered. Big business methods had taken over, and the least important matter was usually handled through a frantic system of indents, channels, authorizations, and dogmatic formality that made little sense. The routine involved in obtaining a simple hold-down bolt was far more complex than the request for a complete Spad in the French Aviation. They soon realized why America had been so long in setting up a visible air arm.

Almost without exception, the pilots of the Lafayette Escadrille were disgusted and indignant. Instead of being allowed to continue to fly as a unit, as they had hoped and requested, the squadron was broken up, and only a few of the original members remained together until the end of the war. Some were shunted off to Paris where they languished and waited for months to get back into a cockpit again.

Raoul Lufbery's experience was especially tragic. One wonders whether he really wanted to make the change. It will be noted that he did not apply for a transfer when Major Hoffman's party appeared at the squadron with its application forms and medical examination routine. Whether he was available at the time, or whether he avoided the issue is not clear, but there are several reasons to believe he dreaded to make the change. Ethnologically, he was more French than American, since he had not put foot in the United States until he was a grown man. He had spent only a short time there and could have absorbed little of the American spirit or American customs. He had no American school background, and English was his second language. As noted in his letters, when he wrote in French, which was later translated into English, his words and phrases were almost poetic. Whether his compositions were improved in translation by Paul Rockwell is a moot question, but the Lafayette's official historian claims that Raoul was a perfect conversationalist, a lover of the pastoral scene, and that when he wrote in French was especially lucid and expressive. Those who remember him during the early days of the Escadrille Américaine insist that Raoul was far more comfortable when he was speaking French.

Rockwell says, "I do not believe it worried Lufbery at all to mingle with young Americans of a more fortunate and cultured class. That strange term, 'inferiority complex,' had not been coined, and I am sure Luf did not feel inferior to any of his comrades or to anyone else. He recognized the fact that some people have more advantages, more background, more education than others, and he was neither bitter nor envious about it. He knew his own values, he knew he was 'tops' in various activities and that no one had more skill, courage, spirit, determination than he possessed. I am sure he was not happy as a major in the U. S. Air Service, or in the company of those rank-heavy tyros who knew nothing about aerial warfare. He should have remained with the French, but he was talked and tempted into the transfer. After all, the pay was much higher, and the prospects of achievement greater. He thought he was getting into a great and budding air corps on the ground floor. Sad disillusionment awaited him.

"Lufbery expressed himself beautifully in French, but poorly in English. I persuaded him to write some of his experiences: he did it in French which I translated for him. I think his sketches were published in the Chicago *Daily News*—in English—and in *La Guerre Aerienne* in French. Some of his writing was most poetic for Luf appreciated a beautiful landscape, and he was a great lover of nature. His greatest joy was to wander alone in the forests and fields around Luxeuil, gathering huge baskets of mushrooms for the *popote*, observing birds and small animals.

"Lufbery was a solitary soul. Had he lived I think he would have made his mark in civilian life; I doubt if he would have remained in a United States uniform. He might have become a good test pilot. He never would have become a 'bum' or in any way a disgrace to the Escadrille of which he was the greatest ace. Of that, I am positive, and I have been told that I am a good judge of my fellow man. Luf was human and had his faults, but he was a fine man and a great flier. I would have trusted him anywhere with anything, including my life."

As Paul explains, there were phases of the higher social life that left him, to say the least, uncomfortable. Whenever he was shipped off to Nice to recuperate from the pain of his periodic rheumatism, he found he was unaccustomed to the pattern of life in a swank Mediterranean hotel, or as a guest at any of the palatial rest homes that were made available to convalescent servicemen. It was because of this that Lufbery often returned before his leave period was over.

When it is stated that Raoul Lufbery was first assigned to the 94th Pursuit Squadron and given a major's commission, it should not be assumed that there was any such squadron for him to command. The 94th Pursuit was chiefly on paper, and as a result Lufbery was sent first to the Instruction Center at Issoudun where he was given an office, a swank desk, some pencils, and told to sit there and allow the non-flying specialists to organize the Aviation Service. Luf knew nothing about paper work, even when there was any. He cared less about the forms, figures, and routine organization a squadron commander was supposed to carry out. But even worse, it was insisted that he wear a complete American uniform, that made him appear and feel like a dressed-up tailor's dummy. All the old free-and-easy glamour of the front-line airman was stripped from him, and it is simple to realize how unhappy he must have been.

Luf knew that he was not earning this new money, a sense most hard-working people experience whenever their fortunes change. He realized that in this silent office he was of no use to anyone, and he resented this kiwi status. He knew, instinctively, that his value was as a combat leader, not an administrative officer. He yearned to be back with a fighting organization.

It must have been a heartbreaking interlude. No one near him spoke his language, nor could understand his impatience. A few may have felt some compassion, and presumed that since this moody man had seen many months of active-service flying, he might relish a rest, a change, and the opportunity to become acquainted with his new associates and surroundings.

But front-line flying men know the dangers of these periodic let-downs, particularly if the rests become too prolonged, or worse still if they do not provide a complete change from the daily war routine. Short breaks from daily patrols that afford complete changes of program are ideal and most valuable. Periods of leave in gay cities, pleasant country homes with good companionship, chances to look on or enjoy contrasting scenes are Mother and Medicine to the war-weary flying man. The British allowed their aviators fourteen days every three months of active-service flying, and such leaves in London, Edinburgh, the Lake District, along the Cornwall shores, or the quiet heather-strewn hills of Scotland were more likely to revive the spirit and nervous system than all the artificial hilarity of the war capitals.

Although the accepted picture is that of wild-eyed air heroes raging and roaring through the bars and hotels of big cities, presumably forgetting what they had left behind them, the situation was more often that of unhurried rambles through country lanes, a change of clothing, quiet nights of pleasant companionship, discussion, and plenty of much-needed sleep. Airmen who pursued these furlough ministrations generally returned with new enthusiasm, interest, keenness, and in full possession of their faculties. The simple life was no assurance of longevity, but it at least kept hundreds of men from breaking down under the strain, and saved them for more important roles in the campaign.

Raoul Lufbery enjoyed no such simple pleasures. He was withdrawn from the line, deprived of most of his companions, placed in a position where he could do nothing but sweat and fume. It was no rest or relief, since from where he sat he could see others taking off and landing, going through their school exercises. It was natural that he would yearn to contribute to the program, but he was not considered an instructor, and any advice or suggestion he might make probably was resented. When he got his own squadron and roster of pilots, he could take over and make use of his experience, but in the meantime "expert" instructors were teaching the students how to fly.

He worked himself into a spirit-fraying frenzy. He begged to be allowed to do *something*, if only to drive some official car about the area. At the front line matters were far from satisfactory. The big German push of March 1918 had hurled back the British and French troops for many miles, the channel ports were again threatened, and only the airmen were holding their own, attempting to stem the tide. Just when experienced pilots were most needed, the men of the old Lafayette Escadrille had to endure the dregs of enforced idleness, wandering about airfields that had no aircraft, and mingling with men who had no idea what was going on.

Finally, Lufbery was moved on to Villeneuve in the Champagne sector where the U. S. 94th and 95th Pursuit Squadrons were being organized. There he found some mild activity, but no war patrols to lead. There were a few decrepit Nieuport-28s lined up in front of the hangars, but they were not armed. There were no machine guns for them, and few armorers to mount them, had any been available.

Raoul took time to study the men who, for the time being, were his pupils, and quickly spotted three in particular whom he predicted would go places in the war. One was an automobile test-driver named Eddie Rickenbacker, another had the colorful Scottish name of Douglas Campbell, and the third was Reid Chambers. All three became outstanding American aces.

Raoul selected Rickenbacker and Campbell to make their first war patrol with him. To the newcomers it was dull and uneventful, but once they were back and making out their patrol reports, they were astonished to learn that their air-blindness had prevented them from seeing four German Albatros fighters and a German two-seater that had stalked them for most of the patrol.

But Luf reassured them that they had done well by staying in formation as long as they had, and he explained that it took some time to learn to "see" in the air.

Lufbery made the best of the circumstances at the field and started formation flying and some primary battle tactics, all carried out well inside the French-American lines, since he could not risk encounters with enemy machines in the air.

He found a few guns here and there, and gradually put together a five-ship formation which he took up the line to patrol the balloon areas, working his men in gradually. When these routine flights were over he usually took off on his own, lone-wolfing about, hoping to add to his score, but luck seemed to be against him, no matter what he tried.

The days and weeks went by, contributing to Luf's despair. He was getting more action fighting with the brass hats of his new service, and it was obvious that he was discouraged and downcast. His old spirit was missing, and he frowned more than he smiled. In all probability his flying skill was being dissipated, for there was no friendly competition to keep his touch and accuracy honed. It was like operating in a vacuum, for there was nothing to contend with.

But he worked with what he had, and after leading several five-ship patrols, decided that his boys had been eased along long enough, and set up a three-ship formation to be led by Captain Peterson who would have Eddie Rickenbacker and Reid Chambers off his wing tips. This threesome took off early on the morning of April 18 with orders to patrol a line between Saint-Mihiel and Pont-à-Mousson. This Peterson was David M. Peterson, ex-sergeant of the Lafayette Escadrille, and he was now flying a Nieuport, not a Spad, and his plane carried a new insignia, the famous Hat-in-the-Ring design that is still associated with Captain Eddie Rickenbacker.

In this first all-American combat patrol, history was to be made. In a suffix to the order, Lieutenants Alan Winslow and Douglas Campbell were to stand by to be available, in case Peterson's flight was chased back to the field. But soon after this patrol took off a sudden fog crept in, and when the three Americans found no activity over the line, they returned Peterson and Rickenbacker got down safely, but Chambers became lost and wisely sat down on a nearby friendly strip By the time the original three had landed, a report came through that there were two enemy planes poking about in the vicinity, so Winslow and Doug Campbell took off when the fog began to dissipate.

It was Winslow who first scored for the 94th by shooting down one of these enemy aircraft only a short distance from his own field. The populace of the town of Toul had seen the fight, and before that thrill had died down, a second enemy plane fell before Campbell's guns within five hundred yards of the 94th's airdrome. Both German pilots were alive, and explained that they had been sent up to intercept three Nieuports patrolling the line, but lost them in the fog. By then they themselves were unsure where they were and while trying to identify the field near the town of Toul, had been set upon by Winslow and Campbell; they were so low as they searched for some evidence of their own field, they were sitting ducks for the two novice Americans.

Toul and the whole surrounding area put on a celebration. Old Moselle wine was brought out, champagne and cognac appeared from the strangest corners, and Colonel Billy Mitchell joined the festivities and sent a most laudatory report back to Washington. It was immediately presumed that American airmen were equally as good as any experienced German, but more important was the psychological effect of this two-plane victory on other Americans who were volunteering for the new aviation service.

Lufbery, of course, was delighted with this initial success, and he did his best to build up the resulting enthusiasm. He held daily talks, answered every question that was put to him, and was in his element again, for he knew most of the answers.

But from all accounts, his main personal concern was the fear of fire in the air. There were no parachutes and all one could do was to put the machine into a sideslip with the hope of preventing the flames from burning away the main spars and wings, and in that manner keep the framework together as long as possible.

Legend takes over much of Lufbery's last flight, which reminds us that history is but fable agreed on. One phase of the legend is that Lufbery was pitifully afraid of fire in the air and on more than one occasion had sworn that he would

never sit it out and die in that manner; he would step out
and take what he considered to be the easier way. He claimed
that he had seen too many poor devils try to sideslip, but
they usually roasted in the end.

Other men who have heard Lufbery talk deny this story,
claiming that Luf always insisted everyone should at least try
to sideslip since in many cases the fire burned itself out within
a short time, and he related incident after incident to prove
his point.

Some airmen who were on the 94th's field at the time declare that Raoul lost his life while attacking an Albatros two-
seater, whereas others insist it was a three-seater, armored
photography plane. Ted Parsons points out that it must have
been an armored airplane for Luf put several telling bursts
into it but his shots had little effect.

At any rate the tragedy came on May 19 when a German
photography aircraft was moving back and forth within sight
of the 94th's field. Everyone raced for a Nieuport, but Luf,
whose regular mount was unserviceable, grabbed the first on
the line, and a crew of mechanics had the prop ticking over in
short time. With Raoul first in the air, it seemed obvious that
no one else need join in. The major would soon dispose of this
intruder.

What happened from this point on must be imagined. Luf
was soon at the level of the photography airplane, and those
on the ground saw him employ all his wiles to gain a commanding position. He moved in and out and then started his
attack. Two long bursts were fired, but they had no effect on
the multi-seater. Another burst from an even closer range
brought no reward, but the enemy gunner popped up from
below and took charge. Some people believe that Luf had
gun stoppage, for he never fired again. He did go back and
make a pass at the enemy ship, but the German gunner stood
his post and poured a series of bursts at the American Nieuport.

Those on the ground saw the plane stagger, wobble, and
fall away. There was a gush of scarlet flame that fanned ou

from the joints of the engine cowling and threatened to wrap a blanket of fire over the cockpit. Luf's friends below wondered what he would do. He did try to get her into a sideslip, for he apparently first pulled up into a stall to lose flying speed. The flames swirled, as if coming from a curved nozzle, and it seemed minutes before the Nieuport began to lose any forward speed. It was at this point that Lufbery was seen to jump, probably forced out by the searing heat as he was trying to lose forward momentum.

One part of the legend is that Lufbery, realizing that he could no longer stay with the burning aircraft, climbed out and tried to maneuver it from a position on the wing root. Another story is that he tried to work the plane to a point over a small stream that wandered through the countryside, hoping that he might, with some luck, break his fall by diving into the water. Perhaps he did, but his luck was not that good. Instead, he fell on a picket fence that surrounded a small cottage garden of a shoemaker on the outskirts of the town of Maron. The shoemaker's wife came out of her kitchen and saw the shattered body of Lufbery draped over the fence. When she tried to pull the airman off she discovered that a length of picket was impaled in Raoul's throat. She stood horrified for a few seconds, and then believing that she would relieve the airman of his pain, boldly pulled out the piece of picket, and carefully wrapped it in a piece of clean paper. When members of the 94th Squadron rushed up to view the final scene of Lufbery's tragedy, she was still standing there holding the offending picket in its wrapping, and her sixteen-year-old daughter was covering the body with flowers.

War's heroes have a strange design for dying.

Chapter XIV

THEY ALSO SERVED

Once the Lafayette Escadrille had been formally taken over by the U. S. Aviation Corps much of the interest in the group of volunteers began to fade. There still were many American pilots scattered through other French squadrons, and it required all of the winter of 1917–18 and much of the spring of 1918 to complete the transfer of those who so desired. Some remained for several weeks and even months on detached service with their former units, others were sent as instructors to the American training schools at Tours or Issoudun. Those who had volunteered late in 1917 and had not completed their training in French aviation schools, were accepted by the United States service as soon as they were ready for active duty. But it was not until June 1, 1918, that the bulk of those who had applied for transfer had received their American commissions and were entitled to wear American uniforms.

All this was of vital importance to the men concerned, but at the time their varied appeals received little attention. The large problem of creating an all-American air service left them a small insignificant group whose former glory was gradually forgotten. Few Americans who followed them across the Atlantic had any idea that 267 volunteers had made the great gesture long before America had actively entered the war. Of these 43 were released before completing their training owing to illness, inaptitude, or injuries received in flying accidents. Those who had served at the front in French uniforms numbered 180, and 93 of these trained pilots were transferred to the U. S. Air Service and 26 to the U. S. Naval Aviation. Five died of illness, 6 by accident in aviation schools 15 were taken prisoner—3 of whom escaped to Switzerland—19 were wounded in combat, and 51 killed in action.

The members of the Lafayette Flying Corps shot down 199 enemy machines, all of which were confirmed officially.

There were several individuals who, because of their special talents, were sought early by American authorities. Frederick Zinn of Battle Creek, Michigan, stands out in particular. He had joined the infantry of the Foreign Legion as early as August 24, 1914, and served in the trenches until February 1916. He was wounded severely at Champagne, and after a spell in the hospital, it was decided that his days as an infantryman were over. He immediately volunteered for the French Aviation, to which he was transferred in the spring of 1916 and started his training at Etampes and went through Cazaux, Pau, and the G.D.E., and was brevetted as a *mitrailleur-bombardier* by August 29. He first served with F.24, flying as an observer aboard Farmans and Sopwith two-seaters from December 12, 1916, to October 21, 1917. Zinn's long experience in this work had taught him a great deal about reconnaissance aviation. He was an expert cameraman, and had carried out dozens of long-range patrols to gather important information. He was bold in the air, and had fought his way back from many dangerous missions, and once back on the ground could complete his task by developing his negatives and making good prints in a very short time. Fred also became an expert in interpreting his photographs for his superior officers.

It is small wonder, then, that Frederick Zinn was the first man the United States mission requested, and he was soon commissioned and attached to the American Air Service headquarters at Chaumont. He had been a sergeant in the French service, but was quickly commissioned a captain, and as such was retained until the Armistice. After the war he was sent into Germany as chief of the American mission for locating the graves of American airmen who had fallen in German-held territory.

Another American volunteer who had trained and flown as an observer was Marius Rocle, a New Yorker. Like Zinn he had served in the Foreign Legion and been wounded in the trenches. He took the regular observation training, and was sent to the front to serve with N.84 which was flying the Nieuport-12, a two-seater model that bore a close resemblance to its single-seater counterpart. Its dimensions were not much greater than the scout and the two could be mistaken at a distance, an error that might be fatal if the gunner huddled low while the enemy attacker was maneuvering to get on its tail. During 1916 this aircraft gave a very good account of itself, but, unfortunately, was kept on active service for too long a time. Eventually it was replaced by Breguet and Salmson machines.

Rocle was next sent to C.46 Squadron and wound up on Breguets with Br.213 where he stayed until February 19 1918, when he was commissioned a second lieutenant and posted to the 13th U. S. Aero Squadron. He had been a corporal with the French. On April 15, 1918, Marius was sent to the 644th Aero Squadron where he remained until the Armistice; by that time he had been on active service for more than four years. Zinn and Rocle were said to be the only two Americans with actual gunner-observer service when the United States entered the war. There, of course, were other who were flying with the British.

Lawrence Scanlan, better known as "Red," came from Cedarhurst, Long Island, and deserves special mention because of his valiant efforts to become a front-line flying man He enlisted in the Foreign Legion on November 26, 1914, was wounded badly in the right leg at Souchez on June 16, 1915 but stayed on until January 1, 1917, when it was discovered that his wounded limb was shorter than the other and he could no longer march as an infantryman.

He volunteered for the French Aviation on February 1917, and started his training at Avord. His shortened leg proved to be somewhat of a handicap, but he managed much of the ground training. Then when he started flying for his brevet he suffered a series of accidents that are still talked about by surviving Lafayette men. Most of them were out-of control drops from great heights, but Lawrence alwa crawled out of the wrecks. In July 1917 he went out of control again, corkscrewed down like a plummet and piled into the roof of the army bakery at Avord.

No one expected him to survive that one, for his machine went straight through until only the tail assembly could be seen. A number of military cooks who had been mixing flour for the next day's batch of bread, managed to escape what to them seemed to be a bomb. The airplane's prop whirled its last, blowing flour in all directions, and through this veritable cloud of white Lawrence clambered out of his cockpit and darted through a nearby window.

The officer commanding the school raced over to the scene and came upon Scanlan, completely covered in flour, walking away from the scene of his crash, and mistaking him for one of the bakers, yelled, "Don't run away. Come into the bakery and help me get the body of the dead pilot!"

"I am the dead pilot, Captain," Scanlan replied, dusting himself off so that he might be recognized.

After three more such fearful crashes, "Red" Scanlan knew that he'd never make it, and when the French offered him his release from the service, he accepted most regretfully. But he went home with the Croix de Guerre, with Star, for his many months of infantry action.

The reader may be wondering who John F. Huffer was. He was recommended for a major's commission by General Pershing, along with like ranks for Lufbery and Thaw. This Huffer was Jean Huffer who had been born in Paris of American parents and had enlisted in the French Aviation on September 28, 1915, and served in four front-line squadrons between April 1, 1916, and February 18, 1918, when he was transferred, and later commanded the 94th Pursuit Squadron after Lufbery's death.

With the French, Huffer flew in pursuit and observation squadrons on the Western Front and in Italy, and during that time was honored with the Médaille Militaire and the Croix de Guerre with three Palms and two Stars.

After spending two months with the 94th, Huffer was assigned to Headquarters, First Air Depot, as Assistant Operations Officer. On July 25, 1918, he took over the command of the 93rd Pursuit Squadron, a post he held until the Armistice.

One of the most experienced airmen trained by the French for the Lafayette Flying Corps was Kenneth Proctor Littauer, a native New Yorker. Although he spent more than two years overseas as a flying man, Ken is perhaps better remembered for the time he was fiction editor of the now defunct *Collier's* magazine. Today he heads a well-known literary agency in New York City.

It is the author's personal opinion that Ken, or Képi, as he was known in the war days, became one of the most valued military airmen wearing an American uniform. Few had his experience and day-by-day accomplishment. He was not a highly publicized ace, nor did he enjoy wide prestige at any time, but his logbook will match any as far as aerial endeavor is concerned; his service record is one that few men in any air force can match.

Ken went to Europe early in 1916 and enlisted in the French Aviation on March 29 of that year. He was brevetted by July 24 and sent to the front as a pilot with Escadrille C.74, flying Caudron reconnaissance planes. This was the famous Caudron G-III, a type widely used through 1915–17. It was powered by a 100-hp Anzani radial engine which was often mounted without benefit of a streamline cowling. It was aboard these almost prehistoric Caudron G-IIIs that the first *organized* ground strafing raid was carried out when on January 1, 1917, an R.F.C. force machine-gunned and bombed the German trenches for more than ninety minutes with the loss of but one Caudron.

With C.74, a combination Franco-Belgian squadron, Ken had scant opportunity for any outstanding work since the duties consisted of routine photo missions, artillery spotting and air reconnaissance. These were all two-way missions; that is to say, to be successful the trip had to be made out and back, or to stay in an area for a definite length of time. A fighter pilot may go out, destroy an enemy photo or spotter plane, and then be shot down himself, but his mission will have been accomplished. The reconnaissance pilot had to go out to his critical point, gather in the photographic record or a visual report, and get back safely with the evidence. If he failed, someone else had to repeat the patrol.

Littauer had more than his share of luck, but he also was a cool, calculating, and skillful pilot, for in more than fourteen months with C.74 he never once failed to bring back his plane and observer safely. On one occasion his gunner was badly wounded, and the Caudron well shot up, but Képi never wavered. On another occasion while flying an artillery shoot, he was attacked by three German fighters, and as he darted about to avoid their fire until some Allied support could drive off the enemy, one German bullet went through the exact center of his little windscreen. How it missed his head, Ken does not know, but he presumes that he must have turned to watch one of the enemy planes, a move that may have saved his life.

During his service with the French he was awarded the Croix de Guerre with Palm and Star, the Belgian Croix de Guerre and the Chevalier de L'Ordre de Léopold, and ended that segment of his war career as a sergeant.

On January 1, 1918, Littauer was commissioned a captain in the U. S. Air Service, and became a flight commander with the 88th Observation Squadron from February 15 to July 1, 1918. On July 1 he was made its commanding officer and served in that capacity until September 20 when he became CO of the 3rd Corps Observation Group, which post he held until October 24, 1918. He then was Chief of Air Service 3rd Army Corps until the Armistice. On November 1 he was promoted to major.

After the war the following citation accompanied the award of the Distinguished Service Cross on January 20, 1919:

For repeated acts of heroism in action near Conflans, France, September 14, 1918, and near Doulcon, France, October 30, 1918. Major Littauer volunteered on a mission to protect a photographic plane for another squadron on September 14 and continued toward the objective at Conflans even after three other protecting planes had failed to start. In an encounter with five enemy pursuit planes, he completely protected the photographic plane by skillful maneuvering, although his observer was wounded and his machine seriously damaged. On October 30 Major Littauer, on duty as Chief of Air Service of the 3rd Army Corps, volunteered and made an important reconnaissance of enemy machine-gun emplacements at a low altitude near Doulcon.

Only a handful of Lafayette Flying Corps airmen had the tactical experience of Ken Littauer.

Dabney D. Horton, registered as a resident of Paris but actually a product of St. Louis, enlisted with the French on August 16, 1916. Like Littauer he became a Caudron pilot and first served with Escadrille C.17 from July 3, 1917, until January 5, 1918. Dabney so enjoyed his associations with the French he decided to stick with them, even after the United States entered the conflict. On January 5, 1918, he was assigned to Sop.255 Squadron, piloting the still active British two-seater for a few weeks. There seems to be a break in his flying career, a break probably to be accounted for by special leave to the United States, but by September 15 he was back on the front flying scouts with Spa.75, and survived the war despite the rigors of so many months carrying out such wide program of air activity.

Warwick D. Worthington was another American who used a Paris address when he enlisted in March 1916, and he, too, was destined for two-seater reconnaissance work, but his flying was marked by a series of unusual accidents and freak breaks of luck. In the first place he spent weeks talking himself into the service, and from the time of his acceptance luck stalked his path. Lesser men would have accepted their fate early in the game.

Worthington endured crash after crash but manfully

crawled out of each wreckage and begged to be allowed to try again. Despite his bizarre experiences he was brevetted finally on an old Farman and when considered to be free of the torment of ill luck, was posted to Escadrille C.53 with which he served from March 3, 1917, until February 13, 1918, attaining the rank of sergeant and being awarded the Croix de Guerre.

An amusing story is told of Worthington which gives some idea of his determination. When he was selected for a Caudron squadron it was deemed necessary that he get in a few hours of G-VI time, but when he reported to a hangar where one lone Caudron G-VI rested, he was told that the type had been grounded.

"Oh, what for?"

"It has been decided that the plane is not safe without a larger tail fin. We have none to replace the old ones."

"I can't fly until such a tail fin is available?"

"That is right."

Worthington went into the hangar, took another look at the plane and walked out. For the next few days he was missing and failed to answer roll call. This was brought to the attention of his superior officers who started a search. At that point Worthington walked into the hangar hauling two of the new-sized Caudron G-VI tail fins. He clumped into the office of the chief pilot, stacked them against his desk and said, "You said, 'no tail fins, no flying.' Here's a complete set. Now may I fly?"

This was no grandstand play; he had gone to Paris and had had two tail fins made up which he paid for out of his own pocket. Nevertheless, he was given a little time in the guardhouse for his trouble—at least long enough to get the new tail fins mounted so that the plane could be used again for training. He eventually went to the front as a G-VI pilot and was promoted to sergeant and awarded the Croix de Guerre. In February 1918 Worthington was transferred and commissioned in the U. S. Air Service, and, as might be expected, denied the satisfaction of flying as a combat pilot.

He served out the rest of the war as an instructor at Tours.

A member of the Lafayette Flying Corps who ended his war as a German prisoner was Paul Frank Baer of Fort Wayne, Indiana. This chubby, happy-go-lucky man was credited with eight victories before he went down, and those who knew him well insist that he might have become America's ace of aces, had he been fortunate enough to fly combat patrols to the end.

Paul Baer enlisted early in 1917 and first went to the front with Spa.80 on August 14, 1917, and fought with skill until January 1918 when, as a corporal with the Lafayette, he was transferred to the U. S. Air Service and commissioned a first lieutenant. He was assigned to the 103rd Aero Squadron on February 18, and was wounded and shot down in combat May 22, 1918, and held prisoner until the Armistice.

Baer must have been an iron man, for he always was in the thick of the fight, and on one occasion made six patrols during one day. He was a natural athlete, lived simply, took regular exercise, and still retained the affection and respect of his comrades.

His last patrol is one of the better stories of the war. He was leading a formation composed of Lieutenants Giroux, Turnure, Wilcox, and Dugan. They crossed the lines at about 15,000 feet in the area southwest of Armentières. Baer soon spotted a flight of five enemy single-seaters some distance inside the German lines. He took his men down and then noticed three more enemy planes above them. With Giroux riding his tail, Baer plunged headlong into the five-ship formation below, and while he selected one, the other four tried to edge him and Giroux out of the play. Then the three jerries who came in from above, nosed into the flurry and a wild melee ensued. Giroux was trapped and killed.

Baer had the good luck to send down one German in flames but as he pulled out of his dive an enemy bullet clipped two of his important control wires. When last seen, Paul Baer was going down fairly well under control, but obviously would have to land in enemy territory. Turnure, Dugan, and Wilcox wriggled out of the fight and returned to their field.

The fact was that Paul, in an airplane that was not in shape for any violent maneuvers, had two Albatros fighters pouring burst after burst into him from twelve thousand feet on down to the ground. He crashed on landing and it was a miracle that he lived through it, suffering only a broken knee. He was soon surrounded by an infantry patrol, the officer of which demanded to know what Paul's Croix de Guerre ribbon stood for. Paul feigned ignorance, shaking his head, but a young German soldier who was standing nearby explained, "That is the French Croix de Guerre, and each of those palms represents a German flier he has shot down." The German officer then became so enraged, he snatched at Paul's ribbons, ripping a large hole in the jacket.

The knee gave Paul much trouble, but at the first opportunity he made a bold attempt to escape and actually got clear of the compound, but after several days of wandering, weather, exposure, and fatigue brought him down. He was captured by a patrol of savage infantrymen who had also picked up two escaped British officers. The captors took their victims to a third-rate beer cellar where more German soldiers were holding a drinking party with a bevy of loose women. The three prisoners were subjected to cruel indignities for hours, and Baer, crippled and half-dead with fatigue and plainly unable to defend himself, was the target for the tasteless gibes, insults, and mauling. He was fortunate to have escaped the ordeal with his life.

Another outstanding member of the Lafayette Flying Corps who elected to remain a sergeant with the French, even though he was offered a captaincy in the U. S. service, was Frank L. Baylies, born September 23, 1895 in New Bedford, Massachusetts. He was educated in the New Bedford public schools, and at the Moses Brown School in Providence, Rhode Island. Well built, and at times quite stocky, Frank was among the top performers in most sports. He was a fine swimmer, and as a schoolboy learned to drive his father's automobile, a facility that got him into the American Field Service.

As an ambulance driver Frank ran up a record that would have satisfied most men, without making further effort as an aviator. He was on the French front early in 1916, saw action along the Somme, at Verdun, and in the Argonne. He drove ambulances in the Monastir sector of Serbia where he was cited for "perfect devotion and fearlessness" in evacuating wounded under heavy bombardment, and was awarded the Croix de Guerre with Palm.

On May 11, 1917, Frank elected to transfer to the French Aviation and trained at Avord, Pau, and Cazaux, and by November of that year was sent to Spa.73, and later on to the Storks squadron. His first war flying was at Dunkirk, and then his outfit was sent back to the Verdun and the Champagne sectors. In a short time Frank Baylies was listed as an official ace. Once he became a member of the Storks, the squadron that produced the great Guynemer, Heurteaux, Dormé, and Deullin, Baylies reacted like a firework. He was a pilot of extraordinary dash and ability, and everyone predicted that he would have a brilliant war career. Had his luck held, there is no knowing how far Frank might have gone. The Storks were in the thick of everything, patrolling one of the most active sectors on the French front, often meeting some of the best of Germany's airmen. Roaming over Noyon, Montdidier, and along their sector of the Somme, the Cigognes had epic battles with the gaudy Fokkers and Albatroses of the new flying circuses. It was here that Frank proved his worth, for his flying was absolutely faultless, his tactics superb, and his shooting deadly.

On one of these occasions, he followed his victim all the way down, and, once he was assured of his victory, attempted to make his way back to his own lines, which meant a mad contour-chase over miles of enemy-held land where the open position put up grim curtains of machine-gun and antiaircraft fire. No World War I aircraft could take such a flailing, and in a short time Baylies' Spad was just a flying skeleton. How he lived through it is a mystery. Eventually, a telling burst broke up the sump of his engine and his lubricating oil flowed away, the Hisso finally seized and his prop stopped. There was nothing for him to do but to stretch what glide he had and hope for the best.

The stretch took him into no man's land between the French and German lines, uncomfortably close to the enemy trenches, but before the Spad had stopped bumping over the shellholes, Frank had flipped his belt and was bounding out of the cockpit like a rodeo performer. Two German soldiers popped up from an advanced saphead and tried to grapple with him, but he sidestepped them and continued on through belts of barbed wire, shellholes, and old parapets, and dove into a French advanced machine-gun pit. He had evaded wild bursts of fire from all directions until friendly hands hauled him to safety.

A pleasant and most companionable man on the ground, Baylies was a cool terror in the air. He now played a new role, moving in close to his enemy before he fired a shot, and in three months scored twelve victories, fully confirmed, with these successful tactics. Many other of his fights may have been victorious, but these usually were staged so far over the line, confirmation was difficult. Although he was now a great favorite with his French companions, and was to receive the Médaille Militaire and the Croix de Guerre with six Palms and one Star, he never lost his quiet, friendly manner with all his associates.

Frank Baylies went west during some bitter fighting along the old Marne salient on June 17, 1918. There is little information on his last encounter when Frank went out with a Spad formation, and some action took place between Greveceour and Lassigny. Ted Parsons, who also was now a member of the Storks, last saw Frank being attacked by four German single-seaters, and before either he or Reginald Sinclair of Corning, New York, then a member of Spa.68, could go to his aid, he was falling in flames.

A few days later a German airman dropped a note explaining that a Frank L. Baylies, an American aviator, had fallen at Rellet and had been buried in a private tomb nearby.

Dr. Gros, who was now a major in the U. S. Air Service, wrote to Frank's mother: "Your son met a glorious death. He was one of the shining lights of our aviation. He was a soldier without fear and without reproach. You must apply to him the eloquent words spoken in the British Parliament with respect to aviators; you must not turn your mind on your sorrow, you must turn it toward all the glory which your son has won and the name which he will leave behind him when the story of this great war is written. He has taken his place by the side of all those heroes who gladly gave up that which is most precious, their lives, for the greatest ideal, the happiness of the human race."

Paul Rockwell also paid tribute to Baylies in a dispatch to the Chicago *Daily News*, which read:

One of the finest and highest-spirited figures that was ever revealed has disappeared from among us. To know Baylies was to like and admire him. His outstanding qualities were those which real heroes possess. Quiet, modest, and reticent on the ground, dashing, fearless and indomitable in the air, Baylies goes down into history as one of the exceptional characters in war aviation.

Baylies' record after reaching the front as a chasing pilot was unique. No other flier in any army gained at the beginning of his career so many official successes in so short a space of time. Baylies destroyed his first German airplane Feb. 19, 1918. On March 7 and 16 he gained his second and third victories; and on April 11 and 12 he had two more official triumphs. May was a wonderful month for this superb air fighter, confirmed victories being won on May 2, 9, 10, 28, 29 and 31, making twelve enemy airplanes officially destroyed.

Mention after mention was awarded to Baylies in the Army orders, and many palms were added to his war-cross and military medal ribbons. Lately he was proposed for the Cross of the Legion of Honor, and also for the rank of Under-Lieutenant.

Another inspiring figure of the Lafayette Flying Corps was David Endicott Putnam of Brookline, Massachusetts, the son of Frederick Huntington and Janet (Hallowell) Putnam. He was born at Jamaica Plain, Massachusetts, on December 10, 1898, a direct descendant of General Israel Putnam of Revolutionary War fame. Young Putnam attended Newton High School and entered Harvard where he became president of his class, and excelled in athletics; he was an expert swimmer, played on the football, baseball, and hockey teams, and was the class orator.

David wanted to fly from the minute he read of Allied aviators on the Western Front, and during his freshman year took and passed an examination for the U. S. Air Service. He was too young to be accepted, so he left Harvard in his sophomore year, worked his way to Europe on a cattle boat, and wound up in the French Aviation. He began flying at Avord on June 10, 1917, and took his acrobatic training at Pau. He was brevetted on October 17 on a Caudron, and by December 12, 1917, was on the front with Spa.94. He never was a member of the Lafayette Escadrille, but still ranks as one of the most colorful and impetuous members of the Lafayette Flying Corps.

Dave did not get over the enemy lines until December 22, but he downed his first Boche on January 19. On April 11 he went through one of his longest and hardest conflicts, engaging four enemy aircraft over a period of thirty-five minutes. He downed one of them and the others withdrew. On the next day he engaged what he termed a German "circus," actually eight enemy aircraft, and succeeded in destroying two of them. On April 23 three more fell before his guns, and then on June 5 he was engaged in the greatest battle of his flying action.

On that day he charged into a pack of ten German Albatros fighters and when that was all over he claimed to have downed five of them, but official confirmation was withheld, and Dave's account was never accepted. He was given credit for three, but the other two were apparently downed so far over the line, it was impossible to check them out completely.

Dave made no complaint and accepted the situation in good grace, but inwardly he seethed for he wanted that record of destroying five enemy planes during one patrol. "You can't shoot them all down in your own backyard," he said laughingly, but never gave up trying to justify his original claim.

His letters home were boyish, full of thrills and gay confidence in his own ability. He wrote on June 16, 1918, giving his version of a typical day with Dave Putnam:

Combat after combat comes my way, and without boasting, I'll say that I generally meet them head on. On Friday, with another fellow, I dove on a bunch of six Germans and three fell. These are not official yet.

Yesterday I was with three other fellows when I saw two Boche biplanes. They saw us at about the same time and started to drive for home. Putting on all the speed I could I gave chase. As my machine happened to be slightly faster than the others of my patrol, I arrived first. With both guns shooting murder, I slowly closed with one of the Boches. Nearer and nearer I drew. One gun stuck but the other rattled on. When I was about ten yards from the German, up came his nose. A perfect target, and just at that moment my remaining gun stopped. The German gunner (I could see him clearly) took one look at me and commenced to fire. A quick turn and I was out of range. I looked back and there was the unlucky Boche falling. Suddenly his left wing broke off and he dashed into the ground. I looked for the rest of my patrol, and there they were some five hundred yards above me watching the fight. We got together again and started to patrol some more. I kept on, for I was able to fix my guns which weren't badly jammed. Suddenly I saw five more Germans and gave chase immediately. As the biplanes had done before them, they too turned for home and in following them I passed through a cloud and lost the rest of my patrol. The Germans, however, went so far that I turned back. I had flown perhaps three minutes toward our lines when a German balloon loomed up ahead of me. "Well," I said, "I've got no incendiary bullets, but there's no harm in shooting at it." No sooner said than done. I pulled both triggers. Pfoof! The balloon burst into flames, and it did look queer. I supposed that there would be just one burst of flame and that would be the end. No; the thing remained in the air, a flaming mass, for about twenty seconds, and then dropped slowly to the ground where it continued to burn. But how the antiaircraft guns did shoot at me. Bang! Bang! Bang! Just a continuous roar. "Flaming onions" also were coming up from the ground. Into a cloud I went. The shooting was even more terrible there, so out I dove. Twisting, turning, circling, I finally reached our lines and made tracks for home. The others arrived about the same time, having witnessed the entire performance. That makes nine official planes and thirteen unofficial for a total of twenty-two in six months.

Putnam's career switched next to the U. S. Air Service, and on June 10, 1918 he was commissioned a first lieutenant and assigned to the 139th Aero Squadron and appointed a flight commander. While with the American forces Dave did not show the skill and dash he had attained while flying as a sergeant with the French. Possibly his new rank brought heavier responsibility, and he had to give more time and attention to the pilots in his care. At any rate, he destroyed only one more enemy aircraft before he went down on September 12, 1918.

His last patrol was in company with a Lieutenant Robertson when they were attacked by at least fifteen German aircraft which apparently caught the two by surprise. Another version is that there were eight machines in the enemy pack. Putnam shot down one of the enemy in flames, and Robertson managed to escape and get to his own lines. One story of the fight is that Putnam went down with two Fokkers shooting him to pieces, while another states that he cleared the initial fight safely, and then saw an Allied two-seater being attacked by eight Germans. He roared in to the rescue and the two-seater escaped, but Dave went down with two bullets through his body. His aircraft fell at Limey, and he was buried with full military honors beside Raoul Lufbery near Toul. In his effects was found a short note to his mother which read:

Mother, there is no question about the hereafter of men who give
themselves in such a cause. If I am called upon to make it, I shall
go with a grin of satisfaction and a smile.

Lieutenant Putnam had been honored with the Croix de
Guerre, the Médaille Militaire, the Cross of the Legion of
Honor, and America's Distinguished Service Cross. In the
final assessment he was credited with twelve official victories.

Even at this late date it is surprising to discover so many
American volunteers who served long and well on the Western Front without making the headlines, or a brief paragraph
in any of the air histories. For many years I have gone over
records and lists of fighting airmen without ever, as far as I
can remember, coming upon the name of Major Charles John
Biddle, but when I began collecting data for this book, this
eight-victory man turned up with a lengthy and interesting
career.

Charles John Biddle was a native of Andalusia, Bucks
County, Pennsylvania, and at last report is still living there,
working as a lawyer with the firm of Drinker, Biddle and
Reath of Philadelphia. In addition to routine legal work, he
has served as counsel for the Drexel Institute of Technology
in Philadelphia, and several other such institutions.

One will find Biddle's name in dusty lists and among vague
mentions of early air fighting, but despite his career he seems
to have attracted the attention of few aviation writers. This
Harvard man was a high-ranking ace at the close of World
War I. After starting as a sergeant pilot with the French, he
became a major in the U. S. Air Service and commanded the
famous 4th Pursuit Group. Like so many more when the
United States appeared to be on the verge of war with
Germany in that fateful spring of 1917, Biddle gave up his
early law practice and made his way to France to take up
the Allied cause. He enlisted on April 8, 1917, and entered
his first aviation school on April 13. He was brevetted on a
Caudron less than two months later, a natural pilot who loved

to fly. As soon as he had completed his course he discovered that he had a month to while away, but unlike most of his companions who rushed off to Paris to "wet their wings," Biddle stayed around Plessis-Belleville and flew anything that was available.

This young man apparently was sage enough to realize that most air-war casualties, whether at the front or during instruction, were the result of inexperience. All too many died in the early school days, or during the first few weeks of combat flying. Biddle stuck to his task and continued to fly, working out his school exercises, week after week, and perfecting every phase of the instruction. As a result, when he was rushed suddenly to Spa.73 about July 28, he was as polished a pilot as practice could make him. He was both a theorist and a man of action, opposite qualifications that seldom combine, but Charlie Biddle was not an average man; he combined them perfectly.

Another almost forgotten man of the Lafayette Flying Corps was Oliver Chadwick of Lowell, Massachusetts, who joined at about the same time. These two men were loyal companions all through their training period for they had much in common. Chadwick also was a lawyer, having represented the house of Stone and Webster, but on the outbreak of the war became restless and filled with a desire to help. He first went to Canada, but the old bugaboo of American citizenship deterred him, so he returned to the United States, and to satisfy his craving joined a Massachusetts artillery battery and saw some service on the Mexican border in 1916. When he returned home he took primary training at Newport News, Virginia, and after gaining some proficiency on a Curtiss biplane, sailed for France and offered his services. He naturally went through the military flying courses with high marks and eventually went to Spa.73.

With all his skill and courage, Oliver Chadwick was shy on luck and was killed in a wild melee on August 14, after being at the front for about two weeks. Biddle tells some of this as follows:

The next morning Oliver and I were not scheduled to fly until the afternoon, but as we were both anxious to get all the practice possible, we went to the field in the hope that they might need an extra man. A patrol was just going out, and being short one man they asked Oliver to fill in. I saw him go off and was a little disappointed that he had gotten the job instead of myself, as he had already had an hour or more over the lines than I. He went out with three Frenchmen and never came back.

They reported that at about 9:45, shortly after they had reached the lines, they had lost track of Oliver while maneuvering near some clouds. Shortly after lunch we received a telephone message that the infantry had seen a machine of the type Oliver was flying shot down in the course of a combat from about 2000 meters, and fall about 1200 meters north of Bixschoote at a place known as the "Ferme Carnot." According to the report, a French machine had gone to the assistance of an English one that was being attacked by a Boche, and at the same time was itself attacked from the rear by two Boche. I had hoped against hope that there might be some mistake; that the machine was merely forced to land, or perhaps it was not Oliver's machine at all, or that he might be only a prisoner."

Later, it was disclosed that Chadwick had fallen between the lines, but very close to the German trenches. When the Spad crashed, patrols from both sides charged out and for a few minutes it was the center of a wild hand-to-hand conflict, but since Chadwick was apparently dead, neither side could either help or capture him, and the infantrymen returned to their slots. Two or three days later, a new French ground attack carried the line forward beyond where Chadwick's plane had crashed, but when friendly hands reached the wreck, Oliver's body was nowhere to be found; only a dead German was sprawled out beside the Spad. It took weeks before Chadwick's death was clearly established, and his burial place found and marked with his name.

Just before Chadwick was killed, he had written to Dr. Gros:

I wish to associate myself as closely as possible with the cause
of France, for I feel that a few Americans scattered here and there
among the French escadrilles can do a greater service to the United
States than if we were all together; but with General Pershing
already here I am well aware that conditions may be different
from the past. Therefore, I wish to let you know of my inclinations
before acting upon them, and should welcome any advice which
you may choose to give. I am more interested in getting into the
fight where I can be of service, than in advancement under either
of the flags which it has been my privilege to serve.

Biddle felt Oliver's death keenly, and he continued to stalk
the enemy, but his chance to avenge Chadwick's loss did not
come until December 5, 1917, when he shot down an Albatros two-seater near Langemarck in Belgium. This was his
only official victory during his five months' service with the
French. This time was not wasted since Charlie used every
minute to study up-to-date combat tactics, and became so
interested in this science, his French companions urged him
to put his findings down on paper. The result was a valuable
monograph on aerial combat which was adopted later for use
in the instruction of all American pilots; a particularly practical contribution to the war effort.

Sergeant Biddle was commissioned a captain in the new
U. S. Air Service on November 7, 1917, but so much valuable
time was wasted awaiting active-duty orders, he remained
with Spa.73 until early in January. A month later he was
shipped on to the Lafayette Escadrille which, legally, had
by then become the 103rd U. S. Aero Squadron. This heady
period of action afforded some satisfaction. For one thing, the
pilots were wearing American uniforms, but were still under
Bill Thaw's command. They had first-class Spads and plenty
of opportunity to fly, and naturally every pilot wished to be
the first to score an official victory for the U. S. Air Service.
While in truth the squadron was neither fish nor fowl, this
honor fell to Paul Baer who destroyed an Albatros near
Rheims on March 11, 1918. Biddle, who was always volun-
eering for extra flights, scored the 103rd's seventh victory on

April 12 when he downed a two-seater Halberstadt, which fell
at Corbeny on the Chemin-des-Dames.

Later on when his squadron was on the Champagne sector,
Biddle was annoyed with the success the Germans were having against French and American kite balloons. They scored
with frequency and apparent ease, for their ammunition
seemed flawless, seldom failing to ignite the gas bags. When
matters had reached a certain pitch, with little being done
about it, Biddle had a conference with a high-ranking French
officer and tried to set up a series of antiballoon shows, but
apparently the French had no incendiary ammunition worthy
of the name, and the proposed balloon "hate" was called off.

On May 15, 1918, a flick of bad luck caught up with Biddle
as he was cruising about over the desolate area between
Langemarck and Ypres. He encountered an enemy plane flying at about 600 meters. To Charlie it appeared to be the
slowest aircraft he had ever seen. "It had a fat, ungainly
body and square tail, the lower wing was much narrower
than the upper, like some British two-seaters. As it turned
out, I was right when I figured it might be some sort of an
armored, ground-strafing machine. He was too much for me
and I flopped into no man's land, but I would have given
something to have downed him so we could have studied
his hide to see how thick it really was and what it was made
of. I have always wondered what a dose of real armor-piercing
bullets would have done to him. As it was, the observer knew
his job. His first burst took out my engine and a slug spattered
off and hit me in the knee, a blow that felt like a smack from
a pitched ball, until I realized that something had penetrated
clean."

Charlie had no choice. This was no time for ruminating on
Junkers armored planes. His engine conked out, and he had
to stretch his glide to make the area between the two front
lines. He piled up in a tangle of barbed wire, shellholes,
stakes, duckboards, and the debris of war. The enemy slot
were less than seventy yards away and the British line
several hundred, but Charlie crawled, ran, and waded to

British observation post under heavy shellfire and machine-gun flailing. Although wounded, he covered the last fifty yards in almost nothing flat.

The hospital held him less than a month, and he was sent back as commanding officer of the 13th Pursuit Squadron, and to celebrate he soon brought down his third and fourth enemy planes at Preny, north of Pont-à-Mousson; both were Albatros single-seaters. On August 16 he downed a Rumpler two-seater by killing the enemy observer and forcing the pilot to land the craft intact inside the French lines near Nancy. A Fokker single-seater went down on the Verdun front and another was shot to pieces over Banthèville in the Argonne sector.

And so it went. By October 25 Biddle was placed in command of the 4th Pursuit Group and promoted to major. On his return, following the Armistice, he wrote a book about his experiences, *Way of the Eagle*, which, unfortunately, is now out of print.

One of the more colorful characters who enlivened the Lafayette Flying Corps was Charles W. "Chuck" Kerwood of Bryn Mawr, Pennsylvania. Chuck's name often comes up whenever World War I airmen meet, and anecdotes concerning him are related from coast to coast. As is usual with such types, legend, often concocted by his admirers, can furnish embarrassing situations to explain, and Chuck's career is cluttered with fables, tall stories, and hair-raisers that he himself had little to do with.

Kerwood would be the last to claim that his war record furnishes any outstanding military accomplishment, but to his credit, he was a volunteer, took his training, and had the bulk of his front-line flying with Escadrille Br.117 (Breguet), carrying out routine reconnaissance and bombardment operations. Such squadrons can provide quick routes to oblivion, but Chuck refused to be blotted out of the picture. He managed a series of strange adventures and developed the gift of telling them. He still survives and time has in no way dampened his enthusiasm for the "tall" tale.

On one occasion when his squadron was ordered on an important bombing raid, there was no Breguet available for Chuck to pilot, so he kidded Manderson Lehr to take him along as his observer-gunner. Lehr was another gay soul who was killed in action near Château-Thierry on July 15, 1918. "Bud," as he was known, was a dreadful mimic who honestly believed he was entertaining his pals when he imitated cows, roosters, and other barnyard habitués. One can imagine the capers Bud and Chuck were capable of.

Lehr reached the general objective on this particular patrol, an important transport artery. Chuck was supposed to drop his missiles one at a time in order to distribute the effect along a railroad, but instead, on seeing a small village where German troops were basking in the early morning sunshine, he "pulled the plug," and released the lot in one grand salvo. So effective was this mass explosion—in Kerwood's eyes—he was convinced he had blown up a complete town, and on his return to the base penned a combat report in which he indicated that he had wiped out a whole city. At least that is the story James Norman Hall culled from the evidence.

At another time Kerwood and Lehr were included in a small formation that was sent out to the Montdidier sector, and Lehr came back with the following report:

Three of us started out on this bombardment expedition. On account of the clouds we were flying at 800 meters, when upon entering a cloud bank we separated for fear of running into each other. When we came out we were far distant from each other. Again, just as we came to the German lines we entered another cloud bank. I came out first and looked around for the others, but could not see them, so I went on to do the work assigned to me, dropped down to 700 meters, and getting over my objective, bombarded the enemy field. Then I went to the right and spotted Kerwood in the distance. I immediately set out and caught up to him. On the way, still at 700 meters, I went through a cloud, and when I came out I saw four Boches come down on him from behind, immediately became engaged in another combat, and when I turned I saw Kerwood below me. He was at about 300 meters *piquing* for the French lines. I could not see any German immediately upon him; he seemed to have his machine under control, but when I started to catch up with him he suddenly dropped. I think a luminous bullet must have struck him, but cannot ascertain whether he was wounded or forced to land on account of motor trouble.

Nothing was heard from Chuck and he was given up for lost, and semi-official reports were sent out that he had been killed. A few weeks later, however, several other American airmen who were prisoners of war, were being passed through a civil prison in Landshut, Bavaria, and one of them came upon the name *"Charles Kerwood,"* scribbled all over the walls of one of the cells. This was the first indication that Chuck had survived, and there was rejoicing among his many friends. Next, it was reported that while being held as a prisoner he had made a desperate effort to escape, and was spotted and shot by a sentry. Other versions of the story is that he was shot when he unknowingly wandered too close to the barbed-wire fence. At any rate the bullet put him in a hospital for a short time.

The wound healed eventually, and Chuck came limping into Paris after the Armistice, replete with a new stock of stories and continued interest in the Lafayette Flying Corps. Chuck was also active in the L'Escadrille Lafayette Flying Corps Association which was organized in New York City in 1928. Today, Kerwood is an executive in the International Cooperation Administration, Civil Aviation Division in Washington, D.C.

Chapter XV

PRISONERS OF WAR

It was Jimmy Bach who had set the pattern. When their luck or engines ran out, many young men who had served long and well closed their war careers behind prisoner-of-war barriers. Although only three members of the Lafayette Escadrille had to endure this indignity—Harold B. Willis, James N. Hall, and Christopher Ford—about a dozen more of the Flying Corps went down on the hostile side of the line before the conflict ended.

In many cases they gave their captors as much trouble as prisoners as they had as active flying men, by attempting to escape and in keeping their jailers continually on the alert. To the uninitiated it may have seemed that while they had it rough, they at least were safe; the war was over for them and with any sort of a break they could go home when it was all over.

But freedom was what these young men had in mind when they volunteered; freedom and independence were the basic stones of their world's structure, and once the shock of being taken prisoner had drained away, the full realization of their spiritual loss overwhelmed them and keyed their first fumbling attempts at escape.

It should be remembered that war was new to those of us who were born just before the turn of the century into a world in which peace had not been broken—except for localized disturbances—for approximately one hundred years. The campaigns of the Crimean, the Civil War in the United States, the Franco-Prussian War, the Boer War, and the Spanish American War had been confined to restricted areas; the last great upheaval threatening civilization had ended with Napoleon's defeat at Waterloo in 1815. We were nurtured in a society, an economy, and mode of life that has not been duplicated, and which cannot be fully appreciated by any historian who has not lived through it. War was something we had read about and had thrilled to its stories and adventures. We knew that men were killed and wounded, but none of us could accept the possibility of being taken a prisoner. We remembered the old steel engravings, the woodcuts, and on-the-spot sketches of prisoners of war who were always downcast, weary-eyed, tragic, and marked with the dirt and disorder of defeat. To die was to make the great sacrifice; it could be heroic and justified. The wounded wore the dressings of heroes who had fought well. But to be eliminated from the great scene as a prisoner of war—nothing could be more hopeless and degrading. There had been no recent conflict with returnees to tell what it was like, how they had endured duress, and planned their escapes. There was little of that to buoy us between 1914 and 1918. Only those who have had to risk the chance of capture by an enemy can understand the inner revulsion and dread of such a misfortune. In my many months on the front I can honestly state that the idea of being killed seldom occurred to me. Although there is a widespread belief that all airmen are fatalists, I never met one front-line flying man who ever referred to the possibility of his being killed, but most men expressed an unholy dread of being captured by the enemy. The subject was discussed often and many of us made routine plans for such a situation, and arranged to leave instructions for the disposal of our effects "in case we were taken prisoner." The thought of capture and loss of personal freedom caused many a restless night.

Considering the hazards of wartime flying, the disposition of engines, and the fact that we generally were well over the enemy's side of the line when trouble arose, we knew what the odds were of our being taken prisoner. That we had such an inner horror of capture may be hard to explain, but we were fighting an enemy who, according to our standards of ethics, was a "swine," as we so frequently expressed. He did not "play the game," as we knew it. The bulk of us had

sprung from Anglo-Saxon forebears, and had grown up obey-
ing the simple rules of proper behavior that guided our lives
at home, in school, on the playgrounds, and in our intercourse
with others in pleasure or business.

This enemy, whom many of us had faced for two or three
years—not a few months—had set a frightful pattern of warfare, beginning with the invasion of Belgium, and his total
disregard for "scraps of paper." In victory he was a tyrant
in defeat he cried, *"Kamerad!"* after destroying hundreds of
villages and poisoning the available wells. As a prisoner he
often cringed and pleaded compassion, tearfully showing
photographs of his mother, wife, and family. The Prussian
type was arrogant, unrepentant, and demanded his rights under the Hague Convention. But if he were the captor, he had
never heard of the Hague Convention. The dignity and right
of the soldier were factors he never respected—except when
they applied to him.

We had no special officers to interpret any of this to us; no
lectures in which we were advised how to act if we were
captured by the enemy. We considered the war news according to our own degree of intelligence, and, after the evidence
it was logical that we should decide that being taken
prisoner by the Germans was about as unfortunate a situation
as we could encounter.

I do not know what warnings or information was available
in American or Canadian training camps. I believe that after
some months a few men and officers who had escaped from
German prison camps went about giving illustrated lectures
on their experiences and offering advice and instruction concerning the various tricks of escape, but none of this came to
us at the front, nor did I meet any of these speakers during
the short time I spent in British training schools.

So, drawing our own conclusions, we did our best to pre-
pare for such an eventuality. Some of us devised small
pocket-sized toilet kits containing a razor, toothbrush, comb
and a small pair of scissors. We usually carried a flat-type
cap, later known as an "overseas" cap to Americans, since

we knew that our leather flying kit would be taken from us and turned over to some fortunate German airman. We carried no papers, letters, diaries, documents, or newspaper clippings of any kind. Our identifications, all that the Hague Convention demanded, were to be found on our military discs provided by the service. In addition most of us had silver identification bracelets which we wore on our wrists. These, of course, were a personal affectation, since the service fiber discs worn around the neck on strong cord were more practical, and virtually impossible to lose.

We obtained small-scale maps of Germany which we stitched inside some section of our tunics. We purchased small compasses in nearby towns, and hid them away by hollowing out a heel of one boot. This trick made us feel quite clever and very E. Phillips Oppenheimish, but I doubt that anyone succeeded with that spy chestnut.

We "borrowed" pieces of hacksaw blades from the mechanics and secreted them in the seams of our jackets. Knife blades of various sorts were saved and added to these "escape kits." Small pieces of mirror "for signaling," but more likely for personal vanity, were included in the collection we hoped to retain should the horror of capture befall us. This pathetic planning was amateurish, but it filled the cold void of our dread. We believed that if we were shot down and penned up, we would immediately start to plan our escape. That we would have to do, for we had no intention of sitting quiet, going to seed, or glorying in the fact that our war was over.

But facing the facts of being a prisoner of war, is not that easy. The psychological strain is almost unbearable, and far more serious than most people can imagine. No man can live for endless months in a prison compound, and not undergo severe mental change. This is the one great dread of the *kriegie*. He has no idea what this limited life might bring, but the possibility of insanity is seldom ruled out. Fortunately, though I may be prejudiced in this, it has been stated time and again that English-speaking peoples, with an instinct

that has served them well in building their civilization, have
a knack of adjusting themselves easily to unpleasant circumstances. Nevertheless, incarceration, because one has fought
for his country and has been captured, leaves an immediate
mark on all but the strongest. It must be remembered that
these men have been cut off from their own country, from
their families, and equally important, from their comrades.
Weeks go by during which doubt and uncertainty of what is
happening at home or on the war front throws a shadow of
fear over them until they are assured that the fight goes well,
a food parcel comes through, or the first letter from home
relieves immediate concern.

It is the canker of not knowing that drains everything from
the prisoner. He loses track of time and season. Worse, he
may lose his self-respect. To many men capture meant personal failure, and the longer they were restrained, the deeper
and blacker became their sense of inefficiency. Some with-
stood the ordeal better than others, but few of them came
out of a prison compound physically and mentally fitter than
when they went in. A mere handful took advantage of this
time to improve themselves by taking courses or adding to
their knowledge of their professions or avocations. These opportunities for study were provided by books from the International Red Cross or from relatives of the prisoners. Much
of the time, however, was spent in remorse and recrimination
—or making plans for a getaway; in all probability the latter
was their true salvation.

James Norman Hall was one of the outstanding member
of the Lafayette Escadrille who ended his war career in
prisoner-of-war camp. It will be recalled that he had been
transferred to the U. S. Air Service, commissioned a captain
and assigned to the 103rd Pursuit Squadron with which he
flew from February 18 to March 29, 1918, when he was made
a flight commander of the 94th Pursuit Squadron. In an un-
derstatement, so typical of Jimmy when referring to himself
he wrote: "On May 7, 1918 during a combat near Pont-à-

Mousson, while diving on an Albatros single-seater, my upper right plane gave way, the fabric covering it bursting along the leading edge. A moment later an enemy aircraft made a direct hit on the motor, and the plane fell out of control near Pagny-sur-Moselle. I was a prisoner in various German hospitals and prison camps until the Armistice."

At the time Hall was flying one of the "discarded" Nieuport 28s with which the 94th was equipped. He was accompanied by Eddie Rickenbacker and Edward Green, and was answering an alert sent out by an infantry post that an enemy formation was approaching Pont-à-Mousson. The Albatroses were not sighted until some twenty minutes had passed, but finally five turned up.

Hall probably was leading and took Rick and Green into the melee when they were at 14,000 feet. At the time they had some altitude advantage, and when Hall began his almost vertical dive attack, he soon sensed he was in trouble, for he was practically out of control. He tested out his stick and discovered that the fabric covering his right upper wing had ripped open all along this leading edge, which naturally acted as brake, and he went into a savage, uneven spin. He had to all off his attack and try to reach his own lines. At the time he had no idea that the search had taken them so far over, but when his plane began to give him trouble, he saw that they had gone a long distance inside the enemy area.

As he flew on, the slipstream fingered under the torn fabric and opened the gap wider. Then strips tore away and fluttered over the trailing edge. Hall cut the throttle as far back as he dared to reduce his speed, but by then enemy antiaircraft guns opened up and there was little hope for fast maneuvers to evade the barrage. Jimmy turned, hoping to see Rick and Green escorting him back, but instead he spotted the Albatros he had dived on, reversing the situation; the hunter was now the hunted.

"He was not dangerously close," Jimmy wrote later, "but would zoom and fire wild bursts in my direction. He

didn't bother me too much but those Archie shells were
really ominous."

He tried to zigzag and change altitude to put off the big
guns, but the Nieuport suddenly gave a lurch, and he saw
the engine cowling change shape and gradually break up.
The rotary engine had been hit, and probably fractured the
master crankshaft on which it spun. He was told afterward
that a small incendiary shell from a quick-firing gun had hit
the Le Rhone motor, but fortunately it had not exploded;
instead it had fouled much of the whirling mechanism
ripping out tappet rods, ignition wires, and the intricate maze
of induction pipes.

"I sat there wondering what the result of this adventure
was to be. I believed at the moment that I didn't much care,
for I had read many stories of the treatment by the enemy of
Allied prisoners of war. Death seemed a preferable fate."

Hall managed a fairly decent landing by pulling out of a
dangerous spin just in time to slither into a large field. The
Nieuport wiped off her undercarriage and thumped along on
her belly for a considerable distance. Jimmy was shaken up
and bashed his face against the small windscreen. He sat
there for some minutes and then watched a number of German soldiers running toward him. He was relieved to hear
one address him kindly in English: "Are you hurt, sir?"

Jimmy explained that he was, and the German soldier
immediately called on two companions and together they
lifted him carefully from the machine and carried him to a
dugout on the edge of a nearby wood. They entered an
officers' mess which was as neat and clean as the proverbial
New England kitchen. He was given a cup of coffee but not
molested in any way. An ambulance man was called, and he
put Hall's right leg in splints and carefully bandaged his
lacerated face. Finally, a German officer came in who showed
no hostility, but referred to "the fortunes of war," and then
asked to see Jimmy's papers.

Since it was near the first of the month Jimmy had about
eight hundred francs in his wallet, an identification card, a

a small typed sheet of squadron orders! He wrote later that during an unguarded moment he chewed this paper and swallowed the pulp. How many captured aviators have since told this "chewing up the squadron orders" tale! At any rate, the officer retained Hall's identification card, but returned all his money.

A short time later a number of German aviators arrived and explained that they were the pilots who had engaged Hall's formation that morning, and one of them confided that one of their planes had been shot down in flames, a victory later credited to Eddie Rickenbacker.

After checking on Hall's injuries, they took him in their open touring car to a hospital in the town of Jarny. On the way they stopped off at the airfield from where the German pilots had flown that morning, and he was given a good meal, during which a jovial senior officer addressed him with: "Well, Hall, what are you people doing over there?"

Jimmy was suspicious of this friendly approach knowing it could lead to some careful questioning, so he decided to play a cagey game. "All right, Major. You know how we Americans love to brag. Ask me whatever you want to know."

The German smiled. "Let's be frank. Didn't you expect rough treatment? We are supposed to cut off your ears or slit your tongue, eh?"

Jimmy said, "Oh, I guess there are good Germans and bad ones. I seem to have fallen in with a group of the best."

They exchanged pleasantries for some time, and then the German major told him what he knew of American, British, and French operations and organization. He showed photographs of Allied airfields, including the one from which Jimmy had taken off that morning. Hall held a dead pan and feigned total ignorance, but he was amazed to learn how much the major knew about Allied activities. Later in the day a small group escorted him to the hospital at Jarny, a short distance from Metz. Once settled there, some of his new associates visited him regularly, brought him his helmet and flying gloves, and later gave him a set of snapshots of his wrecked

Nieuport, a detailed shot of the incendiary shell lodged against the engine, and the famous photograph showing the American sitting in the back seat of the German automobile hugging a dachshund that belonged to one of his captors.

That is how Jimmy Hall went down and was welcomed into Germany.

Everett T. Buckley of Kilbourne, Illinois, had an experience that shows an interesting contrast. He joined the French Aviation in January 1917 and by August 6 was a Spad pilot with Spa.65, Lieutenant Nungesser's noted escadrille, flying from the Senard field. Everett proved to be a valuable pilot and held on for about five weeks on a front that at the time saw heavy air fighting.

On September 6, 1917, Buckley's Spad was damaged seriously by several bursts of enemy bullets during a wild skirmish, and he went down completely out of control near Dun-sur-Meuse. The crash knocked him unconscious, but when he came to he realized he was not badly hurt. However, he was surrounded by a patrol of German infantrymen who roughed him up, and hauled him off to a nearby compound where he was put on a bread-and-water diet for eighteen days for refusing to give reliable information. Once he had convinced his captors that he would not give in, he was taken to the notorious Karlsruhe "Hotel" for another long, drawn-out session of interrogation by German intelligence officers. He refused to comply, so was given up as a bad job and sent on to a prison camp at Heuberg, Germany.

Buckley sat it out for a month or so and then made plans to escape, which he succeeded in doing and getting all the way to the Swiss frontier where he was caught. In all this time nothing was given out by the Germans as to Buckley's whereabouts, or whether he was dead or alive.

He was next sent to a prison farm at Donauschingen and ordered to use a shovel. This was simple for Everett and in two days he was free again, but was captured once more at he tried to cross the Danube. After a wicked going-over by the sentries, he was sent back to Heuberg. When a few days of solitary reflection seemed to convince him that escape was hopeless, he was sent to another prison farm near Waringenstadt. Buckley was a sergeant, which accounts for his being put to heavy manual labor. Officer prisoners were just placed in a compound and seldom ordered to take on any kind of work unless they requested certain jobs to relieve the tedium or improve their prison quarters.

During his first day at Waringenstadt, Everett worked very hard with seven other prisoners—cutting the bars out of a window. Their escape was not noticed until daybreak the next morning and by that time all seven were well away from the neighborhood, but within two days all of them were recaptured and returned to Heuberg and put in solitary confinement for thirty-one days.

Everett Buckley's fourth attempt was successful. He was back on the farm cutting hay with a French prisoner when he made his last try for freedom. He and the Frenchman were immediately chased by a group of German farmers, but a nearby wood furnished cover until the searchers gave up. From that point on, Everett used his previous experiences to get through, and, with his newfound French friend, evaded three lines of German sentries guarding the frontier, but having no real idea where they were, continued their evasive tactics until they were positive they were well inside the Swiss border. They were first picked up by two itinerant musicians who told them they were safely inside friendly territory, and then directed them to the Swiss military police who in turn shipped them on to Berne and Paris.

Thomas B. Buffum, a native of New York City, was another volunteer who suffered the indignities of a prison camp. He first joined the American Field Service in 1917, and after driving an ambulance for several months in Macedonia under hazardous conditions, put in for flying and was accepted

June 15, 1917. He went to the front with Spa.77 on March 24, 1917, and flew his share of the patrols until May 4 of that year when he was shot down in flames behind the enemy lines. For weeks the Germans supplied no information concerning his fate, and he was mourned for dead in many of the Lafayette Flying Corps squadrons, for he was a most popular member at that time.

It was established later that during his last fight in the air with at least ten German machines, Buffum received a bullet through the gasoline tank of his plane and the fuel caught fire. He did a wing-slip and kept the flames from himself until he reached the ground on the enemy side of the line where he landed safely and then jumped from his machine. He was burned, but not seriously. When first attacked he had been flying at about twenty-three hundred feet, and he landed only two kilometers from the front line.

Buffum was finally locked up at Trausnitz Castle at Land shut, Bavaria, where there were several other American avia tors, including Herman Whitmore, Tommy Hitchcock, and Herschel J. McKee. On one occasion Buffum and several othe prisoners escaped from the fortress, but after fourteen night of tramping they were all captured at the Austrian borde:

Louis Leslie Byers was a Philadelphian who somehow go into the French Aviation despite his defective eyesight, passe all his flying tests with good marks, and was posted to Spa.3 on July 13, 1918. Five days later he was shot down in th vicinity of Marquises and taken prisoner, spending the ne: four months behind prison-compound bars until he was r leased by the Armistice.

Another volunteer who had a short front-line experienc was Louis Charton. He was born in France of French parent but later became an American citizen. When war broke out was living in Toul, and immediately enlisted in the Foreig Legion and served as an infantryman until February 1, 191 He transferred to aviation on February 20, 1917, and w: assigned to Spa.97 by August 22, but Charton had only abo two weeks of active-service flying, being shot down over the lines by antiaircraft fire. He became seriously ill in prison camp and was interned in Switzerland until the end of the war.

A man who became a well-known figure in international sport and finance, Thomas Hitchcock, Jr. of Westbury, Long Island, played an outstanding role in the Lafayette Flying Corps. A young man of a renowned family, he seemed destined for a place of prestige amid this unusual company.

Although the United States was already committed to the conflict, Tommy put in his application for, and joined the French Aviation June 25, 1917. On his arrival at Avord he amazed his instructors with his natural ability, daring, and willingness to try anything. A great horseman and sailor, Hitchcock seemed born to fly. No matter how antiquated the aircraft, he could make it perform like a specialty machine tuned for precision acrobatics. He had perfect co-ordination, eyesight, and the touch of the master. With even creaky old school machines he performed maneuvers that astonished his instructors, and a great future was predicted for the young American.

He was brevetted on September 17, passing out on a Caudron, and was soon sent to Escadrille N.87 where he arrived on December 10. He became a star performer in a short time and was credited with the destruction of two enemy two-seaters. Hitchcock was something of a lone wolf, for he went into the air whenever the weather or the condition of his aircraft permitted, roaming far and wide to search out the enemy, and once he spotted a target would stalk his prey until he had exchanged bullets, or his fuel supply necessitated his return.

For a time William A. Wellman, who later became a motion picture producer of note, joined Hitchcock in some of his stalking forays and ran up somewhat a record of his own. On one occasion Hitchcock and Wellman came upon a German two-seater and began a relentless chase, each one taking turns darting in from tight angles to taunt the gunner. Still, the biplace stayed in the air and started to glide for its field near Nancy. Wellman and Hitchcock tried every trick in the bag to torch them, but the rugged two-seater crew hung on, so the two Nieuport pilots turned their attention to the field itself. They shot up aircraft standing on the line, and then dove on hangar after hangar trying to hit something inflammable that would start a good fire. The defense machine guns tried to drive them off, but Tommy and Bill forked the gun teams out of their pits, and when they had driven everyone to cover, pulled out and raced back for their own lines. By the time they returned to their field neither one had a round of ammunition left. They heard later that one of them had killed the German observer in the two-seater.

While flying alone on March 6, 1918, Hitchcock came upon a large flock of Albatros fighters and attacked them boldly, but after his first pass he found himself well trapped by this swarm, and although he made a brave effort to get clear, a German bullet creased his back and another cut an aileron control wire that deprived him of much maneuverability. The Albatros pilots moved in closer and closer until he was finally forced to the ground in German territory.

Tommy's wound was not serious and after a short time in a German hospital he was imprisoned at a compound at Lechfeld. From the minute he was put behind barred gates he planned an escape. He found Herschel J. McKee and several Frenchmen in the same stockade who had made previous tries but with no success. He listened to their stories, learned some of the tricks and mistakes and worked out a new plan. The first one was to huddle in a garbage cart and be covered with a blanket of potato peelings, but unfortunately there were not enough to cover the three men who planned to make this novel exit, and the idea was abandoned.

Then one day Hitchcock, McKee, and Herman Whitmor were told that they were to be transferred to another camp late that afternoon. This was something of a shock for the had spent considerable time devising a series of plans to break out of this particular establishment, and realized that all the hidden equipment such as maps, compasses, food, and extra clothing would have to be left. For the first time in his life Hitchcock said he felt like crying.

However, the three did not give up; the compasses were stuffed in pieces of bread, but the maps were too large to hide and had to be passed on to other prisoners to help some other escaping team. Then Hitchcock, McKee, and Whitmore lined up outside their hut to await the sentry who would march them to the nearest railroad station.

"The minute I spotted our guard," Tommy wrote later, "I began to feel better. He was a simple, good-natured Bavarian farmer who told us he was taking us to Rastatt in Baden. Besides his rifle, he carried a large railroad guide and a time-table which he consulted mile after mile."

Once they were aboard the train Tommy put a number of general questions to their pleasant sentry concerning the towns and countryside through which they were passing. Finally the guard turned the guide over to Tommy who noticed a fair-sized map that had become loose among the pages of the book. He studied it carefully for it had considerable detail, showing bridges, rivers, towns, and contours in the area within about twenty miles of the Swiss border.

"The rest of the area didn't matter," Tommy has explained. "I knew it all by heart. We had studied other maps for weeks."

When the three American conspirators had figured their route and some detail of the time schedule, they decided to make a break and leave the train near Ulm, the nearest point to the Swiss border. They were scheduled to arrive at Ulm at 11:30 P.M., so by 10:30 they began setting the action. Their guard was rather sleepy by now, and had left lying on the seat beside him the map, a packet of money belonging to his three prisoners, and a wad of official papers concerning them, that were to be delivered to the next prison comman-dant.

Hitchcock took the guidebook map and the packet of money

and slipped them into his pocket. A few stations later the
sentry roused up and peered out the window to check the
name of the station, and then looked for his timetable. He
realized that some hanky-panky had been going on, and
Tommy decided it was time to make a break.

The rest of the details have never been made very clear, but
only Hitchcock got away; McKee and Whitmore did not make
it and were held until the Armistice. Tommy ducked out
neatly, hid in the woods, and then moving only at night
crossed the border safely and made his way into Switzerland
just eight days later.

The adventures of "Chuck" Kerwood and Harold Willis
have been related, but another American, seldom mentioned
who had an exciting career was Walter J. Shaffer of Dauphin
Pennsylvania. He was awarded the Médaille Militaire, and
the Croix de Guerre with three Palms, and then had the mis
fortune to be taken a prisoner of war.

Walter Shaffer enlisted with the French in August 1917 and
went to the front first with Spa.156, and then served with
Spa.38. He flew combat patrols aboard the Nieuport, the
Morane Parasol, and the Spad. He served with David Putnam
and the famous Georges Madon; as a matter of fact he made
his first "kill" while flying with Madon. They were engaged
in the Marne sector when the French ace, who was leading
the patrol, discovered a Boche two-seater below them. He
made the initial attack, but his guns jammed. A second pilot
followed down, creating an interesting design with his incen
diary bullets, but missing the two-seater completely. Shaffer
went in next and expended at least one hundred rounds, but
was so new to the game he was unable to tell what had
actually happened.

When they got back to their field Shaffer saw Madon ex
plaining the action to their group commander. "Who was the
third man to make an attack?" Madon inquired of his forma
tion.

Shaffer admitted that he was the culprit.

Madon put out his hand and said as he grinned, "You got him!"

A short time later Shaffer was flying with another pilot. They mistook a covey of enemy fighters for French Spads, and decided that in attacking a German two-seater there would be plenty of protection. The German gunner turned out to be a tartar; first he damaged Shaffer's control stick, and with a second burst grazed his head and almost took off his helmet. At this critical period the four "Spads" above took a hand, became single-seater Fokkers, and made the two American pilots fight like demons to escape.

While attacking a kite balloon ten miles behind the enemy lines on October 3, Shaffer went through a heavy barrage of ground gunfire and had his engine shot to junk. He told this story later:

I had no power. I was ten miles on the wrong side of the line and flopping about at 1800 feet. I knew I was out of luck and would wind up a prisoner, but at the time it was a question whether I would arrive dead or alive. The ground below was a shambles. Nothing but shellholes, barbed wire, and abandoned trenches.

As I glided down, I remembered that aviators were supposed to destroy their planes if they landed in enemy territory. The explicit orders were that we were to burn the plane. Considering everything I wondered whether there would be time or whether there would be anything left to burn. Finally, I decided to wrap it up as best I could in the easiest manner. All I had to do was to go in slowly, tilt her over on one wing tip and let her cartwheel herself to wreckage.

This I did. The effect was amazing. With a splintering of struts and stays, and a ripping of cloth as the lower wing touched the earth, the Spad buried her nose into the ground, smashing the landing gear and the propeller. Considering the fact that this was the first time I had deliberately crashed a plane, I had done pretty well, and I am quite sure our squadron commander would have been most pleased.

On May 29, the third day of the great German advanc south of the Chemin des Dames, a patrol of Escadrille N.g was ordered out to reconnoiter the shifting front and to driv back any German two-seaters that might be trying to fly in portant observation patrols.

Clarence B. Shoninger of New York City, who had been i the French Aviation since May 24, 1917, and a member (N.99 since February 22, 1918, had hoped to go on this fora His engine gave considerable trouble, however, and the patr took off without him. As usually happens, the recalcitrar power plant ran smoothly a few minutes later, and Clarenc begged permission to follow and hope to pick up the patre somewhere near the front line.

Between Rheims and Fismes he spotted them but lost cor tact a minute or so later, and as he curled about seeking h companions he was attacked by a strong force of Albatrc scouts. Shoninger put up a fight and one of the enemy ai craft had to land with a damaged engine, but the fight cor tinued and the American was forced down and crashed wit most of his controls cut away. He piled up beside a Germa antiaircraft battery near Crugny.

It was believed for some time that Shoninger had bee killed, until in the course of time it was learned that he ha been taken prisoner. He had a fairly long period in sever; enemy camps, but was unable to escape and was held unt the Armistice ended hostilities.

Alan F. Winslow, one of America's first great air heroes, ha to endure the indignity of prison camp after being shot dow at the height of his wartime popularity. This most respecte young man from River Forest, Illinois, was recruited into th Lafayette Flying Corps and enlisted in the French Aviatic July 10, 1917. He was brevetted on a Caudron by October 1 and sent to the front to fly with Escadrille Spa.152 on th day before Christmas, 1917. He remained with this Frenc squadron as a sergeant until February 12, 1918, when he wa commissioned a second lieutenant and eventually joined the 94th Pursuit Squadron.

Winslow was disappointed in the initial treatment he received at the hands of the U. S. Air Service officials, and felt that with his experience on Spads, he was entitled to a better deal. In the heat of his bitterness he made an application to join the U. S. Naval Aviation, but a day later wrote to Dr. Gros asking that the naval application be withdrawn. "Please consider my letter of yesterday as hasty," he wrote. "I would not have hesitated to accept an Army commission as first lieutenant. I was, however, a bit rumpled on receiving a second. But if I am not good-enough sport and American to take what is given me, I am no good at all. Therefore I wish to accept my second lieutenancy in the Army."

That was Alan Winslow. He had the spirit of a sportsman, and although many of his countrymen who had not as yet seen France or heard a shot fired, were being commissioned as captains and majors, he realized that there were many others with months of time on the front who were being rewarded with a single gold bar.

We have told previously how Winslow and Douglas Campbell marked the American Air Service's entry into the war by shooting down two enemy planes near Toul on April 14, 1918. From that day on Alan Winslow was engaged almost daily in very active duty, striving to add to his bag. On June 4, with two other pilots of the 94th, he shot down an enemy two-seater well over the lines, but on July 31 during a bitter fight with a formation of German Fokkers he was wounded severely and his plane shot out of action. Alan had a badly shattered left arm and after he landed in enemy territory was rushed to a German hospital where apparently everything possible was done to save his arm, but it had to be amputated above the elbow sometime later. Winslow spent five months in German hospitals and did not return to France until January 9, 1919, one of the last of the American fliers to regain his freedom.

For some time after the war he was an aide to General Billy Mitchell, and lived in Washington, D.C., for many years

where, when last heard of he was writing a book of his ex
periences.

Among the enigmatic figures to filter through the history o
the Lafayette Flying Corps was an American Negro, Eugen
Bullard, probably the only man of his race to attain the breve
of a wartime flying man during the Great War. Only a few o
the volunteers remember Bullard, but those who encountere
him in person, have never forgotten his presence, personalit
and majestic appearance.

At the outbreak of the war Bullard was flitting abou
Europe as a welterweight prize fighter. From all accounts, h
along with Bob Scanlon, another Negro, had started out :
members of Jack Johnson's boxing-carnival troupe which w:
touring overseas. Whenever bouts were available Bullard an
Scanlon took them and both were fairly well known in th
profession in those days. Both were in London at the ou
break of the war, and both hurried across to Paris and tried 1
join the French Foreign Legion. Bullard had no trouble; hov
ever, Scanlon was held up for several months, but eventual
was signed on. For years, Scanlon was mistakenly credit
with being Norman Prince's aerial gunner when Norman w
flying Voisins with V.B.108, and by some it was said he w
the first man to fire a 37-mm air cannon from the air. Aft
much research, this claim failed to stand up. Scanlon w
never a member of the French Aviation although he w
wounded at Caillette Wood when a hugh chunk of sh
smashed his hand.

This injury ruined Scanlon's chances for continuing his l
as a boxer and after the war he wandered about Paris, on t
fringes of the sporting circles and ended up by being sh
and seriously injured by a jealous woman associate.

Bullard served in the Foreign Legion through 1915–16, w
wounded several times at Verdun, and, during one conval
cence, applied for transfer to the flying service. He was :
cepted and began his training by November 15, 1916, and
completion of his courses was assigned to Spa.93 on Aug
27, but remained with that escadrille only until September

when he was sent to Spa.85. Here again, Bullard flew only a short time and was released from that squadron by November 11, 1917.

A short time before his death in New York on October 12, 1961, Bullard explained that he had been taken off Spad flying because of an eye injury received in his Foreign Legion infantry days. I had several long talks with him by telephone and tried to meet him personally, but he was not well enough to sit through any lengthy interview. I wanted to ask him about the report that he had quarreled with his commanding officer and been returned to the Foreign Legion, for according to his record, Bullard was sent back to the 170th French Infantry Regiment on January 11, 1918, and served out the war as a foot soldier. He was awarded the Croix de Guerre with Star for his services in the trenches.

Between the wars Bullard continued his colorful career and was the leader of several dance bands in Paris, operated his own night clubs, and ran a training establishment for prize fighters. During World War II Bullard carried out some secret agent work in French night spots, co-operating with the underground and, again serving with the French Army, was wounded severely at Orléans. When Hitler occupied France, American friends secretly whisked Bullard out of the country and he returned to the United States.

In 1954 Bullard was selected to relight the flame at the Tomb of the Unknown Soldier in Paris from which he again returned to his homeland and for a time was an elevator operator in the RCA building in New York City.

CONCLUSION

With the end of the conflict, an ignominious end in the view of most of the volunteers, the Great Adventure came to a close. Some were obviously relieved, some were outraged at

what they considered an unrealistic conclusion, many wanted
to get out of uniform and take the next boat home. A few sat
around numb, bewildered, unable to adjust to the many new
situations. Some had good homes and important jobs to return to, but most of the volunteers had no idea what lay
ahead for they had left home before they had a chance to
determine their futures or set up any domestic status of their
own.

Many wartime airmen believed that they would be able to
remain with aviation, that a great spread of commercial flying
was only a matter of time. They envisioned air transportation,
airlines, and even transoceanic passenger service. Most of
them were certain that there would be jobs flying the mail,
and those of us who had been so insistent on flying single-
seaters, realized gradually that the more mature types who
had selected twin-engined bombers would be the first in line
for these visionary postwar flying jobs.

A grim handful hung on, hoping that the Armistice was
only a lull in the fighting, and that the enemy would not
agree to the terms the Allies would impose. Others who had
sacrificed their university training, hoped to stay on and become peacetime airmen, retaining their wartime rank and flying pay. Some men begged to stay on, simply because they
loved to fly. Others were equally determined never to leave
the ground again.

Looking back we can all remember the vacuum of inde-
cision; it was impossible to know what to do. We had no
reliable information as to whether the war was really over
We went on long leaves in the hope of coming to some under
standing of our plight. We went to aircraft factories and
took on routine test tasks, merely to "keep our hands in." We
volunteered to ferry aircraft back and forth from France to
Great Britain. Some were fortunate enough to find jobs as
aerial couriers, carrying important documents between London
and Paris, or London and Cologne.

Many of us hounded the repatriation officers for space
aboard the transports to get home as soon as possible: many

more disappeared for weeks at a time and only returned to their squadrons or training bases when their funds ran out. We experienced sudden yearnings to visit Italy, Greece, Scotland, Ireland, Holland, and even Scandinavia. Paris and London, of course, attracted those who were ducking repatriation.

Airmen who had rushed home right after the Armistice, wrote to the rest of us to stay where we were. There was nothing at home to go home for. Civilian life was far from what it used to be. But what could a man do? The war was over and only a mere handful could be accommodated in the postwar air services. The military arms were cut to the bone, and there was no place for second lieutenants; majors would be lucky to revert to first lieutenants. Dozens of colonels with outstanding war records had to drop several grades, if they hoped to remain in the service and be assured of a job when they returned home.

At the end of World War I there were no GI benefits, college educations, allowances, bonuses, or any form of government assistance. We went home to the jobs we had oft months or in many cases, years before. In the early summer of 1914 my pay had been five dollars a week; by 1919 I had learned to fly an airplane, bomb railroad crossings, and fight with a machine gun. Having won a commission in the field, I probably felt that I was worth considerably more, but there were no legal outlets for my particular talents.

Those who had fine homes to return to were certain that everything would be all right, and those who had left the comfort of their mothers' kitchens only a few weeks before, anticipated no hardships on their return. Their problems could not compare with those of us who had been away for more than four years. Frankly, there were few jobs any of us could fill. By 1921 there was a serious depression, an economic letdown that affected ex-servicemen more than any other segment of the population. All the glory, all the medals, all the satisfaction of having served meant little when we appealed for jobs or understanding. In many cases we soon realized that

the sacrifices we had made to volunteer, serve, and fight were
small compared to those we were to endure during the next
five or six years following the Armistice.

"So what are you squawking about?" the stay-at-home demanded. "You had your war, your chunk of glory, you pa-
raded about in fancy uniforms, and got your names in the
paper. The war is over, an' the quicker you forget it, the
better."

Quite true. The war was over, and the volunteers had to
face the horrors of peace.

Jimmy Bach returned from captivity, picked up his medals
and became an American vice-consul in Paris, and later represented an American automobile manufacturing concern in
France.

On November 25, 1921, Lawrence Scanlan died of his old
1915 wounds.

William E. Dugan died in September 1922, following an
operation for septicaemia which he had contracted in the
South American jungles after the war.

Herman Chatkoff, who will be remembered as the Legionaire who requested at least one more month with his infantry
companions after he had gained his aviation brevet, returned
home in 1919, suffered a mental breakdown and had to be
placed in an insane asylum.

Robert Percy, who had acted as Bill Thaw's batman
throughout the war, became a delivery man for a Paris dress-
maker.

Robert Soubiran tried life in the United States for a few
years, and then returned to Paris as the manager of the French
branch of an American electrical corporation.

Bill Thaw had no trouble going into the aeronautical industry in Pittsburgh. He has now passed on, as has Dudley
Hill.

Frederick Zinn worked up a business, manufacturing dairy
and poultry feeds. He never went back to France, preferring

to retain his illusions of his experiences in the Foreign Legion, and as a flying man.

Harold Willis, one of the most gallant of the breed, has had several wearying months of hospital treatment, and still resides in Boston.

Kenneth Marr, whose eyesight is failing, remains cheerful and keeps in touch with many of his old friends.

Frederick H. Prince appears to enjoy a quiet life in Old Westbury, Long Island, and willingly corresponds and offers help whenever requested by the author.

James Norman Hall went to Tahiti in 1920 where he lived and wrote until his death in 1951.

Laurence Rumsey continues a quiet life in Canandaigua, New York, but Edwin C. Parsons is as alert, active, and entertaining as he ever was.

If one should ask them if they would go through their World War I experiences again, they generally are amazed that such a question should be asked. Not one would consider trading that honor for a more concrete return.

At the end of 1918, however, their war was over, and the evidence of having served in what had been the greatest cause for civilization was to be found in their records and logbooks. Those who survived returned to their homes and took up where they had left off. Some succeeded in the world of industry and commerce, some floundered through a hopeless maze of routine toil, just as they would have, had no war intruded into their drab lives, a few made the most of the limited opportunities their experiences had afforded, and full marks for their effort are their just due.

As Paul Ayres Rockwell has penned: "No novel of war or of exotic adventure can compare in interest with the plain, true story of the little group of American citizens who volunteered to fight for France in the early days of the World War. Fiction writers have imagined nothing more thrilling and more splendidly heroic than the deeds of some of these men, nor can be pictured anything greater or more stirring than moments that came to them; words cannot describe fatigue and hardships, and suffering more bitter than they at times knew."

On learning that the author was writing this book, he said in one of his letters:

This sudden revival of interest in the Escadrille Lafayette and World War I flying in general is indeed bewildering. There are eight surviving pilots of the Escadrille, most of them in good health and all willing to help serious and honorable writers. For years just before and following World War II I tried to get well-known authors to write the history of the Escadrille Lafayette, and all found the subject interesting but were already too busy working under contract.

Most of the American volunteer pilots in the service of France were gentlemen (I seldom use the word *gentleman*, for it is grossly overworked and misunderstood in our country), who had ideals and were capable of believing there were things worth fighting for. Almost all came from comfortable homes and gave up good positions, or even lives of ease and luxury, to undergo the hardships and risks of Army life. Many came from families that had been established in America since Colonial times and had helped make this country great, and were better educated than the average young man of the 1914–18 period.

In my opinion, the American volunteers who served France in 1914–17 can best be compared with the Crusaders of centuries ago. Many may have been inspired by desire for adventure, but they also believed in something for which they were willing to offer their lives.

I am writing to you as a fellow volunteer of 1914; you knew and still understand the "spirit of the times." The youth of our generation were not hardened to "wars and rumors of wars," or cynical about patriotism and Causes. We were not afraid of war and death in battle and a large part of idealism still existed. Nationalism was still respected, Americans still loved their flag and were grateful to other nations that had made the flag possible. I think we were better off, spiritually, and happier than the youth of today; certainly more ignorant of the horrible things men are capable of, and by evil men I mean the Communist leaders and such like.

Need more be said?

FREEDOM

They never fail who die
In the great cause: the block may soak their gore,
Their heads may sodden in the sun; their limbs
Be strung to city gates and castle walls:—
But still their spirit walks abroad. Though years
Elapse, and others share as dark a doom,
They but augment the deep and sweeping thoughts
Which overpower all others and conduct
The world at last to freedom.

—BYRON

COMPLETE LIST OF AMERICAN VOLUNTEERS
WHO SERVED WITH THE LAFAYETTE ESCADRILLE

Name	Home	Date of enlistment in the French Aviation	Status
G. Raoul Lufbery	Wallingford, Conn.	Aug. 31, 1914	Killed in action
Didier Masson	Los Angeles, Calif.	October 1914	Died after war
William Thaw	Pittsburgh, Pa.	Dec. 24, 1914	Died Apr. 1934
Bert Hall	Higginsville, Mo.	Dec. 28, 1914	Died Dec. 1948
Norman Prince	Boston, Mass.	Mar. 4, 1915	Killed in action
Elliott C. Cowdin	New York, N.Y.	Mar. 5, 1915	Died Jan. 1933
Victor E. Chapman	New York, N.Y.	Aug. 1, 1915	Killed in action
Dudley L. Hill	Peekskill, N.Y.	Aug. 3, 1915	Died after war
Charles C. Johnson	St. Louis, Mo.	Sep. 2, 1915	Died Oct. 1939
Kiffin Y. Rockwell	Asheville, N.C.	Sep. 2, 1915	Killed in action
Laurence Rumsey	Carthage, N.C.	Sep. 9, 1915	Still living
H. Clyde Balsley	San Antonio, Tex.	Sep. 16, 1915	Died after war
James R. McConnell	Carthage, N.Y.	Oct. 1, 1915	Killed in action
Paul Pavelka	Madison, Conn.	Oct. 18, 1915	Killed by accident
Willis B. Haviland	St. Paul, Minn.	Jan. 26, 1916	Died Nov. 1944
Frederick H. Prince	Old Westbury, N.Y.	Jan. 29, 1916	Still living
Robert L. Rockwell	Cincinnati, Ohio	Feb. 7, 1916	Died in 1958
Robert Soubiran	New York, N.Y.	Feb. 27, 1916	Died Jan. 1949
Ronald W. Hoskier	South Orange, N.J.	Apr. 5, 1916	Killed in action
		Apr. 12, 1916	Died after war

		Apr. 13, 1916	Died after war
Edwin C. Parsons	Osprey, Fla.	Apr. 13, 1916	Still living
Walter Lovell	Concord, Mass.	May 22, 1916	Died after war
Harold B. Willis	Boston, Mass.	May 22, 1916	Still living
Edmond C. C. Genet	Ossining, N.Y.	May 24, 1916	Killed in action
William E. Dugan, Jr.	Rochester, N.Y.	June 10, 1916	Died Sept. 1922
Andrew C. Campbell, Jr.	Chicago, Ill.	July 20, 1916	Still living
Edward F. Hinkle	Cincinnati, Ohio	July 20, 1916	Still living
Kenneth Marr	San Francisco, Calif.	July 20, 1916	Still living
Ray C. Bridgman	Lake Forest, Ill.	July 24, 1916	Died a suicide
Charles H. Dolan, Jr.	Boston, Mass.	Aug. 11, 1916	Still living
Douglas MacMonagle	San Francisco, Calif.	Oct. 3, 1916	Killed in action
David McK. Peterson	Honesdale, Pa.	Oct. 9, 1916	Killed after war
James N. Hall	Colfax, Iowa	Oct. 11, 1916	Died July 1951
James R. Doolittle	New York, N.Y.	Oct. 16, 1916	Died after accident
John A. Drexel	Philadelphia, Pa.	Oct. 27, 1916	Died Mar. 1958
Henry Sweet Jones	Harford, Pa.	Oct. 27, 1916	Still living
Christopher W. Ford	New York, N.Y.	May 9, 1917	Died Apr. 1945

FRENCH AVIATION MEMBERS OF LAFAYETTE ESCADRILLE

Georges Thénault	Paris, France	Called up on outbreak of war	Died after war
Alfred de Laage de Meux	Clessé, France	Mar. 25, 1915	Killed in accident
Arnoux de Maison-Rouge	Paris, France	1915	Killed in action
Louis Verdier-Fauvety	Meaux, France	Feb. 26, 1916	Killed in bomb raid

OFFICIAL VICTORIES
OF LAFAYETTE FLYING CORPS

Gervais Raoul Lufbery	17	Charles Raymond Blake	1
Frank L. Baylies	12	Ellison E. Boggs	1
David Putnam	12	H. Gordon Campbell	1
Paul F. Baer	8	Victor Chapman	1
Thomas G. Cassady	8	Charles W. Chapman, Jr.	1
Gorman deF. Larner	8	Phelps Collins	1
Edwin C. Parsons	8	Elliott C. Cowdin	1
Charles J. Biddle	8	Charles H. Dolan, Jr.	1
William Ponder	7	Donald H. Eldredge	1
James A. Connelly, Jr.	6	Robert G. Eoff	1
David McKelvey Peterson	5	Andre Gundelach	1
William Thaw	5	David W. Guy	1
Charles G. Grey	4	Willis B. Haviland	1
Bert Hall	3	Robert B. Hoeber	1
James Norman Hall	3	Charles Chouteau Johnson	1
Jean Huffer	3	Henry S. Jones	1
Sereno T. Jacob	3	Hugo N. Kenyon	1
Norman Prince	3	Schuyler Lee	1
Reginald Sinclair	3	William F. Loomis	1
George E. Turnure, Jr.	3	Walter Lovell	1
Charles H. Veil	3	Kenneth Marr	
Charles H. Wilcox	3	Alan Nichols	
Wainwright Abbott	2	Charles B. Nordhoff	
James Baugham	2	David S. Paden	
Edward J. Corsi	2	Leonard M. Reno	
Austen B. Crehore	2	Leyland L. Rounds	
Edwin B. Fairchild	2	Glenn N. Sitterly	
Christopher W. Ford	2	Robert Soubiran	
Thomas Hitchcock, Jr.	2	Joseph C. Stehlin	
Walter D. Rheno	2	Henry E. Stickney	
Kiffin Y. Rockwell	2	Benjamin Stuart Walcott	
Harold Y. Saxon	2	William E. Wass	
Walter J. Shaffer	2	Joseph V. Wilson	
Alfred H. Stanley	2	Wallace C. Winter	
William A. Wellman	2	Houston Woodward	
Alan F. Winslow	2	Walter R. York	

Total 199

COMPLETE LIST OF LAFAYETTE
FLYING CORPS PILOTS
IN ORDER OF ENLISTMENT
IN THE FRENCH AVIATION

1914

:. Raoul Lufbery	Aug. 31
)idier Masson	Oct.
ames J. Bach	Dec. 10
Villiam Thaw	Dec. 24
ert Hall	Dec. 28

1915

azier Curtis	Feb. 28
orman Prince	Mar. 4
lliott C. Cowdin	Mar. 5
ictor E. Chapman	Aug. 1
udley L. Hill	Aug. 3
arroll D. Winslow	Aug. 19
harles C. Johnson	Sept. 2
iffin Y. Rockwell	Sept. 2
aurence Rumsey	Sept. 9
. Clyde Balsley	Sept. 16
mes R. McConnell	Oct. 1
ul Pavelka	Oct. 18

1916

an Huffer	Jan. 1
illis B. Haviland	Jan. 26
ederick Prince, Jr.	Jan. 29
bert L. Rockwell	Feb. 7
ederick W. Zinn	Feb. 14
bert Soubiran	Feb. 27
arwick D. Worthing-	
on	Mar. 9
nnis Dowd	Mar. 28
nneth P. Littauer	Mar. 29
nald W. Hoskier	Apr. 5
phen Bigelow	Apr. 13
omas M. Hewitt,	
r.	Apr. 13
win C. Parsons	Apr. 13

Norman L. Barclay	May 22
Walter Lovell	May 22
Harold B. Willis	May 22
Pierre Boal	May 24
H. Lincoln Chatkoff	May 24
Edmond C. C. Genet	May 24
Marius Romain Rocle	June 5
William E. Dugan, Jr.	June 10
Andrew Courtney	
Campbell, Jr.	July 20
Edward F. Hinkle	July 20
Kenneth Marr	July 20
Ray C. Bridgman	July 24
Archibald Johnston	July 28
Charles H. Dolan, Jr.	Aug. 11
Dabney D. Horton	Aug. 16
George A. McCall	Sept. 1
Douglas MacMonagle	Oct. 3
David McKelvey Pe-	
terson	Oct. 9
James Norman Hall	Oct. 11
James Ralph Doolittle	Oct. 16
Leland L. Rounds	Oct. 16
John Armstrong Drexel	Oct. 27
Henry Sweet Jones	Oct. 27
Bennett A. Molter	Nov. 2
Robert L. Donzé	Nov. 7
Eugene Bullard	Nov. 15
Granville A. Pollock	Dec. 24
Walter D. Rheno	Dec. 24

1917

Everett T. Buckley	Jan. 6
Oliver M. Chadwick	Jan. 17
Daniel Huger	Jan. 26
Lawrence Scanlan	Feb. 8
John Joyce Whitmore	Feb. 8
Charles H. Wilcox	Feb. 8

George E. Turnure,		Robert L. Moore	May 2
Jr.	Feb. 16	Clarence Bernard Sho-	
Charles W. Kerwood	Feb. 18	ninger	May 2
Alfred D. Pelton	Feb. 19	Julian Cornell Biddle	May 2
Joseph C. Stehlin	Feb. 19	Clarence H. Faith	May 2
John Russell Adams	Feb. 20	Henry Brewster Palmer	May 2
Paul Frank Baer	Feb. 20	Stephen Tyson	May 2
Louis Charton	Feb. 20	George Gale Willard	May 2
Caleb James Coats-		Lester Strayer Brady	May 2
worth, Jr.	Feb. 20	Phillip P. Benney	May 3
Edgar G. Hamilton	Feb. 27	David E. Putnam	May 3
Charles Trinkard	Mar. 13	Glenn N. Sitterly	May 3
André Gundelach	Mar. 20	Arthur Bluthenthal	June
Sereno Thorp Jacob	Mar. 20	Schuyler Lee	June
Theodore de Kruijff	Mar. 20	Vernon Booth, Jr.	June
Edward J. Loughran	Mar. 20	Cyrus F. Chamberlain	June
Leonard M. Reno	Mar. 20	Roger Harvey Clapp	June
Harold E. Wright	Mar. 20	Fearchar Ian Ferguson	June
Charles T. Malone	Mar. 21	David E. Judd	June
Charles Maury Jones	Mar. 26	Manderson Lehr	June
Marcellus E. Wild	Mar. 29	William Henry Meeker	June
Wainwright Abbott	Apr. 2	Charles B. Nordhoff	June
Charles J. Biddle	Apr. 8	Benjamin Stuart Wal-	
Donald E. Stone	Apr. 8	cott	June
Herschel J. McKee	Apr. 12	William E. Wass	June
Alfred Holt Stanley	Apr. 12	Charles Raymond	
Russell F. Stearns	Apr. 12	Blake	June
Charles Herbert Veil	Apr. 12	William Thomas	
Carter Landram		Ponder	June
Ovington	Apr. 20	Philip Washburn Da-	
Austin G. Parker	May 2	vis	June
Philip N. Bush	May 9	Sidney Rankin Drew	June
Stuart Emmet Edgar	May 9	Eric A. Fowler	June
Christopher W. Ford	May 9	Clarence M. Glover	June
Dudley G. Tucker	May 9	William F. Loomis	June
Meredith L. Dowd	May 14	Leo E. Benoit	June
Edgar J. Bouligny	May 15	Charles W. Chapman,	
Edward J. Corsi	May 15	Jr.	June
Hugh Terres	May 15	John Rowell Cotton	June
Phelps Collins	May 17	George Dock, Jr.	June
Frank L. Baylies	May 21	Joseph Francis Gill	June
Nathaniel Duffy	May 24	Warren Tucker	
Robert M. Hanford	May 24	Hobbs	June

Walter B. Miller	June 10	Alan H. Nichols	July 1
Harold Young Saxon	June 10	Hugo N. Kenyon	July 5
Clifton B. Thompson	June 10	Arthur Lawrence Cun-	
Louis Leslie Byers	June 13	ningham	July 7
Donald Herbert El-		James Henry	
dredge	June 13	Baugham	July 10
Henry Forster	June 13	James Alexander	
Norman Grieb	June 13	Bayne	July 10
Earl W. Hughes	June 13	Thomas G. Cassady	July 10
William J. McKerness	June 13	Robert B. Hoeber	July 10
Charles M. Kinsolv-		G. de Freest Larner	July 10
ing	June 13	George Clark Moseley	July 10
Robert E. Read	June 13	Kenneth Albert Roth-	
Upton Sullivan	June 13	armel	July 10
William A. Wellman	June 13	Dumaresq Spencer	July 10
Herman Whitmore	June 13	Alan F. Winslow	July 10
Alan N. Ash	June 15	Dinsmore Ely	July 13
Thomas B. Buffum	June 15	Cedric Gerald Faunt	
James A. Connelly,		LeRoy	July 13
Jr.	June 15	William Graham Bull-	
Reginald Sinclaire	June 15	en	July 14
Charles Chester Bas-		Robert Grimshaw Eoff	July 14
sett, Jr.	June 17	David Sheldon Paden	July 14
Charles G. Grey	June 17	Houston Woodward	July 14
Jasper C. Brown	June 19	Austen Ballard Cre-	
Linn Palmer Cookson	June 19	hore	July 16
David Wilbur Lewis	June 21	Frank Elmer Starrett	July 19
Alvin Alexander Cush-		John F. Randall	July 20
man	June 22	Alan A. Cook	July 21
Benjamin H. Baird	June 25	Russell B. Corey	July 21
Thomas Hitchcock,		David W. Guy	July 21
Jr.	June 25	Ralph Lane Loomis	July 21
Harry F. Johnson	June 25	Henry Elmer Stickney	July 21
James H. McMillen	June 25	William Hallet Tailer	July 21
William B. Rodgers,		Elmer B. Taylor	July 21
Jr.	June 25	William Carey	
Leslie R. Taber	June 25	Van Fleet, Jr.	July 21
Wallace Charles Win-		Joseph Volney Wilson	July 21
ter	June 25	Rufus R. Rand, Jr.	July 26
Walter R. York	June 25	Henry Batchelor, 3rd.	Aug. 1
H. Gordon Campbell	June 27	James Murray Grier	Aug. 1
Edwin Bradley Fair-		Walter John Shaffer	Aug. 1
child	June 27	Ellison Converse	
George Marion Kyle	June 27	Boggs	Aug. 4

LIST OF VOLUNTEERS
RELEASED BY THE FRENCH GOVERNMENT
BEFORE SERVING AT THE FRONT

Sidney T. Allen, St. Louis, Mo.	Defective Eyesight
W. K. Appleton, Jr., Nice, France	Inaptitude
Arthur M. Aten, Brooklyn, N.Y.	Deserted to United States
Clarence M. Bosworth, New York, N.Y.	On leave in America
Algernon Boyesen, New York, N.Y.	Inaptitude
Stafford L. Brown, Newton Center, Mass.	Disciplinary reasons
Richard N. Bullen, Chicago, Ill.	Injured in training
Joseph M. Carrère, New York, N.Y.	Inaptitude
Edward M. Collier, Bass Rivers, Mass.	Ill health
Isadore Court, New York, N.Y.	Inaptitude
Lowell R. Dulon, New York, N.Y.	Inaptitude
Sherburne Eaton, Boston, Mass.	Inaptitude
Chester A. Elliott, Akron, Ohio	Transferred to U.S.A.S.
John Endicott, Boston, Mass.	Disciplinary reasons
Joseph Flynn, Philadelphia, Pa.	Dishonorable conduct
Tod Ford, Pasadena, California	Ill health
William Frey (no address)	Deserted to United States
William W. Gibson, Savannah, Ga.	Inaptitude
Reginald G. Gouraud, Paris, France	Inaptitude
David Porter Guest, Richmond, Va.	Released at own request
John B. Harrison, Bloomfield, N.J.	Inaptitude
John Heilbuth, Paris, France	Defective eyesight
Leslie Hickson, New York, N.Y.	Released at own request
Minton W. Holden, Camden, N.J.	Injured in training
Edwin A. Hough, Edgemere, Mass.	Inaptitude
Mark Leslie Hull, Mamaroneck, N.Y.	Inaptitude
William F. Kirkwood, Boston, Mass.	Inaptitude
John Robert Kowall, Roxbury, Mass.	Injured in training
Henry S. Lee, Cornwall, N.Y.	Inaptitude
Leslie Ludlam, Montclair, N.J.	Ill health
James B. McCreary, Buffalo, N.Y.	Ill health
William McGinn, Cincinnati, Ohio.	Released at own request
Gordon B. Macke, New York, N.Y.	Released at own request
Guy Bertram Magley, Joplin, Mo.	Inaptitude
Harold L. Manierre, Chicago, Ill.	Inaptitude
Alvin Ford Miller, New York, N.Y.	Defective eyesight
George Miller, Kansas City, Mo.	Inaptitude
Gordon R. Mills, Chicago, Ill.	Ill health
Oscar Mouvet, New York, N.Y.	Inaptitude
Curtis B. Munson, New York, N.Y.	Released at own request

Nathan Oakes, Jr., Providence, R.I.	Released at own request
Thomas Potter, Westchester, N.Y.	Inaptitude
Hugh O. J. Ridlon, Chicago, Ill.	Released at own request
George Rockwell, Waterbury, Conn.	Released at own request
John F. Rolph, Centerville, Md.	Released at own request
Raymond T. Ross, Crawfordsville, Ind.	Defective eyesight
Joseph Roe Saul, Lancaster, N.H.	Disciplinary reasons
Edwin Booth Schreiber, Anaconda, Mont.	Released at own request
Horace Seaver, Hartford, Conn.	Injured in training
Walter B. Shipley, Page, W. Va.	Released at the front
Samuel W. Skinner, Cincinnati, Ohio	Died during training
Wallace C. Speers, Montclair, N.J.	Ill health
Gerald S. Stone, Spencer, Mass.	Ill health
Neal Wainwright, Boston, Mass.	Released at own request
Westel R. Willoughby, Baltimore, Md.	Released to U. S. Army
Pierre M. Wilson, Marseilles, France	Ill health

ACKNOWLEDGMENTS

Approaching the closing pages of this book I realized
that whatever merit or interest it has attained is due chiefly
to the help and practical contributions of so many friends and
others who had learned of this project. Without their assistance and encouragement I could not have presented so much
information on the history of these American volunteers. The
book might have been written eventually but it could not have
offered such a complete and interesting story without this
unstinting aid.

First and foremost I must thank Colonel Paul Ayres Rockwell of Asheville, North Carolina, for his generous contribution. No man alive could have provided the data, photographs, letters, clippings, and records which he so kindly
turned over to me. Colonel Rockwell, brother of Kiffin Rockwell, had long acted as chief historian of the Lafayette Escadrille. He knew every member personally and kept in touch
with them or their families for years. He was a goldmine of
reminiscences, facts, dates, and addresses, but more important, from the day he was advised that I had undertaken to
write this history, he kept up a continued correspondence
offering advice, new thoughts, suggestions and sheafs of
newly uncovered material. He gave full permission to use his
earlier book, *American Fighters in the Foreign Legion* as a
source book and all other pertinent documents in his possession. His lively recollections of Raoul Lufbery, backed up by
many original copies of the personal writings of this air hero

helped considerably in forming a complete reassessment of Lufbery's true character. Without Colonel Rockwell's aid, this work would have been a wearisome chore instead of the fascinating experience it turned out to be.

Edwin C. Parsons, now Rear-Admiral Parsons of the United States Navy (Ret.), was another cheerful enthusiast. His contribution was most valued and filled in much of the action so necessary to a book of this kind. Ted, who had shot down more than his share of enemy aircraft, drew not only on his personal memories, but gave access to his many stories of the Lafayette Escadrille which had been printed in adventure magazines all through the English-speaking world. He also provided much squadron information, granted me permission to quote from his book, *The Great Adventure* and cheerfully answered all my letters with their pages of what must have seemed dreary and pointless questions. Parsons, too, continued months of correspondence, providing a most arousing spirit of enthusiasm which kept me buoyed up throughout the writing of this book.

Mr. Frederick H. Prince, Jr., of Old Westbury, New York, patiently responded to all my letters and requests and although not in the best of health, gave unstintingly of his time and knowledge. He provided the names and addresses of dozens of valued contacts.

Mr. H. Hugh Wynne of Santa Ana, California, the editor of *Cross & Cockade Journal,* provided many of the photographs presented here and full use of certain information concerning the Lafayette Escadrille which had appeared in his organization's publication.

Mr. Charles W. Kerwood of Washington, D.C., although denying that he played any important role in the Lafayette Flying Corps, willing helped in compiling data and put me in touch with others who had valuable information.

Mr. LeRoy Prinz of Los Angeles, California, contributed the photograph of the garden fence on which Raoul Lufbery fell to his death, and several others which could not be reproduced in this volume.

I am indebted to William Wickham Hoffman, former U. S. Army major, who contributed the valued material on the transfer of Lafayette Flying Corps airmen to the U. S. Air Service.

Major James F. Sunderman, Chief Book Branch, Office of Information, Department of the Air Force, again came to my aid and provided many valuable photographs.

In conclusion I am also grateful to Charles Scribner's Sons of New York for their permission to reproduce Alan Seeger's poem which appears at the opening of this book.

BIBLIOGRAPHY

For the reader who would delve deeper into the history of the Lafayette Flying Corps, or more specifically into the story of the Lafayette Escadrille, we can offer only a very limited list of books covering these subjects. Not too many volumes were written about these men, for their lives and deeds were overshadowed, after the Armistice, by the over-all picture of America's part in the Great War. Also, since many were transferred to U. S. Army Air Service squadrons early in 1918, much of their history and accomplishments were absorbed into the official histories of the units to which they were assigned. The following, if they can be obtained, will satisfy most readers and we heartily recommend every one.

American Fighters in the Foreign Legion, by Paul Ayres Rockwell, Houghton Mifflin Company.

The Great Adventure, by E. C. Parsons, Doubleday, Duran & Company.

High Adventure, by James Norman Hall, Houghton Mifflin Company.

Flying for France, by James R. McConnell, Doubleday, Page and Company.

War Letters of Edmond Genet, edited by Grace Ellery Channing, Charles Scribner's Sons.

New England Aviators (two volumes), Houghton Mifflin Company.

The Lafayette Flying Corps, (two volumes) by Hall and Nordhoff, Houghton Mifflin Company.

History of the World War, (five volumes) by Frank H. Simonds, The Review of Reviews Company.

The Great Events of the Great War, (seven volumes) edited by Charles F. Horne, National Alumni.

Air Aces of the 1914–1918 War, by Bruce Robertson, Harleyford Publications, Ltd.

Aircraft of the 1914–1918 War, by D. A. Russell, Harborough Publishing Company, Ltd.

Falcons of France, Nordoff and Hall, Little, Brown and Company.

En l'Air, by Bert Hall, The New Library, Inc. (1918).

Norman Prince, by Babbitt, Houghton Mifflin Company.

Victor Chapman's Letters from France, The Macmillan Company.

The Story of the Lafayette Escadrille, by Georges Thénault, Small Maynard & Company.

INDEX

Aero Club of America, 126
Aero Club of California, 126
Albatros aircraft, 34–36, 185, 187, 190, 211, 219
Albert, 231
Allard, Sergeant, 98
Allen, Frederick, 22
Alpha Delta Phi, 70
Alpha Tau Omega, 70
American Express Company, 56
American Field Service, XIII, 16, 20, 22, 66, 153, 173, 200, 201, 220, 278, 301
American Fighters in the Foreign Legion, 326
American Volunteers:
  Members of Lafayette Escadrille, 319
  Released before service at front, 324, 325
Ames, George Preston, 69
Amiens, 141
Anglo-American Hospital, 109
Antoinette monoplane, 122
Antwerp, 14
Anzani engine, 26
Arabic, R.M.S., 24
"Archie," pet dog, 188, 189
Argus engine, 35
Arlington National Cemetery, 203
Armengaud, Colonel, 248
Armentières, France, 276
Armistice, 149
Arras, 71, 231
Asheville, N.C., 109
Atlanta *Constitution*, 108
Atlanta *Journal*, 41

Atlantic Monthly, 207, 209
Aviatik aircraft, 5, 6, 74, 106, 120
Avord, 26, 27
Ayres, Major Enoch Shaw, 42

Bach, James J., 1, 4–14, 18, 19, 292, 314
Bacon, Robert M., 23
Baer, Paul Frank, 253, 276–79
Ball, Captain Albert, 37
Balloon busting, 212, 213
Balsley, H. Clyde, 25, 30, 61, 77–84, 86, 87
Bar-le-Duc, 48, 55, 88, 103
Barrés, Colonel, 20, 67, 132
Baylies, Frank L., 105, 277–80
Beauchamp-Proctor, Captain Andrew, 213
Becherau, M., 192
Belfort, 39
Bentley engine, 246
Bernstorff, Count J. H. von, 132, 133
Bertaud, Captain, 133
Besnard, M. René, 23
Besseneau hangars, 48
Bethune, 231
Biddle, Charles, 253, 284–89
Bigelow, Stephen, 162
Bishop, Captain William A., 37
Blériot, Louis, 27
Blériot aircraft, 200
Bliss, Robert W., 17
Bliss, General Tasker H., 249
Boal, Pierre, 24
Boelcke, Oswald, 35, 67, 68, 75, 105, 106
Boer War, 149, 153

Bolling, Lt. Col. Raynal C., 248
Bonnell, Brooke, XIII
Bordeaux, 15
Bouligny, Edgar John, 1
Bourgeous, Leon, 23
Bouttieaux, Colonel, 18, 23
Breguet aircraft, 29
Brest-Litovsk, 24
Bridgman, Ray Claflin, 198, 199, 210
Bristol Fighter, 182, 185
Brocard, Lieutenant, 3, 57
Brussels, 14
Buc, 19
Buckley, Everett T., 300, 301
Buffum, Thomas B., 301, 302
Bullard, Eugene, 310, 311
Bullecourt, 202
Burgess Flying School, 16
Byers, Louis Leslie, 302

Cachy-sur-Somme, 130, 132, 134, 138
Calais, 14
Calderon, José García, 71
Cambrai, 36, 204
Camel, Sopwith, 182, 185, 190
Campbell, Jr., Andrew Courtney, 193–96, 242, 243
Campbell, Douglas, 174, 263–65, 309
Campbell, H. Gordon, 244
Canadian Contingent, First, 173
"Carranza," pet dog, 91
Carranza, Venustiano, 125
Carstairs, Stewart, 1, 2, 14
Casey, Jack, XIII
Caudron aircraft, 4, 29
  C-III, 57; C-IV, 57; G-2, 19; G-3, 272; G-VI, 275
Cavell, Edith, 24
Chadwick, Oliver, 285–87
Chambers, Reid, 174, 263, 264
Chandler, Robert, 17
Chapman, John Jay, 69, 157
Chapman, Victor, XII, 25, 30, 69–76, 79, 83–87
Charton, Louis, 302
Châteauroux, 27
Chatham Bar, 28
Chatkoff, Herman Lincoln, 160, 314

Chaudun, 202, 245
Chaumont, 201
Chicago Daily News, 260, 280
Chipilly, 186
Ciecomski, Lieutenant, 196, 197, 232, 233
Civil War, The, 149
Clinton, Cornelia Tappen, 157
Clinton, Governor George, 157
Coffyn, Frank, 198
Cohan, George M., 181
Coiffard, Lieutenant Michael, 213
Collier's, magazine, 272
Collins, Phelps, 253
Collishaw, Major Raymond, 190
Compiègne Forest, 150
Confederate Army, 42
Constantinesco gear, 89
Cooper, Captain H. A., 37
Cooper bombs, 232
Coppens, Major Willy, 213
Corcieux, 127
Counani, Republic of, 139
Cowdin, Elliott, 18–20, 24, 30, 67, 68, 136, 255
Cross and Cockade Journal, 327
Curtis, Frazier, 16–19, 21, 107
Curtiss, Glenn, 198
Curtiss biplane, 122

Daniels, Josephus, 159
Dannemarie, 39
Daytona Beach, Florida, 222
Dean, Tommy, 122–25
Deane, Silas, 15
DECORATIONS:
  American: Bronze Star, 109; Distinguished Service Cross, 224, 273, 284
  Belgian: Croix de Guerre, 273; Chevalier de L'Ordre de Leopold, 273
  French: Croix des Blesses, 109; Croix de Guerre, 13, 31, 51, 55, 62, 73, 84, 87, 109, 110, 143, 145, 167, 171, 201, 271, 272, 275, 277, 279, 284, 306, 311; Legion of Honor, 13, 22, 55, 62

87, 109, 110, 129, 162, 172, 280, 284; Médaille Militaire, 13, 20, 51, 84, 87, 271, 279, 284, 306

de Havilland-2, 32, 36

de Havilland-4, 193

de Laage de Meux, Lieutenant, 31, 61–64, 88, 127, 136, 142, 172, 188

de Lafayette, Marquis, 15

de Lesseps, Jacques, 17, 198

de Lesseps, Paul, 17

Delta Kappa Epsilon, 70

de Maison-Rouge, Lieutenant Arnoux, 62, 64, 65, 188, 189, 196

Deperdussin aircraft, 19, 57

de Sillac, M. Jarousse, 18, 21, 22

Dodd, Major T. F., 247

Dominguez airfield, 152

Donauschingen prison, 300

Doolittle, James Ralph, 224, 225

Douaumont Fort, 24, 53, 103, 106, 134

Douchy, 165

Douhet, Guilio, 204

Dover, England, 237

Dowd, Dennis, XIII, 1, 160, 161

Dressy, Private Jean, 62, 187, 188

Drexel, John Armstrong, 198, 199

Dugan, Jr., William E., 24, 172, 173, 210, 218, 276, 314

Dunkirk, 14, 130, 225, 237

Dun-sur-Meuse, 241

Escadrille Américaine, 25, 30, 31, 36, 38, 39, 102

Escadrille de la Garde Cherffienne, 108

Escadrille des Volontaires, 133

Esther, pet skunk, 91

Etain, 63

Etonian, R.M.S., 139

"Explosive" bullets, 114, 115

Farman, Maurice, aircraft, 46, 97

Farnsworth, Henry, XII, 70

Felix, Lieutenant, 58

Festubert, 146

F.E.2b, aircraft, 36

Flanders, Battle of, 227, 228

Fleury, 66

Flying Aces, magazine, 189

Flying Circus, 229

Flying for France, 66

Foch, General Ferdinand, 149

Fokker, Anthony, 32

Fokker D-2, aircraft, 35

Fokker triplane, 35, 87

Fonck, Captain René, 107, 155, 191

Ford, Christopher, 24–26, 245, 292

Ford, Henry, 24

Foreign Legion, XIII, 14, 23, 42, 43, 57; Third Regiment, 43, 69

Forest de Hesse, 175

Foster, Sergeant, 37

Foulois, General Benjamin D., 249

"Fram," pet dog, 91

Franklin, Benjamin, 15, 69

Frechon, Mr., 21

Free French Forces, 109

French Air Service, XIII, 2

French Red Cross, 137

FRENCH REGIMENTS: 8th Hussars, 65; 14th Dragoons, 62; 36th Infantry, 126; 107th Infantry, 179; 109th Infantry, 126

Froids, 76

Gallipoli, 24, 180

Garros, Roland, 32, 198

Genet, Citizen, 157

Genet, Edmé Jacques, 157

Genet, Edmond C. C., XII, 70, 157–61, 163–72, 188

Georgetown, S.C., 15

Gerstner Field, 225

Gibbs, Sir Philip, 203

Gilbert, Eugene, 32

Giroux, Lieutenant, 5–7

Grahame-White, Claude, 198

Great Adventure, The, 151, 327

Green, Edward, 297

Grinnell College, 206

Gros, Dr. Edmund L., 21–23, 67, 77, 108, 110, 132, 133, 137, 144, 173, 208, 245, 250, 280, 309

Groupe des Divisions d'Entrainement, (G.D.E.), 28, 29
Guerre Aerienne, magazine, 103, 175, 240, 260
Guynemer, Captain Georges, 107, 155, 161, 191

Habsheim, 115
Hague Convention, 294
Halberstadt aircraft, 229
Halifax, Nova Scotia, 138, 139
Hall, Bert, 4, 18, 19, 30, 48–52, 60, 87
Hall, James Norman, 49, 108, 174, 205–12, 214–20, 292, 295–300, 315
Ham, 64, 165, 170–72, 181, 186
Handley-Page bomber, 185, 239
Hanriot aircraft, 229
Happe, Captain, 31, 139
Hartmannsweilerkopf, 40, 166, 167
Harvard University, 201, 281
Haviland, Willis B., 130, 131
Henry's Bar, 28
Heuberg prison, 300
Hewitt, Thomas, 172, 202
High Adventure, 209
Hill, Dudley Lawrence, 48, 89, 144, 145, 156, 188, 314
Hill, 79, 305
Hindenburg Line, 165, 184
Hinkle, Edward F., 162, 172
Hirschauer, General, 23
Hispano-Suiza engine, 162, 190, 192, 246
Hitchcock, Jr., Thomas, 302–6
Hitler, Adolf, XV, 149
Hoffman, Major William W., 247–50, 328
Horton, Dabney, 274
Hoskier, Herman C., 156
Hoskier, Ronald Wood, 156, 163, 164, 187, 188
Hôtel de la Bonne Rencontre, 29
Hôtel des Invalides, XII, 96
Hôtel Palais d'Orsay, 17
Hoxsey, Arch, 198

Huerta, General Vitoriano, 122, 12?, 125
Huffer, John F., 271, 272
Hughes, Charles Evans, 168, 181

Immelmann, Max, 102
Indian Head insignia, 38, 60, 17?, 253
Issoudun, 261

Jacob, Eugene, 70
Jay, John, 69
Johnson, Charles Choteau, 25, 30, 4?, 61, 77, 90, 118
Johnstone, Ralph, 198
Jones, Harry S., 174, 198, 200
Junkers aircraft, 204

Kappa Alpha, 70
Karlsruhe prison, 300
Kenly, Brigadier General William ?, 248
Kerwood, Charles W., 289–91, 3?, 327
Kirschner prints, 186
Kitchener's Mob, 207

Lafayette cocktail, 59, 137
LAFAYETTE ESCADRILLE, XI, XII, ?, 19, 52, 55, 133, 150, 161
  Bonus for Decorations, 197; me?, bers transferred to U. S. For?, 252, 254; rate of pay, 137, 1?, uniforms, 156, 157; vict?, scores, 136
Lafayette Flying Corps, X, 15, 20?,
Lafayette Flying Corps, The, 108
LAFAYETTE MEMORIAL, 62
La Fère, 170
Lakes Gerardmer, 40, 128
Laon, 10, 11
Latham, Hubert, 198
Laurens, Captain, 72
Le Bourget, 19, 88, 89, 112
Lechfeld prison, 304
Leelanaw, S.S., 24
Legion of Garibaldi, 18
Lehigh University, 200

Lehr, Manderson, 290
Le Plessis-Belleville, 25, 29
Le Rhone engine, 5, 35, 111, 246
Letord aircraft, 29
Lewis gun, 33, 37
Lincoln, U.S.S., 250
Littauer, Kenneth Proctor, 272–74
London, 24
Loos, 146
Lorraine-Dietrich engine, 192
Louis XVI, 158
Louis XVIII, 157
Lovell, Walter, 162, 201, 218, 233, 234
Lufbery, G. Raoul, 38, 48, 59, 61, 77, 78, 85, 92–103, 112, 113, 121, 127, 128, 161, 162, 170–72, 175–79, 208, 210, 233, 234, 239, 240, 243, 249, 259–67, 283
Lufbery Circle, 102
Luke, Lieutenant Frank, 213
Lunéville, 19
Lusitania, R.M.S., 3, 20
L.V.G. aircraft, 86
Luxeuil-les-Bains, 30, 48, 63
Lydon, Joseph, XIII, 70

McConnell, James R., 25, 30, 31, 39, 60, 65, 66, 79, 87, 90, 103, 164–67, 208
McCudden, Major James, 64, 155
McKee, Herschel J., 302, 304–6
MacMonagle, Douglas, 174, 205, 220–22
MacMonagle, Mrs., 220, 222
Madon, Georges, 155, 306
Mangeot, Sergeant-Pilot, 7–10
Mannock, Major "Mickey," 102, 144, 155
Marie Antoinette, 158
Marone, 267
Marr, Kenneth, 172–75, 315
Martainville, 142
Massengale, St. Elmo, 43, 44
Masson, Didier, 38, 48, 60, 91, 122–27, 136, 137, 153, 255
Mauser factory, 88, 112, 126, 127
Meissner, James, 174

Men Against the Sea, 206
Menier, Senator, 23
Mercedes engine, 6, 34, 35
Messines, 36
Metz, 99, 299
Mexican Aviation Corps, 152
Meyrowitz goggles, 29
Mézières, 5
Millerand, M. Alexander, 17
Mitchell, Colonel William, 182, 183, 193, 245–47, 265, 309
Mock, R. L., 41, 42
Moisant, John B., 198
Morane, Leon, 198
Morane Parasol, 29, 96, 186
Morane Saulnier aircraft, 4, 8
Moses Brown School, 277
Mount Pleasant Academy, 158
Mouy, 170
Mulhouse, 176
Mutiny on the Bounty, 206

Nancy, 19
National Cathedral, Washington, D.C., 129
Nationalist China, 51
Nedim Bey, 71
Neuve-Chapelle, 146
Nieuport aircraft, 28–30, 32, 34, 36, 37, 88
Nieuport-28, 192, 193, 263
Nivelle, General Robert Georges, 202
Nock, Ivan, XII
Nordhoff, Charles B., 108, 206
Norton-Harjes Ambulance Corps, 156, 225
Now It Can Be Told, 203
Nungesser, Lieutenant Charles, 49, 107, 135, 155
Nuremberg, 12

Oberndorf, 122
Oberursel engine, 35
Obregón, General Alvaro, 122, 123, 125, 152
Oscar II, S.S., 24
Ostend, 14
Outlook magazine, 66

Paris Air Guard, 17, 72, 77

Parsons, Edwin C., 91, 102, 108, 125, 137, 151–55, 163–65, 188, 194, 195, 210, 218–20, 230, 232–38, 241, 242, 251, 254, 266, 279, 315, 327

Pau, 16, 19, 27, 28

Pavelka, Paul, 48, 138–44

Penguin (Bleriot) aircraft, 4, 26

Percy, Robert, 314

Peronne, 230

Pershing, General John J., 202, 224, 246, 247

Pétain, General Henri Philippe, 202, 230

Peterson, David McKelvy, 174, 205, 222–24, 264

Petit-Detroit, 167

Phélizot, René, 14

Phillips Exeter Academy, 152

PILOTS, Complete list of Lafayette Flying Corps, 321–23

Pitcairn's Island, 206

Poperinge, 146

Porto Corsini, 130

Pourpe, Marc, 95–97, 103

Pozières, 180

Prieur rockets, 212

Prince, Jr., Frederick H., 129, 130, 162, 255, 315, 327

Prince, Norman, 16–21, 25, 30, 48, 66, 78, 87, 89, 107, 119–21, 127–30, 159

Prinz, LeRoy J., 327

Psi Upsilon, 70

Putnam, David E., 205, 281–87, 306

Ravenel, 162, 221

Regnier, Colonel, 24

Renault engine, 46

Richthofen, Baron Manfred von, 35, 148, 190, 228

Rickenbacker, Captain Eddie, 174, 263, 264, 297

Riff War, 108

Rochambeau, S.S., 159

Rockwell, Captain Henry, 42

Rockwell, Kiffin Yates, 1, 24, 30, 40–48, 63, 66, 71, 72, 78, 87, 89, 113–20, 326

Rockwell, Noadiah, 42

Rockwell, Paul Ayres, 1, 40–42, 108, 109, 156, 208, 209, 243, 259, 315, 326

Rockwell, Robert Lockerbie, 109–11, 188, 232, 233

Rockwell, William, 42

Rocle, Marius, 24, 269, 270

Rodel, Mme., 29

Roisin, Commandant, 97

Roller (aircraft), 26, 27

Rolls-Royce engine, 246

Romorantin, 27

Roosevelt, Theodore, 168

Royal Air Force, 205

Royal Canadian Air Force, 205

Royal Flying Corps, 25, 139, 182

Royal Fusiliers, 207

Royal Naval Air Service, 17, 112, 115, 127, 130, 190

Rumsey, Laurence, 25, 30, 48, 144, 315

Saint-Cyr-l'Ecole, 19

Saint-Just, 138

Saint-Mihiel, 79

Saint-Pol-sur-Mer, 227

Saint-Quentin, 165, 166, 170

Salmson engine, 246

Salonika, 143

Samson, chef, 137, 188

Scanlan, Lawrence, 270, 271, 314

Scanlon, Bob, 310

Seeger, Alan, IX, XII

S.E.5, aircraft, 182, 185

Senard, 238

Shaffer, Walter J., 306–8

Shoninger, Clarence B., 308

Sigma Phi Epsilon, 70

Sinclair, Reginald, 279

Snipe (Sopwith), 192

"Soda," pet lioness, 92, 165, 216, 23, 254

Somme, 134, 147

Sopwith aircraft, 29, 36, 127, 24, 243

Sopwith-Kauper gear, 36
Sopwith triplane, 36, 190
Soubiran, Robert, 1, 24, 130, 131, 314
Spanish-American War, 149
Spad-7, 36, 162, 182, 189–90
Spad-12, 191
Spad-13, 191, 245
Spad-17, 191
Spad-XI-A2, 192
Spandau-Maxim gun, 75
Spencer, Sarah, 62
SQUADRONS:
  American: 13th, 270, 289; 22nd, 200; 88th, 273; 93rd, 272; 94th, 174, 220, 222, 261, 267, 271, 309; 95th, 223; 103rd, 55, 110, 132, 145, 172, 173, 200, 201, 222, 253, 276, 287; 138th, 145; 139th, 145, 283; 644th, 270; Third Corps Observation Group, 273; 4th Pursuit Group, 289; Fifth Group, 145
  British: No. 11, 37; No. 19, 191; No. 22, 38, 39; No. 24, 191; No. 56, 38, 39
  French: Br.117, 289; Br.213, 270; C.11, 61, 160; C.17, 274; C.18, 126; C.30, 62; C.34, 61; C.42, 19, 57, 61; C.46, 270; C.53, 275; C.74, 272; D.6, 19, 57; F.24, 269; MS.38, 4, 50; N.3, 140, 150; N.15, 135; N.49, 199; N.65, 135; N.67, 64; N.68, 126; N.84, 135, 270; N.87, 303; N.88, 135; N.99, 308; N.103, 51; N.124, 25, 30, 52, 55, 58, 68, 88, 127–29, 132, 135, 145, 150; Sop.255, 274; Spa.3, 254, 255; Spa.38, 306; Spa.65, 64, 65, 300; Spa.73, 278, 285; Spa.77, 301; Spa.78, 64; Spa.85, 311; Spa.93, 310; Spa.94, 281; Spa.97, 302; Spa.102, 130; Spa.112, 208; Spa.124, 65, 205; Spa.152, 308; Spa.156, 306; Spa.163, 65; V.97, 77; VB.101, 72; VB.106, 97; VB.108, 20, 71, 310; 13th Chasse Group, 135, 150

Stinson Flying School, 225
Sukuna, S. L. V., 71
Sunbeam engine, 246
Sunderman, Major James F., 328
Sweeny, Charles, 1, 2

Tank Corps, 204
Thann, 40
Thaw, William, 1–4, 14, 18, 19, 24, 30, 31, 38, 48, 52–61, 76, 87, 89, 112, 136, 162, 164, 165, 185, 208, 210, 216, 248, 314
Thénault, Captain Georges, 30, 39, 49, 61, 62, 78, 84–86, 88, 115–18, 164, 202, 232
Thénault's Tribute to Kiffin Rockwell, 116–18
Thiamount, 66
Toul, 265
Trenchard, General Sir Hugh "Boom," 147, 184
Trinkard, Charles, 1
Turnure, Jr., George E., 253, 276

United States Air Service, XI, XIII, 193, 247
U. S. Army, 94, 102
U. S. Army Air Force, 109
U. S. Congress, XI
U. S. First Tactical Air Force, 109
U. S. Naval Aviation, 130
U. S. Navy, 159
University of Chicago, 206
University of Pennsylvania, 152
University of Utah, 13

Vadelaincourt, 83
Vailly, 3
Vanderbilt, William K., 22, 137, 138
Verdier-Fauvety, Lieutenant Louis, 61, 64, 65, 196, 216
Verdun, 47, 48, 79
Verne, Jules, XI
Vickers gun, 89
Victories, Complete list scored by Lafayette Flying Corps, 320
Villa, Francisco "Pancho," 125
Villeneuve, 263

Virginia Military Institute, 40
Voisin aircraft, 20, 29
Vosges Mountains, 31

Waller, Corporal J. H., 148
Wallingford, Connecticut, 94
Waringenstadt prison, 301
Warren, Mrs. Whitney, 153
Warsaw, 24
Washington, General George, 42
Way of the Eagle, 289
Weeks, Kenneth, 76
Wellman, William A., 303, 304
Wells, H. G., XI
Wheeler, Dr. David E., XII, 70
"Whiskey," pet lion, 89–93, 165, 216,
    239, 254

White, Dr. William, 23
Whitmore, Herman, 302, 304–6
Wilcox, Charles, 253, 276
Willis, Harold B., 108, 109, 162, 17
    187, 230, 233–35, 241, 242, 29
    306, 315
Wilson, President Woodrow, 41, 16
    168, 170, 171
Winslow, Alan F., 174, 264, 265, 3
Worthington, Warwick D., 274, 2
Wright biplane, 152, 225
Wynne, Hugh H., 327

Ypres, 36, 146

Zinn, Frederick XIII, 24, 269, 314

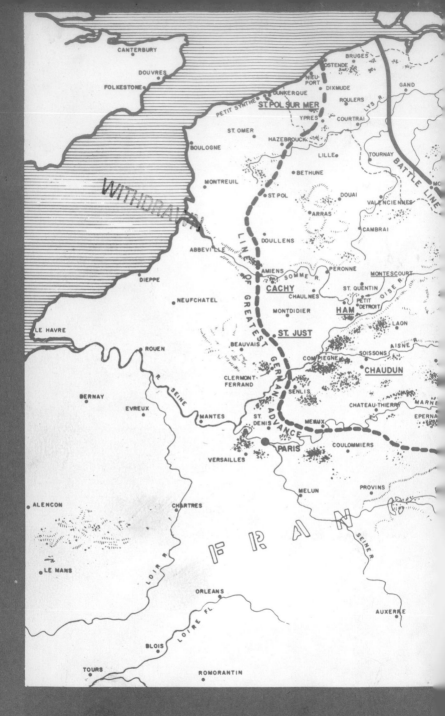

THE WESTERN FRONT · SHOW